SIMPSON

IMPRINT IN HUMANITIES

The humanities endowment
by Sharon Hanley Simpson and
Barclay Simpson honors
MURIEL CARTER HANLEY
whose intellect and sensitivity
have enriched the many lives
that she has touched.

AMERICAN BREAD

CALIFORNIA STUDIES IN FOOD AND CULTURE

Darra Goldstein, Editor

AMERICAN BREAD

A History

ANDREW COE

UNIVERSITY OF CALIFORNIA PRESS

University of California Press
Oakland, California

Library of Congress Cataloging-in-Publication Data

Names: Coe, Andrew (Andy) author
Title: American bread : a history / Andrew Coe.
Other titles: California studies in food and culture 90. (bcp47)
Description: Oakland, California : University of California Press, [2026] | Series: California studies in food and culture ; vol 90 | Includes bibliographical references and index.
Identifiers: LCCN 2026017293 (print) | LCCN 2026017294 (ebook) | ISBN 9780520397507 cloth | ISBN 9780520397514 ebook
Subjects: LCSH: Bread—United States—History Classification: LCC TX769 .C552 2026 (print) | LCC TX769 (ebook)
LC record available at https://lccn.loc.gov/2026017293
LC ebook record available at https://lccn.loc.gov/2026017294

Manufactured in the United States of America

GPSR Authorized Representative: Easy Access System Europe, Mustamäe tee 50, 10621 Tallinn, Estonia, gpsr.requests@easproject.com

35 34 33 32 31 30 29 28 27 26
10 9 8 7 6 5 4 3 2 1

The publisher and the University of California Press Foundation gratefully acknowledge the generous support of the Simpson Imprint in Humanities.

For the Bread Bakers

Contents

Illustrations

INTRODUCTION

I WROTE THIS BOOK because I love bread. In America it is made from grain, water, salt, and leavening and then cooked, usually by baking in an oven. It is the plastic-bagged loaf stuffed on the shelf in the supermarket aisle. It is the hand-crafted sourdough *pain de campagne* pulled from the wood-fired oven at a one-man bakery in the mountains of northern Vermont. It is the cornbread dished out at a Nashville cafeteria, each slab crisp at the edges and fluffy inside, perfect for mopping up the liquor from collard greens. It is the whole wheat no-knead loaf cooling on the rack in a home kitchen. Depending on where we live, we also may consume sweet Hawaiian rolls, Milwaukee rye, Southwestern fry bread, New York bagels, and oat porridge boules made with four different heritage grains. *American Bread* is my attempt to tame this multitude and tell the story of our many bread traditions from the arrival of the first European settlers around 1600 through today. I explore where these traditions came from, what they are now, and how they help us understand our nation's culinary heritage.

This book is about more than just bread. When the first Europeans settled on the shores of North America, they were constrained by scanty food supplies, inadequate equipment, limited knowledge of how to feed themselves, and profound ignorance about the ecology of this foreign land. They encountered Indigenous peoples who had mastered the art of surviving off the native flora and fauna, but so different were their ideas about how to live and eat that Europeans learned little from them—except the crucial art of growing corn. Over the decades, however, the settler-colonists learned to survive and even thrive, a process that I illuminate through the story of bread. They discovered how to grow wheat and rye on alien soil and moved westward to claim rich farmlands. This expansion came at a grave human cost, of Native tribes who were pushed out of their lands and of enslaved Africans brought in to till the fields. To feed the growing population, the settlers mastered the art of producing leaven and processing grain in the most efficient mills the world had ever seen. Through the simple act of kneading together homegrown flour, water, salt, and yeast, they helped produce our national identity and diet. Bread made us Americans.

I tell this story through the lens of thirteen representative American loaves. Most of them are still eaten today but not always in their original form. I chose these loaves not just because they are some of the most widely consumed breads, but because their stories resonate. They illustrate important advances in the history of baking ingredients and techniques, helping us understand the development of American agriculture and the food industry and highlighting the evolution of American cuisine from the hardscrabble days of the early settlers to today's industrial food system. We may no longer receive the bulk of our calories from bread, as we did during colonial days, but we retain a deep emotional attachment to the staple. In some essential way bread endures as a synonym for all food.

Each chapter looks at the origin and development of one signature American loaf, beginning with the early New England settler "Rye and Indian" and going right up to today's artisan bread. The chapters begin with the people, either groups or individuals, who felt the necessity to make a particular loaf. I discuss the ingredients, techniques, and equipment needed for each bread. I give representative recipes for nearly every loaf, from early cookbooks through the formularies of professional bakeries. I follow the loaves as they develop through time in the hands of both home and professional bakers, continuing to the present day. For instance, Boston Brown Bread, which is still made in eastern New England, is a direct ancestor of the crude rye and cornmeal loaves thrown together by the Pilgrims and their descendants four centuries ago.

Each loaf in this book is linked to larger narratives in American culinary and industrial history. The first centers on the encounter between European expectations about proper diet and American Indian foodways. Loaf bread made from wheat and rye was the staple of early seventeenth-century colonists who came to the New World. They produced it using the traditional ingredients, tools, and methods that had been used for centuries in England: stone-ground flour, brewer's yeast, hand-mixing, slow rise, and baking in domed, wood-fired ovens. Unfortunately, the settlers were singularly ill-equipped and often incompetent at finding ways to grow wheat and rye and establish bread production on these shores. Their savior was corn, or maize, the staple of Indigenous cultures all the way from Central America north to present-day Canada. Native American groups along the East Coast of North America placed corn at the center of their belief system, becoming experts at growing and processing the grain. In order to survive, Europeans had to learn from Indigenous informants how to grow the crop and turn it into food. Corn produces far larger crops than wheat or rye. However, as an ingredient for bread, it has one great drawback: corn lacks the gluten that would allow it to rise. Colonists managed not only to figure out how to incorporate corn but to make it a centerpiece of their diet. Down-home Southern cornbread is just one of the end products of their efforts.

The colonists who landed at Plymouth, Jamestown, New Amsterdam, and other sites were largely immigrants, and it is the immigrant story that has shaped nearly all the loaves in this book. Over the centuries wave after wave of foreigners have landed on US shores hoping to re-create the culinary customs of their homelands, including breads. Early settlers were mostly from Great Britain, but beginning in the mid-nineteenth century the United States received thousands of migrants from Ireland, Germany, France, Austro-Hungary, Italy, and Eastern Europe. They quickly made their mark on American culinary culture, bringing French sourdough to California, European ryes to both urban and farm communities, and Jewish bagels to New York and other cities. Some loaves were adopted so readily that they soon became "American"—one ancestor of supermarket white bread is the fine Vienna loaf. Italian bread took much longer to gain acceptance due to prejudice against migrants from southern Italy. Immigrants changed not only American cuisine with their loaves but also the baking industry as a whole. In the late nineteenth and early twentieth century, for example, the majority of urban bakery owners and workers in the United States were from countries like Germany, Austro-Hungary, Italy, France, and Russia. They introduced new varieties and baking techniques that continue to be used today.

Nearly every store-bought loaf on American tables today shows the impact of industrialization on the bread-making process. From the late eighteenth century on, American bakeries have been intent on manufacturing larger quantities of bread more quickly and cheaply. Farmers harvested more wheat than was needed for mere subsistence and found markets for grain throughout the mainland colonies and the Caribbean sugar islands. The first bottleneck was the flour industry, with its inefficient mills needing large numbers of workers. The breakthrough came shortly after the American Revolution, when the inventor Oliver Evans introduced his fully automated flour mill. For bakers the problem was leaven, traditionally made from unreliable and bitter brewer's yeast. The introduction of the Fleischmann brothers' compressed yeast cakes around 1870 helped bakers achieve consistent and better-tasting batches of loaves. The next challenge was mechanization, building machines that could replicate every step of the complicated baking process and eliminate the need for large workforces. Finally the largest flour mills installed Hungarian steel roller mills, giving them the ability to produce huge amounts of cheap white flour stripped of many of its nutrients. The new bread factories used that flour to bake thousands of loaves a day, deploying the new arts of advertising and marketing to put them on every American table. The country's dietary staple became the industrial white pan loaf that crowds today's supermarket aisles.

The backlash against industrial flour and bread began almost as soon as they were introduced. The most colorful personality in this book is the temperance orator Sylvester Graham, who in the 1830s campaigned against the evils of bakery bread made with cheap white flour and bad leavening. It not only tasted foul but, according to Graham, was slowly killing consumers. He advocated a diet based on loaves made from home-ground whole wheat flour, clean water, good leavening, and a mother's love (because women would be doing all the baking). That belief in the essential goodness of whole wheat was picked up by health food apostles and the counterculture of the 1960s. For antiestablishment activists, baking your own wheat bread was an act of defiance against the military-industrial–Wonder Bread complex (at a time when the brand was owned by a major defense contractor). White bread was also enriched with artificial vitamins, while in wheat the good things were naturally part of the grain. Some counterculture bakers went to Europe and fell in love with Old World artisan loaves. They learned European sourdough techniques and appreciation for stone-ground flours and came back to bake handmade baguettes and giant French village loaves in wood-fired ovens. The artisan bread movement remains strong today, while the largest baking corporations are trying to win part of their market by selling "artisan" whole grain sourdough breads produced in their fully mechanized factories.

The relationship between home bakers and commercial bakeries is one of the most interesting story lines I follow through this narrative. During the colonial era and the early decades of the American republic, almost all bread was produced by women at home. However, the rise of cities, the shrinking of apartment space, and the entry of women into the workplace made it harder for housewives to fit in their weekly baking day. At the same time, bakeries became larger, more technologically advanced, and productive. They hired advertising agencies to convince women to *stop* home baking—Why toil? Have more time for your children, for yourself!—and buy their bakeries' loaves down at the grocery. By 1955 only 5 percent of US families regularly consumed bread they had made themselves. The tide began to turn in the 1970s as consumers began to question the health value of supermarket breads and rediscover the joy of baking at home. This was not a fad. Home cooks found that their loaves tasted better and were healthier than store-bought. This trend soared during the enforced idleness of the COVID-19 pandemic. While the boom has subsided since many people have returned to work, home baking remains a part of many Americans' cooking routines.

What a reader will not find in this book is a discussion of every American bread. I do not include ship's biscuit, pizza, biscuits, muffins, croissants, focaccia, brioche, donuts, challah, babka, pretzels, scones, tortillas, pancakes, Cuban bread, fry bread, keto, gluten-free, or paleo. The reasons vary. Some are too regional; others aren't breads as I define them. Some fall more into the category of viennoiserie (enriched, often sweet breads); and paleo, keto, and gluten-free are simply too new. I also didn't cover some issues, such as industrial bread as an ultra-processed food, which are very much in the realm of current events. In the end this is a personal selection of loaves that interest me. The rest will have to wait for a much-needed encyclopedia of American bread.

If there is one loaf that could be defined as the "American bread," it is the factory-made white pan loaf, as exemplified by Wonder Bread, with its squeezably soft texture, gummy mouthfeel, and faintly acrid aroma. It reflects the deep-rooted belief, going back to Roman times, that the whiter the crumb, the finer and better it is. The white pan loaf has been sold to us as high quality, sanitary, healthy, and energy-boosting—and your children will love it! For well over a century, this style of loaf has dominated grocery shelves and filled lunchboxes. However, uniform legions of white pan loaves marching out of semitruck-sized ovens represent only one strand of American culinary culture. What really marks our bread is its diversity, based on wheat, rye, corn, and other grains, leavened with yeast, sourdough, or chemicals, baked in a pan or directly on an open hearth, and prepared at home or in an odorless industrial plant. My intent in writing this book is to celebrate American bread in all its glory and complexity, not only to record how bread fits into the larger history of American cuisine but to encourage bakers to explore and enjoy this essential part of our heritage.

1

RYE AND INDIAN

ON A BLEAK NOVEMBER DAY in 1620 an English ship carrying more than a hundred cold, seasick, and scurvy-ridden passengers dropped anchor in what is now Provincetown Harbor at the northern tip of Cape Cod. The *Mayflower* had embarked in early September from Plymouth, on the south coast of England. The ship spent more than two months at sea, fighting through one bitter North Atlantic storm after another. The battering knocked the mainmast askew and caused so many leaks that caulking them was a full-time job. One passenger died; another washed overboard and only saved himself by catching a rope that someone tossed after him. The passengers, most of them Protestant separatists who called themselves "Pilgrims," had originally planned to settle at the mouth of the Hudson River (today's New York Harbor). However, they were so worn out by the voyage that they decided to land at Cape Cod—the first part of North America that they saw. When the *Mayflower* came to rest in the harbor, they fell to their knees to give thanks for a safe arrival. Then they rose from the deck to examine the land around the harbor. They found no "friends to welcome them, nor inns to entertain or refresh their weatherbeaten bodies, no houses or much less towns to repair to, to seek for succor." Their new home, a range of sandy hills thickly covered with trees, appeared to the Pilgrims to be a "hideous and desolate wilderness, full of beasts and wild men."[1]

Leery about exposing themselves to danger, they decided to wait before staking claim to dry land. The *Mayflower* carried a shallop, a thirty-foot boat designed for coastal exploration, that had been damaged during the rough passage. The ship's carpenter had to repair it before they could set out to explore where to plant their new settlement. However, a man named Myles Standish was not willing to wait the weeks it might take to fix the boat. He was one of the passenger list's "Strangers"—artisans, servants, and others who had been hired to help the Pilgrims establish their colony. Standish was a tough English soldier whose task was to defend the group from Native Americans, Spaniards, pirates, and whoever else might attack them. Anxious for adventure, he volunteered to take a party of men and explore the nearby hills to look for fresh water and whatever foodstuffs they could forage.

Sixteen heavily-armed men landed on the harbor shore and marched single file down the beach. A few hours into their trek, they noticed off in the distance five or six Indigenous people, whom they called "savages," and gave chase. The Native Americans fled into the woods; the Pilgrims trotted after them along a forest path that took them south down the peninsula. After a trek of ten miles or so, night began to fall. The men made camp on a hilltop and supped on "biscuit and Holland cheese," washed down with a little "aqua vitae," or brandy. The next morning they continued on the path, which eventually led to an open field that showed signs of Native American plantings and mounds of sand that looked like graves. The expedition also stumbled across a house foundation and a great iron kettle. Was this a sign that some shipwrecked European had lived here? Nearby rose a mound of sand that looked freshly piled. Sensing that some kind of booty lay beneath, the Pilgrims began to dig. They unearthed something that turned out to be far more valuable to them than a cache of Native American gold or pirate's treasure: two "finely woven" baskets filled to the brim with "fair Indian corn."[2]

The Pilgrims scooped up handfuls of the grain and let the hard yellow, red, and blue kernels run through their fingers. For them "corn" meant wheat, rye, oats, and barley—their accustomed grains of home. These kernels looked and felt altogether different. Nevertheless, one of their leaders, William Bradford, wrote that "it seemed to them a very goodly sight." Aware that they were stealing someone's precious supplies for the winter, the Pilgrims filled the kettle with corn and stuffed more into their capacious pockets. Lugging their booty, they staggered back toward shore to signal the *Mayflower.* Upon seeing the haul, the passengers were "marvelously glad and their hearts encouraged." Bradford declared that the discovery of the cache was sign of a "special Providence from God."[3] (Another sign of such "providence," he announced, came when smallpox wiped out a large Indigenous village but spared the English settlers.)

Despite their faith in their holy mission, the Pilgrims knew that the odds were they would not survive a year in the New World. Scurvy was getting worse among them. Supplies were already low, and the earliest planting season was four or five months away. Then it would be at least two or three months until harvest (assuming that their seeds grew in this alien soil). Come spring, the *Mayflower* would set sail again for England, and the Pilgrims would be left alone among the "savages" and wild beasts until the next supply ship came—if they lasted that long. Pilgrim leaders sat down with Captain Jones to go over the list of stores that filled every inch of the *Mayflower*'s hold: barrels, casks, and crates holding ship's biscuit, oat and rye meal, salt beef, salt pork, ham and bacon, salt cod, cheese, butter, dried beans and peas, vinegar, gin, brandy, and beer. Some of that would have to stay aboard to feed the crew for the return voyage. The bulk would be off-loaded wherever they decided to plant their settlement to support the Pilgrims through the long winter and beyond. It was clear that these stores were not enough.

Yet now they looked at about ten bushels of a grain they called "Indian corn." The fat, shiny kernels were utterly unknown to them. They had no idea how to prepare the grain or how it tasted. But they knew that if they wanted to survive, out of Indian corn they would have to make their bread. The Pilgrims had likely heard of Indian corn before their trip, but they probably had never seen it. Rembert Dodoens, the Flemish botanist who compiled the era's most important encyclopedia of edible plants, called "Turkie Corne or Indian Wheat" a "marvelous strange plant, nothing resembling any other kind of grayne." When Dodoens was writing in the mid-sixteenth century, there was still much confusion in Europe about the corn plant. He thought it originated in Turkey, while New World explorers knew it was endemic to the Western Hemisphere. Some people claimed that it made palatable bread, but Dodoens had his doubts: "The bread that is made thereof is drye and hard, having very small fatnesse or moysture, wherefor men may easily judge, that it nourisheth but little, and is evill of digestion, nothing comparable to the bread made of Wheat, as some have falsely affirmed."[4]

For the Indigenous peoples of southern New England, corn (*Zea mays*) was the staple. They believed it had come to them from the Southwest, realm of their paramount god, the first kernel carried in the ear of a crow. (The first bean was carried in the crow's other ear.) To the Southwest also lay the great civilizations of Mesoamerica, the land where corn had first been domesticated around nine thousand years ago. Corn arrived in this part of North America after 1,000 CE and became central to Native diet and culture. Their entire year was oriented around the life cycle of corn. In early spring and again in late autumn, it was the men's job to prepare the land for corn planting using the techniques of slash-and-burn agriculture. They would set fires to clear away brush and scorch the tree trunks before felling them with stone axes. Filled with stumps, holes, rocks, and mounds, Native planting grounds looked nothing like the carefully cleared and plowed fields of England. However, they were remarkably productive, thanks to the wood ash that acted as fertilizer and the Indigenous farmers' highly advanced system of agriculture.

It was the women's job to plant and tend and harvest the corn. When oak tree leaves had grown to the size of mouse's ears, they knew it was time to plant. The women would go into the fields wielding a sharp stick and carrying a bag full of seed corn on their shoulder. Every four feet or so, they would poke the stick into the ground and then drop four or five kernels into the hole. They would then push the earth into a mound above the hole to protect the seeds. Along the coast every spring schools of alewife, a kind of shad, would run up the rivers. Native Americans would trap and net the fish and use them as fertilizer, burying one in every mound in their fields. After a few weeks, when the first green leaves were pushing out of the dirt, they would go through the field again and poke a hole or two into the mounds and drop a couple of beans in each. This planting ritual would be repeated again in a month or two, because the Native Americans sowed both early and late crops of corn. Through the summer the women were constantly in the fields (as well as tending children and preparing meals) to hoe out weeds and protect the crops against marauding birds by day and raccoons and other invaders at night.

The first harvest occurred in August, the season of green corn. Its arrival was celebrated in a great feast when green ears were plucked from stalks and placed still husked onto the fire. Native Americans consumed them with gusto amid dances and thanks to the gods for the bounty. Larger harvests took place in September and October when the corn was fully mature. Every plant produced two or three ears, each holding 250 to 500 kernels. If the crop wasn't damaged by rain or drought, a good crop would yield not only enough to support the community for the next year but also excess that could be used for trade. Women would strip off the husks and sort the dried cobs and kernels for their various uses, some to be consumed immediately, others for winter stores, seed for the following year, and the most perfect ears to be used as ritual offerings.

Women did the arduous work of preparing the corn kernels for consumption. They pounded the kernels in mortars made from the tops of tree stumps that had been burned and then scraped with stone axes to form a wide bowl. For travelers the echoing sound of big wooden pestles thumping into these mortars was often the first sign that they were approaching a village. The problem with this method is that the resulting meal contains bits of the hard pericarp, or outer coating of the kernel, and thus had a gritty texture. Women usually treated the grain with some kind of alkali to soften it. Originating in Mesoamerica (where corn was initially domesticated), this process was known as nixtamalization. The word comes from the Nahuatl words for "ashes" and "uncooked corn dough." In Mesoamerica women soaked corn kernels in a mixture of water and either lime (calcium hydroxide) or lye (potassium hydroxide) made from wood ashes. Along the eastern coast of North America the principal method was to add some wood ash (containing potassium hydroxide) to a pot of boiling corn and let the mixture seethe for hours. Both methods dissolve the pericarp and soften the endosperm, causing the corn to puff up into what we know as hominy. The women then rinsed the kernels and rubbed off what remained of the outer shell. What was left was soft, tasty, and much easier to grind into meal. A happy side effect of this process is that it also releases the niacin (vitamin B3) in the grain so that the body can absorb it. Native Americans thrived on their diet of alkali-processed corn. Other groups who relied on corn as a staple, including European settlers, but didn't have access to this technology, were not so lucky.

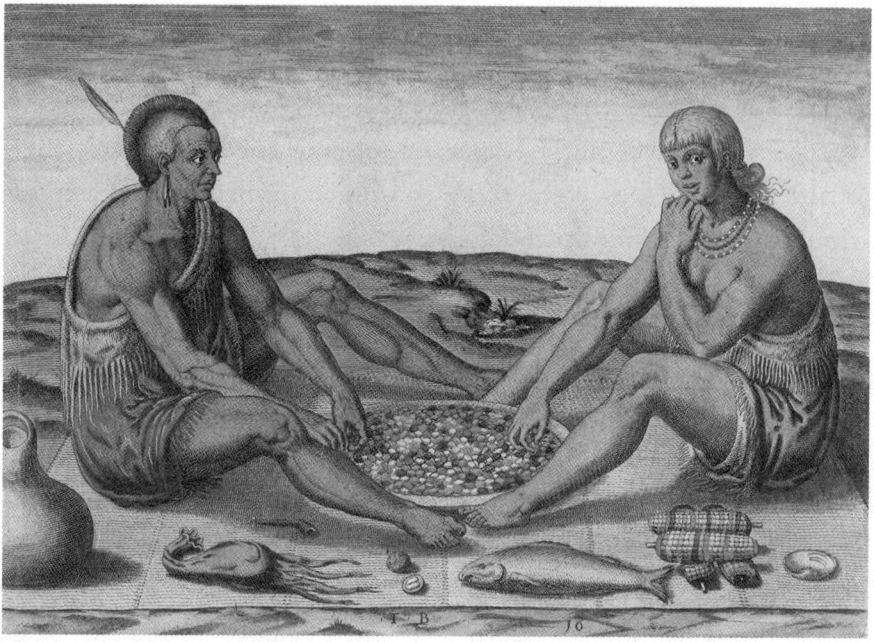

Figure 1. A Native American couple from the Outer Banks, off the coast of North Carolina, and a basket of colorful corn kernels. This Theodor De Bry engraving is based on a painting by John White, from Thomas Hariot's *A Briefe and True Report of the New Found Land of Virginia*, 1590. *Source*: This engraving is in the public domain, from the Harvard Library.

The principal corn dish was a big bowl of boiled meal. The Narragansett called it *Nasàump*, described as "Indian corn, beaten and boiled." Indigenous women would often mix beans into the corn mush to produce the ancestor of the dish we know today as succotash. This could be seasoned with fish, clams, various kinds of meat, or dried fruit. The dish was eaten communally, the shared act serving to reinforce ties of family, village, and tribe. Women would also parch the cornmeal so men could carry it as they went out on fishing or hunting trips. A little water would turn the powder into a simple staple.

Native Americans did not have "bread" in its modern dictionary meaning as a "baked or leavened food made of a mixture whose basic constituent is flour or meal." They did not use ovens as we know them or employ either chemical or bacterial leavening when preparing it.

They did knead their nixtamalized cornmeal, form it into masses, and then apply heat. To prepare their "bread," women would sift ground grain to extract the finest meal. They would then add water and knead it into a dough. Unlike wheat, corn does not have any gluten that could impart the ability to stretch, so the dough would have been a dense and heavy product. The women could roll the dough into balls that would be boiled until firm, making them perfect provision for carrying on journeys. Or they could pat the meal into thick discs that they would cook either directly in the coals or wrapped in corn leaves or husks and covered with hot coals. If they didn't have corn, as often happened on long hunting trips, they could pound chestnuts, acorns, or various kinds of roots into meal to make similar fire-cooked "breads."

This corn-based diet evidently agreed with the Indigenous peoples of southern New England. When the Pilgrims first encountered them, they noticed their fine physiques, powers of endurance, and ability to withstand cold and hunger with equanimity (in contrast to their own sickly and fractious community). As for the Pilgrim settlers, they equated good health with their ability to live as Englishmen in the New World. That included consuming the food and drink that defined them as English—mainly bread, beer, and pottage. In 1857 the cookbook writer Eliza Acton stated: "Bread is a first necessity of life to the great mass of the English people; being in part the food of all—the chief food of many—and almost the sole food of many more."[5] This was even more true in the early seventeenth century than in Acton's time.

The English lived on bread. The lower they were on the economic ladder, the more likely they were to rely on bread for most of their sustenance. Fine white bread was reserved for the elite. The highest status loaf was manchet, made from sifted white wheat flour and often enriched with eggs, butter, and sugar. The next steps down were the loaf called cheat, baked with half white and half whole wheat flour, and then "brown bread" from 100 percent whole wheat. In rural areas the

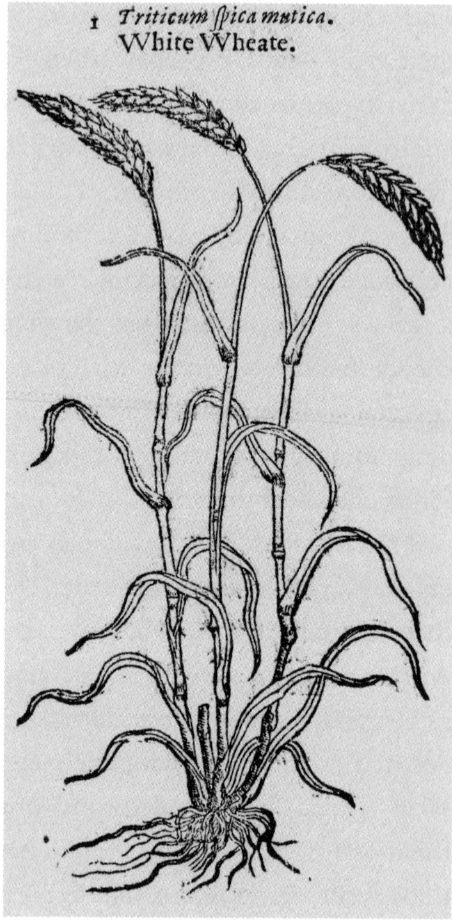

Figure 2. White or common wheat. *Source*: John Gerard, *The Herball* (A. Islip, J. Norton and R. Whitakers, 1636).

most common bread was maslin, made from mixed wheat and rye flour. Lowly servants and laborers had to subsist on brown bread, which could be made from any coarse meal, including wheat, rye, barley, malt, and even ground dried peas. All of these breads were leavened, usually with liquid yeast. In northern England and in Scotland many people also ate unleavened flatbreads called bannocks made from oat or barley meal mixed with water and salt. These flatbreads were cooked on stone or metal griddles set on the fire—a technique that the settlers would embrace in their new surroundings.

The English liked to eat their bread with pottage, the gruel that was at the center of most daily meals. Pottage was made of a cereal or pulse (peas or beans) softened with a liquid, either water, milk, or broth. These gruels could be flavored with meat, preferably beef or mutton, vegetables, saltfish, fruits, nuts, cream, and so on. (Larger pieces of beef, mutton, or game were usually reserved for feast days.) Eaters would drop slices of bread into their pottage to thicken it and also use it as a sop to wipe the bowl clean. Pottage was eaten by all levels of society, from the aristocracy on down. Simpler fare, particularly for the poor who didn't have access to a hearth, centered around bacon, salt meat, bread and cheese, or bread and fish, usually salted or pickled herring. English men, women, and children washed down their bread and pottage with beer. Water was considered poisonous. Due to raw sewage draining into most rivers and streams, a cup of water could easily cause cholera and a host of other fatal diseases. Although commercial breweries had begun to appear in the sixteenth century, many housewives still made beer at home. These were generally low-alcohol ales made from barley malt. (Hops was just coming into fashion as a flavor agent and preservative.) The "alewives" would turn the brewing by-products, including the froth and the lees at the bottom of the barrel, into ale barm. This was the precious liquid yeast that they would use to leaven their breads.

In the early seventeenth century, Europeans had only two types of leaven to raise their breads: sourdough and yeast. In England by far the most common method for leavening doughs was using yeast made from beer, although some bakers did know how to use "sour leaven" or a portion of old dough to raise their breads. The active ingredient in ale barm was the yeast known as *Saccharomyces cerevisiae*, which translated means something like "sugar fungus of beer." When added to a mixture of flour, water, and salt, the yeast converts the sugars in the grain into carbon dioxide, ethyl alcohol, and other compounds. The CO_2 bubbles permeate the dough, stretching the glutens and causing the dough to rise and lighten. During the baking process, the chemical components produced by the yeast are changed by the heat and produce the distinct aroma of yeast bread. Today almost all bakers use various kinds (liquid, compressed, or dry) of factory-produced yeasts that are highly reliable—they make bread rise. The liquid yeast used four hundred years ago was a very different product—capricious, prone to turning bitter or putrid, or simply going flat. Seventeenth-century English baking was much more an art than a science—the housewife's swine grew fat from eating the remnants of failed loaves.

When the *Mayflower* arrived in Cape Cod Bay at the end of 1620, the ship's stores of beer and other supplies were running low. The captain was anxious to offload his hundred or so ailing passengers as soon as possible so he could return to England. After a month of reconnaissance around the bay, the Pilgrims decided to plant their settlement on two hills on its western shore, near a freshwater stream. This was the site of an abandoned Native American village whose inhabitants had been killed in an epidemic, probably smallpox brought by European sailors. The Pilgrims called it New Plymouth and immediately began building a twenty-foot-square "common house" to shelter them from the cold and frequent winter storms. By this time dozens of them were deathly ill with scurvy and other diseases. Of the 102 colonists who landed, 45 died during that first winter. Only a dozen or so men were healthy enough at any time to bury the dead, build shelters for the living, and forage for food.

The Pilgrims lived on their scant stores of ship's biscuit, cheese, butter, dried peas and beans, salt meat, and whatever fish and game they could find. They had run out of beer so they had to drink water from the nearby stream, which they considered a great hardship. They had "bake-kettles," or Dutch ovens, with which they could make bread, but without leavening they could not make proper English loaves. They probably made do with oat or barley pottage and flatbreads cooked in the ashes of their communal hearth. The Pilgrims also must have experimented with their cache of Indian corn, but their first challenge was to find some way to process the hard kernels. They had brought over a few brass mortars and pestles, but these would have been inadequate for grinding large quantities of grain. Perhaps they found an old Native American tree stump mortar nearby or even used the most primitive method of all—crushing them between two rocks. Their situation nevertheless remained precarious, and the odds were that they would not survive that first year in the New World. The Pilgrim community was saved by two Native Americans whom they encountered in the middle of March 1621.

Up until then the Plymouth colonists had seen Indigenous peoples in the distance but had no direct contact with them. They were shocked one day when a tall Native American man, nearly naked despite the cold, strode right into their little cluster of houses and said, "Hello, Englishmen." He was Samoset, a chief from a Maine tribe who had learned a bit of the language from visits by English fishermen. Responding warily to Samoset's desire for friendship, the Pilgrims fed him biscuit, butter, cheese, pudding, and "a bit of mallard." In return, Samoset described the various tribes who were their neighbors, saying that they would willingly trade furs for European knives and other goods. Samoset explained that the Plymouth settlement was on the site of a Patuxet village whose population had all died in a "plague" a few years earlier. A few days later, Samoset introduced them to Squanto, the last survivor of the Patuxet, who spoke even better English. Squanto had escaped his tribe's fate because he had been kidnapped and sold into slavery in Spain. Samoset and Squanto helped the Pilgrims negotiate a peace treaty with the Massachusett, the tribe just to the north. Afterward, Squanto decided to stay in Plymouth to help the colonists adapt to life in the New World.

It must have been obvious to Squanto that the Pilgrims had no idea how to harvest the foods of the forests, fields, and waters. His first act was to go down to the mouth of a nearby stream and stir up its muddy bottom with his feet. This roused a whole school of eels that congregated there and were so easy to catch that Squanto quickly filled a bucket with them. That night the Pilgrims feasted on "fat and sweet" eels—one of their favorite foods back in England.[6] With the first warm days of spring, the colonists planted an acre or two each of "wheat and pease," but Squanto evidently saw that this would be inadequate. They needed a good crop of corn to survive the year. Squanto showed them how to plant corn Native American–style, with little mounds arranged every few feet, the whole field covering twenty acres.

This was also the time of the alewife run, and Squanto helped the colonists net the fish and instructed how to bury an alewife or two in every corn-hill to act as fertilizer. That September brought their first harvest in the New World. William Bradford, Plymouth's governor, wrote that the wheat and peas "came not to good," but the corn harvest gave the settlers a peck (about two dry gallons) of meal a week. They supplemented that with stores of dried fish and fowl (mainly ducks and wild turkeys) as well as venison and other meat. In letters to their English brethren the Pilgrims boasted about how fat were their larders. What they omitted to tell potential colonists was how they prepared their bread. Was it made of wheat—the preferred grain of "civilized" peoples—or Indian corn?

The apparent success of the Plymouth Colony drew other settlers to the land they called "New England." Some were religious dissenters like the Pilgrims, while others were simply adventurers looking for a new start. In 1630 a group of English Puritans founded the Massachusetts Bay Colony, centered on Boston, while others established settlements in what became New Hampshire, Rhode Island, and Connecticut. Their relentless expansion pushed the Indigenous peoples out of their tribal lands along the coast and further inland. Realizing their very existence was threatened, in 1675 the New England tribes united in war against the English settlers. Led by the chief Metacomet, aka King Philip, they raided towns and burned thousands of homes but were unable to prevail against superior arms. By the end of "King Philip's War" in 1678, New England's Native population had been reduced by more than half, and many tribes simply disappeared. The English colonists were now in sole possession of the land and could transform it as they saw fit.

Their goal was to live as Englishmen and -women. Their settlements grew from little villages with a few dozen thatched-roof huts to proper towns with such English names as Reading, Gloucester, Lancaster, and so forth. Each community centered on its village green, with a neighboring church that doubled as meeting house. Their businesses included at least a tavern, store, and blacksmith, while residents now lived in one- or two-story homes with central chimneys, glass windows, clapboard siding, and big kitchens doubling as dining rooms where they could prepare their meals. Housewives did most of their cooking over the wide kitchen fireplace, while they baked their breads in beehive ovens of clay or brick either built into their fireplace wall or set out in their yard. Most women no longer had to grind or pound their own grain. Back in the 1630s, the first immigrant millers had arrived in the colonies to set up water- and wind-powered grist mills. Farmers from miles around would bring their grain to be ground; the miller's fee was a portion of the meal. After the farmer brought the meal home, his wife would bolt (sift) it using a cloth or horsehair sieve to separate fine bread flour from coarser parts suitable for mush. Unlike back in England, however, her loaves were much more likely to be made of corn and rye than wheat.

New England colonists could not easily enjoy their customary wheaten loaves, because the grain suffered in the sandy soils of chilly New England and was regularly blighted by black fungus. Luckily they discovered that rye (*Secale cereale*) grew well in poor soil and tolerated the region's harsh winters. The biggest crop, however, was corn. Puritan leader Edward Johnson stated: "The chiefest Corne they planted before they had Plowes was Indian Graine, whose increase is very much beyond all other."[7] Acres and acres of cornfields surrounded nearly every town. So important was the grain that in 1631 it was recognized as specie: one could pay their taxes with sacks of corn. Nevertheless, many new arrivals were unhappy when they discovered that they would have to subside on "Indian" bread. When a group of Puritans ventured into the wilds to found the Massachusetts town of Concord, wrote Johnson, "the want of English Grain, Wheat, Barly and Rie proved a sore affliction to some stomacks, who could not live on Indian bread and water."[8] But only wealthy landowners and merchants could afford a regular diet of wheat bread. Everybody else not only ate corn dishes at every meal but (eventually) learned to like them.

In 1660 the scientist Robert Boyle, a founder of the Royal Society of London, asked John Winthrop Jr., a visiting leader of the Massachusetts Bay Colony, to write an article on the food value of Native American corn. This was a thorny topic in England, because top botanists debated whether or not corn was a worthwhile crop. Like Rembert Dodoens, the eminent herbalist John Gerard claimed that "Turky wheate doth nourish far lesse than either Wheate, Rie, Barly or Oates. The bread which is made thereof . . . is of hard digestion and yeeldeth to the body little or no nourishment; it slowly descendeth and bindeth the belly."[9] In his article John Winthrop Jr. made clear that he disagreed, asserting that "it is now found by much Experience, that it is wholesome and pleasant for Food of which great variety may be made out of it." Winthrop extolled the form and multicolored glory of "this Beautifull Noble Eare of Corne" and described how it is grown, harvested, and made into bread: "The English make very good Bread of the Meale, or flower of it being Ground in Mills, as other Corne, but to make good bread of it there is a different way of ordering it, from what is used about the Bread of other Graine."[10]

After much trial and error, colonists had realized that bread dough made from corn had to be treated differently from wheat or rye dough. According to Winthrop, housewives mixed cornmeal and water into a loose dough slightly thicker than pancake batter. They would put about two quarts of this onto a shallow wooden dish attached to a long handle and then pour the mixture onto the clean-swept floor of a hot oven. The dough would spread into a big thin disc; they would quickly repeat the process by dumping a second batch of dough onto the first to make a thick disc. After sealing the oven, they would let the bread bake for hours or even overnight until it was a "good darke yellow Colour." These discs were often so large that housewives had to break them into pieces before removing them from the oven. Winthrop added that New Englanders made a second "very goode Breade" by mixing cornmeal with a half or a third the quantity of rye or wheat meal. They would add yeast leavening to the dough and let it rise before baking. Winthrop admitted, however, that the "best sort of Food which the English make of this Corne is that they call Sampe," the anglicization of *Nasàump*, or cornmeal mush, but mixed with very English milk and sugar.[11]

New Englanders' common bread evolved from the two shapes that Winthrop describes: the disc and the loaf. The *unleavened* discs were descendants of the cornmeal cakes that the Native Americans baked in their fires. Mixed from just cornmeal and water, the colonists' "ash cakes" were essentially the same thing, either placed directly in the coals or first wrapped in oak leaves or corn husks. Another version was called "journey cake" (presumably because it could be carried while travelling) and later "jonny cake" or "johnny cake." This was cooked by sticking the meal and water dough onto a wooden plank that was propped up before a bright fire. New Englanders' favorite *leavened* breads were variations of the rye and cornmeal loaf described by Winthrop. Their staple was called "Rye and Indian," more simply "Ryeaninjun," and also "brown bread" (not to be confused with the English wheat loaf). It was made from half cornmeal that had been scalded with hot water, half rye meal, liquid yeast, and salt. After the housewife kneaded the dough until stiff, the bread was allowed to rise, then baked for hours or even overnight. Made with fresh cornmeal and prepared by a knowledgeable cook, these breads would have been sweet and redolent of corn. Due to cornmeal's lack of gluten and the low gluten content of rye, Rye and Indian loaves were dense and their crusts often as chewable as old leather.

During the late eighteenth and nineteenth centuries the popularity of unleavened breads gradually dwindled (except in Rhode Island, where johnnycakes remain a local specialty today). At the same time, Rye and Indian's importance grew, helped in part by its link to a second New England staple. Due to restrictive laws protecting the sanctity of the Sabbath, housewives could not cook on Sundays. Every Saturday evening, housewives would slide into the oven a big loaf of Rye and Indian and a pot of beans. This was made from white beans and salt pork and was a direct descendant of English pottages. The next morning they would pull them out for the Sabbath breakfast. In big towns like Boston this task was often performed by commercial bakeries, so that Sunday mornings would see streets filled with citizens trooping home carrying beanpots and loaves of bread. According to the *Northampton Courier*, "a man's origin and primitive descent is known to be Yankee when he advocates and defends brown bread and bean pot. . . . A man who will not uphold these wholesome and nutritious compounds, would sell his birthright for a mess of pottage,—he has no real Yankee principle of life in him, and should be driven out of paradise into the land of musquito [*sic*] nets and nullifiers [i.e., the American South]."[12]

Some commentators identified Rye and Indian as not just a New England dish but part of an identifiably "American" diet (as opposed to those effete wheaten loaves associated with the English elite). In 1788 a commentator suggested that all citizens should make Rye and Indian bread a central part of a "Federal Diet." Both nutritious and economical, the homegrown loaf would help lay the foundation for a new nation.[13] Said a writer in the *Massachusetts Ploughman*: "No bread is more agreeable to the unsophisticated palate; none is more healthy and friendly to the constitution; and none will sustain the laborer longer than well-made brown bread."[14] As an added boon, farmers could also crumble the loaf and feed the crumbs to the hogs, who would fatten quicker than on a diet of simple grain.

Here is one of the earliest printed recipes for Rye and Indian, from *The American Farmer* in 1821. One can hear the discursive quality of a housewife's voice in its prose. This recipe is obviously meant for an experienced home baker:

> RYE AND INDIAN BREAD
>
> An equal quantity of rye and Indian meal, *meal from the best mellow corn*, sifted so as to separate the meal from the bran, stir it well together and mix it with water as hot as the hand can be borne in it, *knead it faithfully*, much depends on that, after which put half the quantity of good yeast allowed for the same quantity of yeast or flour bread—it must not be made as hard or stiff as flour bread, and does not take so much time to rise, it requires a hotter oven, and will not bake in less than six hours, and is improved by standing eight or even ten hours from the time it is first put in—we use in this part of the country for this kind of bread, iron pans, shaped something like a flower pot—the shape may not be material to the quality of the bread, but that form gives the best slices for brown bread toast.[15]

Many early descriptions of this loaf emphasize that the dough should be made of corn and rye meal and *not* wheat flour, which doesn't produce as flavorsome a finished product. As the nineteenth century progressed, cooks began to add molasses—New Englanders' favorite sweetener—to the bread, first just a couple of spoonsful but then increasing to a cup of molasses or more for a cloying two-pound loaf. As wheat became more affordable, housewives added wheat meal or flour to soften the loaf. Rye and Indian became "three-third" or "thirded" bread, made from equal parts corn, rye, and wheat. Some recipes removed rye entirely to produce loaves like "Amidama" bread, which was invented in the 1880s at Mrs. Johnston's Gloucester, Massachusetts, bakery. Amidama bread was a "brick" or pan loaf made with cornmeal, wheat flour, molasses, yeast, baking soda, butter, salt, and water. Over the years its name changed to "Amadama" and then "Anadama" bread. By the 1930s, Anadama bread had become associated with an origin myth: A fisherman's wife always makes him cornmeal and molasses mush for dinner. Furious, he yells, "Anna, damn her!" then mixes some flour and yeast into it and throws it back in the oven. Pulling it out later, he discovers that it has become a delicious bread. Anadama bread remains a specialty of the Gloucester and Cape Ann area north of Boston.

In the mid-nineteenth century, with the spread of cast-iron cooking stoves, housewives discovered a new way to prepare their Rye and Indian: steaming. This was less labor-intensive than firing up a brick oven and produced loaves with some of the qualities of Indian pudding, another favorite food. Rather than yeast, they leavened it with an alkali such as baking soda, which gave a better outcome. Still, they would finish the bread in the oven to give it a proper crust. The loaf's popularity spread outside New England, where the name "Rye and Indian" was replaced by "Boston Brown Bread." Noting the bread's sales in New York City, one Boston newspaper commented, "Had we known how near they were to a state of starvation, we would have sent them a loaf long ago."[16]

Seeing the market, stove manufacturers promoted steaming as the new convenience way to cook. "Save Money, Health, Fuel," promised one. "SPEIR'S COOKER cooks Vegetables, Puddings, Meats, Fish, Beans, Brown Bread, Custard, Fruits at the same time, and one will not flavor the other."[17] Boston canneries saw opportunity in steamed breads and began producing canned brown bread. Somehow this led home cooks to a tradition of steaming their own brown breads in cans, although a loaf pan does just as well. Today only B & M of Portland, Maine (founded in 1867 as Burnham & Morrill Company) still manufactures canned brown bread (containing mostly whole wheat flour with only small amounts of rye flour and cornmeal).

2

CORN BREAD

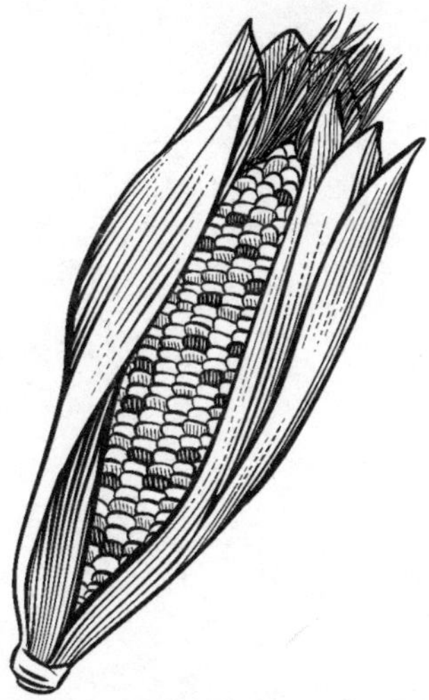

FOURTEEN YEARS BEFORE the first Pilgrim voyage, an English trading company sent an expedition to the New World. The goals of the Virginia Company of London were to spread the Gospel, to provide new lands for England's growing and restive population, and to provide a plentiful and profitable source of raw materials. The band of 105 adventurers was all male, a mix of "gentlemen," artisans, laborers, and servants, including a couple of boys. Like all voyages to the New World at the time, this was a high-risk venture. Company directors were well aware of all the expeditions that had failed before, particularly the disastrous Roanoke Colony of 1585 that had disappeared without a trace. Before their ships departed, they prepared a detailed list of instructions, covering everything from where they should build their fort to how to interact with the Indigenous peoples. They knew that the 1607 expedition could not rely on the regular arrival of supply ships from England. The colonists

Figure 3. An early engraving of maize, also called "Turkie Corne" or "Turkie Wheat." *Source*: John Gerard, *The Herball* (A. Islip, J. Norton and R. Whitakers, 1636).

would be bringing a supply of English seeds, probably including wheat, oats, peas, and barley, for planting at their settlement. However, they were also instructed to avail themselves of Indian corn: "To avoid the danger of famine, use and endeavor to store yourselves of the country corn." The only source for corn was the Native population, so it was essential to keep on good relations: "You must have great care to offend the naturals if you can eschew it and employ some few of your company to trade with them for corn and all other lasting victuals."[1]

The Powhatans who made their home in coastal Virginia prepared their corn much like the Native Americans encountered by the

Pilgrims. In late summer they feasted on green corn. The main harvest occurred a few months later, when the Powhatans reaped the grain that would support them until the next growing season. After pounding the corn in mortars, they would stew the meal with beans or pat it into cakes that they would either bake in hot ashes or boil in hot water. This type of bread was called "apone" or "appon," out of which sprang the word *pone*, or corn pone. The English settlers tasted these foods as guests of neighboring chiefs. Back at their little fort on Jamestown Island, however, they lived off their imported provisions of wheat, oats, dried peas, wild game, and whatever they could forage from the bay, which was filled with shellfish and sturgeon. None of the Englishmen had any farming experience, but they managed to plant a small field of English "corn" (i.e., wheat) to see if it would grow. It thrived, but the crop was too little to be of much use.

The colonists at first neglected their instructions from the Virginia Company to find and store corn, expecting they would soon receive a new shipment of supplies from England. Meanwhile, they scoured the countryside for exploitable resources (of which they uncovered few) and any signs of an El Dorado such as the Spaniards found in Peru and Mexico. In early August, however, one of their party came down with the "bloody flux" (probably dysentery) and soon expired. This marked the onset of five months of disease during which almost two-thirds of the original party died. Those who lived barely had the energy to forage, and a mere twenty days of provisions remained in their stores. Their daily ration was a few ounces of wheat or barley mush and water. The Englishmen's pitiable state, and the loud moans of the sick and dying, caught the attention of Native people in a nearby settlement: "It pleased God, after a while, to send those people which were our mortall enemies to relieve us with victuals, as Bread, Corne, Fish, and Flesh in great plentie, which was the setting up of our feeble men, otherwise wee all had perished."[2]

One of those who survived the "dying time" was Captain John Smith, a professional soldier who had been named a leader of the expedition.

Realizing that they were at risk of starvation, he visited nearby Indigenous settlements to barter beads, metal tools, and sheets of copper for precious corn. The English did not realize that area was in the midst of one of the worst droughts in hundreds of years. The Native Americans were loath to trade for corn with these interlopers, but the indefatigable Smith nevertheless managed to keep on good enough terms with the surrounding chiefs to keep the Englishmen alive for the next two years. However, their situation further deteriorated when a Virginia Company ship arrived with more hungry colonists but few supplies. Declaring that "he that will not work shall not eat," Smith forced each settler to pull his own weight, including "gentlemen" who had never held a hoe. From two Indigenous prisoners the English learned how to plant corn, which was less labor intensive than wheat and produced much more weight in grain. The settlers' existence remained precarious, especially after a plague of rats consumed most of their crop. Seeing that the colony would starve if they remained together, Smith ordered eighty men to go downriver to live on oysters and water and a second group into the hills to hunt for food. Archaeologists have recently dug up English graves from this period and discovered some skeletons that bear the marks of cannibalism.[3]

Injured by an explosion, Captain Smith returned to England in late 1609 to publish two widely read books about his experiences. Despite the harsh conditions he described, they spurred continued interest in the settlement. It nevertheless took several years for the Virginia Company's investment to begin to pay dividends. The turning point came in 1611, when John Rolfe, who gained fame for marrying Pocahontas, planted a crop of sweet South American tobacco near Jamestown. In 1613 the first shipment of Rolfe's tobacco found a market in London, and the Virginia colony was reborn as a tobacco plantation. Settlers planted tobacco on every clear spot of land, including on Jamestown's streets and cemetery grounds. When a privateer arrived in 1619 with "20 and Odd Negroes" captured from a Spanish ship, they were bought by Virginia's governor, becoming the first enslaved people in the

British colonies, toiling as servants and laborers on tobacco plantations. Focusing on quick profits, many farmers ignored the fact that they also had to grow edible crops. In response to frequent food shortages, the governor ordered that any farmer wishing to grow tobacco had to also plant corn and contribute some of the crop to a public granary.

Over the next century the southern coast from Maryland to Georgia evolved into a highly stratified and exploitative plantation system based on growing tobacco in the North and rice in the South. After a series of bloody conflicts, the region's Indigenous population was decimated, the survivors pushed back into the hills. The colonists who occupied their lands formed large estates modeled on the holdings of the English rural aristocracy. They built sprawling manor houses tended by dozens of enslaved men, women, and children and enjoyed probably the most refined and sumptuous food found in the North American colonies. The dishes came out of spacious "big house" kitchens usually presided over by an enslaved cook (who managed to sneak African foodstuffs such as okra and black-eyed peas onto the family table). The plantation owner's diet was based on the cuisine of seventeenth-century and early eighteenth-century England, including roasts, stews, puddings, and many varieties of Old World fruits, vegetables, and herbs. They followed recipes from family cookery manuscripts or from English cookbooks, such as Eliza Smith's *The Compleat Housewife; or, Accomplished Gentlewoman's Companion*, that were sold by American printers. For extra richness cooks would bake "French bread," a type of enriched loaf made with milk and eggs. In Carolina rice country, where rice was a staple of every meal, plantation kitchens turned out soft loaves of mixed wheat and rice, either rice flour or whole rice cooked into a mush. However, these delicate white loaves faced stiff competition from breads made from Indian corn.

In 1705 the plantation owner Robert Beverley published his *History and Present State of Virginia* as an advertisement for further investment and settlement in the colony. He boasted about how English crops grew far better in Virginia than in New England to the north. However, he did not hide the fact that most Virginians, like New Englanders, preferred corn to wheat as their staple food:

> The Bread in Gentlemen's Houses, is generally made of Wheat, but some rather choose the Pone, which is the Bread made of *Indian* Meal. Many of the poorer sort of People so little regard the *English* Grain, that though they might have it with the least trouble in the World, yet they don't mind to sow the Ground, because they won't be at the trouble of making a Fence particularly for it. And therefore their constant Bread is Pone, not so called from the Latine, *Panis,* but from the *Indian* Name *Oppone.*[4]

Part of this was simple economics: tobacco was the money crop, while growing wheat was labor intensive and produced a relatively small harvest compared to corn. To make good wheat flour, one also needed a mill, of which there were few in Virginia compared to New England. Most plantations either owned querns (hand-turned grindstones) or horse-powered mills for grinding their wheat. Less well-to-do Virginians found it much easier to simply plant corn and crush the grain using their trusty wooden mortars. But even the upper classes had a taste for corn. In the late eighteenth century, George Washington was probably the most successful wheat farmer in the state, and his many guests enjoyed wheat bread at his bountiful dinner table. At his breakfast, however, Washington preferred a frugal repast of "two small cups of tea and three or four cakes of Indian meal."

Early recipes for corn pone call for the same ingredients as ash cakes, hoe cakes, and johnnycakes: cornmeal, water, and maybe salt. The difference between them was how they were cooked. Ash cakes were wrapped in leaves and put in the coals; hoe cakes were cooked on a metal sheet; johnnycakes faced the fire on a plank; and corn pone (aka pone bread) was cooked in a bake kettle or an iron pan with a lid. This 1847 recipe is credited to "a lady friend of ours in Virginia, than whom we know no better housekeeper":

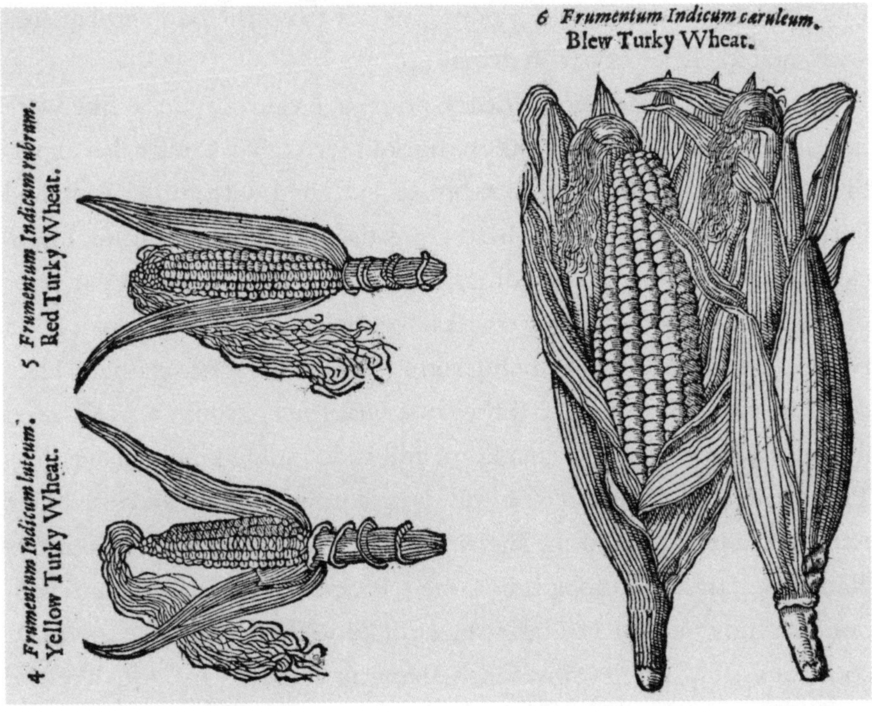

Figure 4. Fat cobs of corn, illustrating the promise of rich crops for European settlers. *Source*: John Gerard, *The Herball* (A. Islip, J. Norton and R. Whitakers, 1636).

TO MAKE CORN PONE

One quart sifted corn meal, as much hot water in winter and cold in summer as will make it the consistence of thick mush; add a teaspoon of fine salt; set the dough to rise in a warm place in winter, and bake it in an iron skillet the top of which must be well heated. Corn bread requires stronger heat in baking than wheat.[5]

The dough for this pone was usually left to sit overnight, although any rise would have been minimal. Up in New England housekeeping experts insisted that all breads must be allowed to cool before eating, because "mastication of hot bread reduces it to a tenacious, gummy mass" that gastric juices cannot digest. In the South everyone knew that the best way to eat corn pone was hot from the pan and covered with melted butter or bacon drippings.

By the early nineteenth century, pone, hoe cakes, and the like were not the only baked corn dishes on the Southern table. Cooks also experimented with "improved" corn breads enriched with milk, eggs, and butter. These ranged from batter breads (essentially cornmeal pancakes) to spoon breads, puddings, and loaves made with wheat flour mixed into the dough. They didn't have the deep corn flavor of a good pone, but they made up by being softer, richer, and more refined. They could be made even lighter if the cook beat the eggs into a froth, used finely sifted cornmeal or corn flour, and added some kind of leavening. The earliest published recipe for risen cornbread appeared in Mary Randolph's 1824 cookbook, *The Virginia House-Wife*. Born into a famous plantation family, Randolph became a Richmond boardinghouse proprietor renowned for her table. Her cookbook—the second American cookbook after Amelia Simmons's *American Cookery*—includes a recipe for "Corn Meal Bread": "Rub a piece of butter the size of an egg, into a pint of corn meal—make it a batter with two eggs, and some new milk—add a spoonful of yeast, set it by the fire an hour to rise, butter little pans, and bake it."[6]

Over the next decades risen cornbread of various types challenged pone for dominance of Southern tables. They all contained white cornmeal enriched with milk or buttermilk, eggs, butter, and salt. Fried pork skins—cracklings—could be added for flavor. "Crackling bread" became as popular as plain cornbread, particularly in rural districts. As the leaven, yeast was soon replaced by saleratus, also known as "sal aeratus" (Latin for "aerated salt"). Early nineteenth-century chemistry texts identified this alkaline compound as potassium carbonate, which, like sodium bicarbonate, or baking soda, was used to leaven dough. There were no government standards for food ingredients in that era—saleratus could have referred to both chemical leavens. The new miracle ingredient for nineteenth-century housewives, saleratus provided a quicker and much more reliable rise than yeast. After the batter was mixed, the cook poured it into an iron skillet greased with either butter or bacon fat and popped it into the oven until it was set and brown and crispy around the edges. Some cooks experimented with replacing white cornmeal with yellow, softening the texture with added wheat flour and adding sugar.

Mixing sugar into cornbread was controversial south of the Mason-Dixon line. In 1921 a popular home economist named Rose Michaelis gave a well-attended cooking demonstration in Houston's City Auditorium. One of the dishes she featured was a cornbread made with four cups of cornmeal, salt, baking powder, shortening, milk, two eggs, and three-quarters of a cup of sugar. This prompted a columnist for the *Houston Post* to protest this "crime of cornbread":

> Dear Miss Michaelis, about that cornbread recipe, which includes three-fourths of a cup of sugar. Tell them not to do it. Sugar in cornbread is an abomination. It ought to be made a crime. It violates every tradition of the South. It insults the palate. It mocks the art of cookery. When the Lord made corn, He put all the sugar in it He intended it to have. This cornbread with sugar in it was an idea born of the devil, planted in New England and sent South by our enemies. It is threatening the life of real cornbread right in the land of its birth. It has done and is doing worse. It makes men trifling and women frivolous. It is responsible for most of the murders and divorces. It is the mother of bolshevism and the germ of anarchy.[7]

And so on. According to purists, a true "Southern" cornbread should be made with only stone-ground white cornmeal and no flour or sugar. It also could be baked in muffin or gem pans, but it was better made in a well-seasoned iron pan. And it must be put on the table fresh from the oven, because "corn bread never was intended to be eaten cold."

Cornbread was more than just a staple of nearly every meal. It was part of the pantheon of foods—including collard greens, biscuits, ham, fried chicken, black-eyed peas, and so on—that defined Southern identity. For white folks that was the identity that has its roots in "Dixie," an idealized vision of the pre–Civil War era of magnolia trees, blushing belles, and great cotton plantations worked by docile slaves. In 1907, Florence Williams Brantley, a Georgia journalist then working in New York City, published a song called "Longing for Dixie" that ends:

I'm sick mos' ter death of Yankee beans—
Lawd, how I long fer some collard greens!
An' pone corn bread an' sweet tater yams,
Wid good brown gravy from country hams—
I'm all out of sorts, an' I'm down in the mouth,
Jes' a-longin' an' longin for the der sunny south.[8]

Nearly a decade later, a Maryland poet named Folger McKinsey (aka "The Bentztown Bard") wrote "The Cornbread Country," extoling the link between cornbread and the rural Eden that was the Old South:

Men of the cornbread country—
Waken and dream again,
Of the vales of the old Virginia land
So bright in the dreams of men!
Waken and walk with fancy
Back to the house 'neath the trees
And the hollyhocks in the garden,
And the golden drone of the bees:
Oh, for the cornbread country,
The jasmine land I see
Down there in the dreams of Jackson,
Down there with the friends of Lee.[9]

The poem goes on to stipulate that the cornbread must crunch when eaten, presumably because it's been cooked in a well-greased iron pan.

What these verses do not acknowledge is that, from the eighteenth century on, the hands that made most Southern cornbread belonged to

African American cooks (many of them enslaved) using recipes they themselves had invented. At the start of the Civil War a third of the region's population was enslaved African Americans, and in states such as South Carolina and Mississippi the percentage was more than half. Enslaved African Americans toiled in the cotton, rice, and tobacco fields; they worked as servants in the big plantation houses and ran the kitchens that produced food for the white owners' tables. In 1853 and 1854, Frederick Law Olmsted, later known as the greatest American landscape architect, toured the "Seaboard Slave States" as a journalist. He often stayed at plantation houses and meticulously reported on the food served at the master's table and how it was prepared, like at this meal in Virginia:

> We dined in a room that extended out, rearwardly, from the house, and which, in a Northern establishment, would have been the kitchen. The cooking was done in a detached log cabin, and the dishes brought some distance, through the open air, by the servants. . . . A stout woman acted as head waitress, employing two handsome little mulatto boys as her aids in communicating with the kitchen, from which relays of hot corn-bread, of an excellence quite new to me, were brought at frequent intervals. There was no other bread, and but one vegetable served—sweet potato, roasted in ashes, and this, I thought, was the best sweet potato, also, that I had ever eaten; but there were four preparations of swine's flesh, beside fried fowls, fried eggs, cold roast turkey, and opossum, cooked, I know not how, but it somewhat resembled baked suckling pig.[10]

Corn was not a novelty to enslaved Africans who had been taken to North America. In the sixteenth century the Portuguese had brought corn to the West African coast, where it quickly became one of the principal grains. The slavers bought stores of corn (and rice and yams) and loaded it onto their ships to feed their human cargo, usually in the form of mush or fried cakes. In the New World plantations it was the enslaver's responsibility to feed his workers and their families. At first, the enslaved Africans were fed in communal mess halls, but within a few decades the enslavers found it was cheaper to simply allot rations to their workers, who in any case preferred to prepare their own meals. The staple was corn, along with rice in South Carolina, supplemented with a scant amount of salt pork or salt fish.

Never the most generous enslaver, George Washington gave his adult enslaved workers a typical weekly ration for his time: a peck (10–12 pounds) of cornmeal, two pounds of salt herrings, some pork fatback "now and then," and milk and butter. This was barely enough for a man or woman working in the fields from dawn to dusk to stay alive. They had to supplement their meager diets by hunting and fishing, usually at night, and Washington also allowed them to tend their own little gardens, which were often far better kept than their enslavers' fields. Plantation owners often noted that their enslaved workers seemed tired and occasionally displayed swelling of the limbs, "black tongue," bow leggedness, and other conditions but wrote off those symptoms as simply laziness or "Negro" conditions that had nothing to do with poor diet.

Despite their deprivations, enslaved workers nevertheless strove to prepare food to their own taste, even out in the fields: "The slaves go to the field in the morning; they carry with them corn meal wet with water, and at noon build a fire on the ground and bake it in the ashes. After the labors of the day are over, they take their second meal of ash-cake."[11] Along the South Carolina and Georgia coast, enslaved workers on the rice plantations added to their cornbread benne, or sesame seeds, a traditional African flavoring. Back in their quarters, they pounded out their corn using big wooden mortars and pestles rather than use the meal from their enslavers' millstone—the flavor was better. Their workday was usually eleven or twelve hours long, most of it in the hot sun. A meager meal was the most that they had energy for: "They then make a fire . . . and cook their own supper, which will be a bit of bacon fried, often with eggs, corn-bread baked in the spider after the bacon, to absorb the fat, and perhaps some sweet potatoes roasted in the ashes. Immediately after supper they go to sleep, often lying on the floor or a bench in preference to a bed."[12]

From small farms to big plantations to such cities as Charleston and Richmond, enslaved men and women also performed most of the work for preparing the enslavers' food. They stoked the fires, tended the kitchen gardens, scrubbed the pots, turned the spits, swept out the baking ovens, and created all the dishes for the table, including the bread. African American cooks introduced white people to ingredients native to Africa such as okra, field peas, and watermelon and to preparations, including rice and peas (aka Hoppin' John) and gumbo, that became Southern staples. In bread, however, there remained a strict racial hierarchy: enslaved workers were only given cornbread; wheat bread was reserved for white people. Two verses of an African American work song protested: "We raise de wheat /Dey gib us de corn; /we bake de bread, /Dey gib us de crust."[13] To protect wheat flour from pilferage, the (white) mistress of the house kept it under lock and key in the kitchen storeroom, doling it out with a stingy hand. Their "faithful" enslaved servants avenged themselves by stealing loaves whenever they could. The boy who swept the kitchen floor probably ate as much white bread as the master of the house.

Some enslaved cooks became celebrities in their own right, including George Washington's chef Hercules and James Hemings, who prepared the most *à la mode* French cuisine for Thomas Jefferson. In the majority of Southern kitchens, however, women were the cooks. They enjoyed high status among the enslaved workers, but this did not necessarily protect them from harsh treatment from their employers. Here's a memory from a Virginia woman who grew up enslaved: "When mother was in pregnant stage, if she happened to burn de bread or biscuits, Missus would order her to the granary, make her take off all her clothes. . . . After she had stripped her stark naked she would beat mother wid a strap. . . . She beat all de slaves cruelly, dat 'hell pigeon' did."[14] Even Hercules and James Hemings, despite all their privileges, did not accept their enslaved status. Much to Washington's consternation, Hercules absconded to Philadelphia and was never seen again, while James Hemings negotiated his freedom from Thomas Jefferson.

The end of the institution of slavery upended the social and economic system of the South. During the Reconstruction era that followed, freed workers could leave their plantations, bargain with potential employers, and vote. In response, Southern plantations adopted a contract labor system under which farm workers (often illiterate) would sign an agreement to till the cotton or tobacco fields from early spring planting season to autumn harvest. The plantation owner would provide the necessary seeds, tools, housing, and food supply for the worker and his family (who were also expected to toil in the fields). In lieu of money, the farm worker would receive a share of the crop as his pay. "Sharecropping" looked like an advancement over slavery, because in theory workers could hire out to whichever plantation paid the most. In reality, it was in many ways worse. The plantation owner was only required to feed his workers for nine months a year. After the bounty of harvest season, the cropper family's food gradually ran out, so by the time of planting they were usually half-starved. And even during the growing season, the "plantation ration" was usually limited to three ingredients: pork fatback, cornmeal, and molasses—known as the "three m" diet ("meat, meal, and molasses"). Owners operated plantation stores selling flour, coffee, lard, and other ingredients, usually on credit. Somehow it was impossible for workers to ever pay off their store debts, so they would have to sign up for another year's contract, again and again. In essence, sharecropping became another form of enslavement.

In 1895 the scientist Wilbur O. Atwater, the founder of nutrition science in the United States, traveled to Tuskegee, Alabama, to study the local diet. Those who lived in the town of Tuskegee consumed adequate amounts of fresh meat, vegetables, eggs, and dairy products;

those who worked on the farms lived on "fat salt pork, cornmeal, and molasses." Most of their cooking was done over open fires:

> The daily fare is prepared in very simple ways. Cornmeal is mixed with water and baked on the flat surface of a hoe or griddle. The salt pork is sliced thin and fried until very brown and much of the grease tried out. Molasses from cane or sorghum is added to the fat, making what is known as "sap," which is eaten with the corn bread. Hot water sweetened with molasses is used as a beverage. This is the bill of fare of most of the cabins on the plantations of the "black belt," three times a day during the year.[15]

If they had any buttermilk, they crumbled dried pone in it and stirred it to make a kind of mush. In the summer they augmented this meager fare with collard and turnip greens cooked in bacon fat and an occasional stewed opossum. Atwater concluded that the "meat, meal, and molasses" regimen gave Black farm workers only a fraction of the protein deemed necessary but too much "fuel" (i.e., fats and carbohydrates). It was decades before scientists fully understood that this diet could cause a deficiency of niacin (vitamin B3) and lead to pellagra and other potentially fatal diseases of malnutrition. Rates of these illnesses among poor Black (and white) people only began to drop during World War II, when the Food and Drug Administration ordered that most commercial cornmeal be fortified with minerals and vitamins, including niacin. By the 1950s pellagra was essentially eliminated from the United States.

Those formerly enslaved who were able to escape from the plantation did not face the same threat from a limited, cornbread-heavy diet. At the end of the Civil War thousands of men, women, and children moved to towns and cities across the South, or made the trek North or West to places with more opportunities. Many found work in domestic service, hotels, and boarding houses as well as in the food trade. Some were able to open their own restaurants and catering businesses. The largest bakery in Jackson, Mississippi, was the Black-owned Risher's, employing a dozen workers. A few of those food professionals began to publish cookbooks as a way of promoting their business. The first to contain cornbread recipes was 1881's *What Mrs. Fisher Knows About Old Southern Cooking*, by Abby Fisher, who is believed to have been born into slavery in Alabama. She moved to San Francisco, where she ran a store selling her prizewinning pickles, sauces, jellies, and preserves. Her cookbook includes a "Plantation Corn Bread or Hoe Cake," presumably as a nod to the Old South, but her other cornbreads emphasize lightness and delicacy. She makes the "Breakfast Corn Bread" with well-cooked rice as well as cornmeal for a soft, smooth loaf. Fisher's recipe for "Corn Egg Bread," also containing baking soda, sour milk, and lard, instructs the reader to "beat eggs very light," producing a fluffy bread more to the taste of her urban market.

Many of the cookbooks that followed also navigated the line between the foods of the plantations (i.e., those prepared by enslaved cooks) and the modern era. A number of the titles published in the first half of the twentieth century featured the recipes of African American cooks, usually called something like "Mammy Lou" or "Aunt Priscilla," but were actually compiled by white authors. *Mammy Lou's Cook Book* (1931), written by Betty Benton Patterson, collected the recipes of "all the negro mammies we known, loved, and lost awhile" for a white audience nostalgic for food before the modern era of "vitamining" and dieting. Its cornbread recipes included hoe cake, corn pone, and crackling bread. In contrast, *Lena Richard's Cook Book* (1939), self-published by a famous New Orleans chef (one of the first to host a television cooking show), highlighted the food that she and her customers preferred to eat. "Lena's Corn Bread" mixed its cornmeal with an equal amount of flour and added two tablespoons of sugar for a touch of sweetness—both ingredients anathema to defenders of traditional Southern skillet cornbread.

African American diners did not forget the cornbread dishes that had sustained their ancestors. In the 1960s and 1970s a new trend of "soul food" cookbooks sought to rescue traditional African American Southern cookery from the "Mammy" tradition. They usually contained recipes for corn pone, ash cakes, and hoe cakes. However, their cornbread recipes reflected more modern tastes, made with wheat flour as well as cornmeal (allowing both white and yellow) and sugar. In her 1989 cookbook *Iron Pots and Wooden Spoons: Africa's Gifts to New World Cooking*, the food historian Jessica B. Harris included what she called "a basic recipe for the purists" with equal amounts yellow cornmeal and flour mixed with sugar, baking powder, salt, milk, egg, and peanut oil. Today, according to culinary historian Michael Twitty, the dish is "the sweet, cakelike cornbread that is everywhere, . . . half flour in form and invitingly golden and paired with jelly, honey, chili or chicken." If you wanted, he writes, you could still make the ash cakes that sustained enslaved workers on the plantation, but it would taste more of ashes than corn:

> It's white cornmeal mixed with water, and (if you are lucky) a pinch of salt, molded into a ball that you press into a cake. Then you find a leaf of the tulip poplar tree (coincidentally also called the "toilet paper tree") or perhaps a large maple, or failing these, a cabbage or collard leaf, and wrap that around and have a fire of embers and coals ready to bake it. Twenty minutes later, or when it's capable of destroying your dental health permanently, presto! You can now enjoy the hardtack of life under King Cotton.[16]

3

WHEAT BREAD

IN MARCH OF 1624 a ship called the *New Netherland* departed from the Amsterdam docks. Commanded by Captain Cornelis May, it carried more than sixty passengers, most of them young couples, French-speaking Walloons from the vicinity of Leyden—the same city where the Puritans had stayed. They were heading for the mouth of what they would name the North River, now known as the Hudson River, situated on the coast of North America between Plymouth Colony and Jamestown. The ship belonged to, and its crew and passengers were employees of, the Dutch West India Company, which had been granted rights to trade in and colonize the region. Unlike the Jamestown settlers and the Pilgrims, these settlers were well prepared to make homes in the New World.

Dutch exploration of the Hudson River began in 1609, when Henry Hudson, under the employ of the rival Dutch East India Company, sailed his ship the *Half Moon* up the river looking for the Northwest Passage to China. He noted the waters full of fish, ample land suitable for cultivation and the diet of the Native Americans: "Their food is Turkish wheat [corn], which they cook by baking, and it is excellent eating."[1] A few years later, a Dutch explorer built a small trading center up the river (at the site of today's Albany) where his employees exchanged European goods for valuable beaver, otter, and other skins. Over the next decade, more than a dozen Dutch ships made their way to this portion of the coast, nearly all of them bringing back lucrative cargoes of furs. Dutch traders built good relations with the various Indigenous tribes they encountered and, in addition to furs, purchased supplies such as venison and corn to sustain themselves. Native Americans taught the traders how to boil coarse cornmeal into a porridge called *sappaen*, also called *sapan* or *samp*, which they preferred doused with good Dutch butter—if they had it.

Like the English settlers in Jamestown and Plymouth, the Dutch intended to consume their accustomed foods in the region they called New Netherland. The Dutch Republic was then one of the richest and most powerful nations in the world, and that wealth was reflected on the table. One of the favorite subjects for that era's Dutch painters was a still-life showing a sumptuous table spread with their favorite foods and drinks: bowls of fruit, plates of glistening oysters, hams with large chunks carved out, meat pies, fried herrings covered with capers, mounds of yellow butter, great discs of Goudas and other cheeses, cracked nuts, shimmering glasses of wine, flagons of beer, and white bread, usually crusty rolls. From the evidence of elegant table linens, silver salt cellars, and fine wine and beer glasses, it is clear that these are the tables of the wealthy (who would have been the intended patrons of the artists). There are far fewer paintings depicting the foods of the less fortunate. From the early sixteenth century the painting *A Poor Man's Meal*, attributed to Hieronymus Francken the Younger, shows a plain wooden table covered with ceramic vessels holding the typical foods of Dutch workers and peasants: some kind of porridge, herring, thick pancakes, a clay flagon of beer, and a big loaf of rye bread.

Figure 5. *The Baker Oostwaard and His Wife*, by Jan Steen, 1658. The boy at lower right blows a horn to signal that the family's loaves are for sale. *Source*: Rijksmuseum, Amsterdam.

Like the English, the Dutch made their breads from white wheat, coarse wheat, and rye flour. Beer was a near-universal drink on Dutch tables, so bakers had ample supplies of brewer's yeast with which to leaven their loaves. Most bread was baked in the ovens of professional bakers. When their loaves were ready, they would open the windows of their shops and blow a cow horn to signal to the neighborhood. Housewives came to buy and also to bring their own doughs to cook in the baker's now-empty oven. A 1658 painting by Jan Steen shows the smiling Leyden baker Arent Oostwaard and his wife displaying their wares, including big round ryes, white bread rolls, decorated breads (probably spiced and slightly sweet), and pretzels, at the door of his shop while a boy blows the horn in the background.

In their New World colony the Dutch would have to toil and sacrifice before they could establish their Dutch way of living and eating. The aim of the Dutch West India Company's 1624 expedition was to enforce its license to trade and colonize the land by planting settlers along the Hudson, Delaware, and Connecticut Rivers. The *New Netherland* entered New York Harbor that May and landed first at Nut Island, now known as Governor's Island. Eight settlers stayed there to assist in trading operations, while the rest were dispersed to build forts inland on the three rivers. They had signed six-year contracts with the Company, their primary task being to expand the fur trade with the Native Americans. However, they were more than indentured servants; they also had the right to hunt, fish, grow their own crops, and trade, but they could only sell their goods to the Company. Until their farms were producing, they were "provided with the necessary supplies and clothes from the Company's storehouses and that at a reasonable price." The following year, three ships arrived in the harbor carrying forty-five more settlers, horses, cattle, hogs, sheep, agricultural implements, and seed. One of the settlers' first tasks was to plant grain, probably mostly wheat with some rye and buckwheat. By August "the grain was nearly as high as a man" and almost ready for harvest.[2] Unlike in Jamestown and Plymouth, in New Netherland at least a few of the settlers soon were able to enjoy loaves of American-grown wheat.

Unfortunately the Dutch were forced to abandon their ambitions for a larger colony. In 1626 their fur traders up the Hudson had inserted themselves into a war between the Mohican and Mohawk tribes, and three Dutchmen were killed. Local Company director Pieter Minuit ordered all inhabitants of the far-flung trading posts to return to New York Harbor. The new plan was to establish a larger Dutch settlement, called New Amsterdam, at the southern tip of Manna-hatta, the large island just to the north of Nut Island. The center of this community was Fort Amsterdam, built at the island's southern tip as protection against Native American raids and attack by competing European powers. Just outside the fort's stockade, they built a shed housing a horse-powered grist mill. The animal would have been tethered to an arm protruding from the top millstone, turning the stone as it walked to grind the grain. Wheat and other grains were grown in fields covering at least 120 acres on the east side of Manhattan in the vicinity of today's East Village and Lower East Side. The grist mill burned in 1628, and the Dutch had to rely on hand-powered querns and even mortar and pestles until it was rebuilt.

The colonists at New Amsterdam did not starve during those first few years. Neither, however, did they enjoy the abundant tables seen in those Dutch still-life paintings. The Rev. Jonas Michaelius, the settlement's ailing and bad-tempered Dutch Reformed minister, complained that he couldn't find horses, cows, or laborers to work his land—and that the prices of milk and butter were so exorbitant that he would be forced to spend the winter without butter! Instead, Michaelius had to rely on "poor and hard rations" from the Company commissary: "this hard fare of beans and gray peas, which are hard enough, barley, stockfish, etc., without much change. . . . The summer yields something, but what is that for any one who does not feel well?"[3] Bread evidently was not on his table. Other settlers enjoyed samp, made from corn either grown by themselves or bought from local Native Americans, but Michaelius never mentions it. He was recalled to the Netherlands as soon as his three-year term was up.

For the first few decades of New Amsterdam's existence, bread baking and flour milling were controlled by the Dutch West India Company. The horse mill was replaced by a Dutch-style windmill situated on the Hudson River just west of the fort where it best could catch the prevailing winds. Numerous period views of the settlement show the windmill standing proud with its four blades. However, the reality was that it was often in disrepair, with two blades in tatters and the other two barely generating enough force to turn the millstone. Anyone could bring their grain to be ground, but the Company always got its wheat ground first because it had many more mouths to feed. By 1633 the Company had moved its bakery out of the fort into its own building just south at the corner of Pearl and State Streets. Back in the Netherlands, most townsfolk bought their bread from a baker rather than make it at home, and it's likely that housewives did the same on Manhattan Island. They prepared such Dutch specialties as pancakes, waffles, and *olie-koecken*—fried balls of dough seasoned with spices and dried fruit, the ancestors of doughnuts. For their bread staple they went to the baker, who would announce its sale by blowing on a cow horn just like in the old country.

In 1639 the Dutch West Indies Company ended its monopoly on the economic life of New Amsterdam and encouraged tradesmen of all kinds, including bakers, to move to the settlement. Its farms were finally producing enough grain to ensure that colonists could enjoy bread year-round and even have a surplus left over to sell to the West Indies. At least four private bakers are mentioned in the records of the 1640s; they not only baked bread but farmed, traded furs and tobacco, and occupied positions in the local government. Before this time there had been no need to regulate bread, because the Company controlled its production. The grumbles began in the fall of 1649, a year when a bad harvest led to low supplies of grain. The bakers, however, still found a way to make money, which the townsfolk discovered by "the meagerness of the coarse bread as well as the underweight of the white bread."

The Council discovered that bakers were selling all their finest white bread to the local Native Americans, because they had acquired a taste for bread and cake made from fine white flour, and because they had the best wampum. While prices in New Amsterdam were noted in stivers, the actual currency was wampum made of white and purple clamshell beads. Native Americans had access to high-quality strung wampum with the more valuable purple beads, while the Dutch only had loose beads frequently mixed with bone, glass, and other detritus. As a result, "the Indians and barbarous natives are furnished with the best in preference to the Christian nation from a desire and inclination for the highest profit." The Council's answer was to bar bakers from selling any fine white bread and instead only produce "common bread" made from pure wheat or pure rye in eight-, four-, and two-pound loaves until conditions improved.[4]

Two years later, further complaints reached the Council "respecting the excessive exaction and usurious profits imposed" by some bakers. In Europe, and particularly the Netherlands, governments had for centuries regulated the price and weight of the bread staple. If the populace could no longer afford bread, the threat of riot was always there, so even the most authoritarian ruler had to respond. In 1651 the Council established the first assize of bread, fixing its price and size: Loaves of coarse wheat and coarse rye should be sold in eight- and four-pound loaves, with the wheat bread fixed at fourteen stivers and the rye twelve stivers (one stiver = one-twentieth of a Dutch guilder). Bread made of fine white flour couldn't cost more than three stivers a pound and had to be sold in one-pound, half-pound, and quarter-pound loaves. The ordinance further noted that bakers were refusing to produce the rye bread eaten by New Amsterdam's poor and threatened them with fines and loss of license if they continued.[5] Bakers frequently complained that the assize made it hard to earn a profit, particularly in years of bad harvest when the price of grain rose; they appealed to the Council to get the price of loaves increased. Determined to make a profit, some unscrupulous bakers also sold on the Sabbath, sold underweight loaves, and added coarse wheat and rye bran "unfit for bread" into their product. The Council eventually hired an inspector to check prices and quality and required all bakeries to stamp each of their loaves so they could identify anyone selling inferior bread.

Despite settlers' industriousness, the New Amsterdam colony did not return as much profit as investors in the Dutch West India Company had hoped. In 1629, Company directors adopted a proposal to increase development in the colony by allowing members to purchase large tracts of land that they could use for farming and trading. The largest of these patroonships, as they were called, was bought by Company director Kiliaen van Rensselaer and comprised 960 square miles of land up the Hudson River around Fort Orange (now Albany, New York). Van Rensselaer was required to purchase the land from the Mohicans and bring in at least fifty settlers to farm, tend cattle, bake bread, trade with the Native Americans, and so forth. The great question was, how to turn a profit? Although van Rensselaer never actually visited the New World, he was in constant mail contact with his agents in New Amsterdam and in Rensselaerwyck, as his patroonship was called. The land along the river had rich soil relatively free of stones and easy access to the Indigenous peoples who trapped beavers. Patroon van Rensselaer determined that the two main commodities produced by his estate would be beaver pelts and wheat.

Wheat grew so plentifully—at least in years when there was no drought or flood—that it replaced wampum as the main currency. Tenant farmers who grew the crop had to pay rent to their patroons in wheat, and the patroons in turn shipped their taxes, in the form of schepels of wheat (one schepel equals about three-quarters of a bushel, or about sixty pounds), down to the governor in New Amsterdam. Most years the farms produced enough wheat so that the patroon could sell the grain to other Dutch settlements or even back in Amsterdam itself. After the English took over New Netherland in 1664, the farmers could market their crops in all the North American colonies and also in the West Indies, where wheat fetched high prices from wealthy sugar plantation owners. In the seventeenth and eighteenth centuries the big Dutch and English landlords who owned vast tracts of Upstate New York were plantation owners in their own right. Far fewer enslaved Africans than in the Caribbean worked their acreage, but they had a similar focus on a monoculture crop that they marketed in any port where they could find buyers. Aside from the weather, disease, and pests, their principal challenge came from competitors who were always trying to take a bite out of their wheat trade.

New York farmers planted two wheat crops—the first in early spring and the second at the end of the summer for harvest just before the first frosts. They also grew rye and buckwheat, but wheat was the big cash crop. It's unclear what variety was the wheat; the original seeds likely came from either Netherlands farms or from the Baltic region where the Dutch bought most of their grain. We also don't know what was the difference between the "summer" and "winter" wheats, except that the winter variety was more valuable: four Dutch shillings a bushel compared to three shillings a bushel for summer wheat. Based on the price difference, it's likely that the winter wheat was more suitable for making the delicate white breads favored by the local elite. The spring wheat may have been better for making coarse wheat breads and ship's biscuit, which was one of the major products of New Amsterdam bakers.

For the first few decades Upstate farmers grew, milled, and packed their own grain for sale down the river and overseas. They imported millstones from Holland, built wind or water mills, and hired professional millers who were paid in wheat. Business remained profitable until 1680, when Governor Andros and the council issued a proclamation that began: "Whereas several Complaints and abuses have been represented and made appear concerning ye Bolting and Packing of flower for Exportacion [*sic*] to ye Great Detriment and hazard of soe Considerable a Pairt of our Trade."[6] As a result of supposedly substandard flour being shipped, Andros and the Council banned all bolting except in the city of New York—as New Amsterdam had been renamed. Bolting is the process of sifting ground wheat through a fine fabric sieve to remove all bran and other coarse bits. This effectively barred Upstate merchants from marketing their own grain abroad. Now they had to sell their wheat and flour to New York City merchants, who were obviously in Andros's good graces. Within months flour became the city's dominant trade. Maria van Rensselaer, daughter-in-law of Kiliaen van Rensselaer, complained to a relative back in Amsterdam: "Much money has been spent on the new mill, as I thought it would produce some revenue, but now bolting is also forbidden, so that I am at a loss to know where a stiver [a Dutch coin] is to come from to be sent over."[7]

Flour milling and packing was so important to city revenue that in 1686 the municipal seal was designed to include four windmill vanes flanked by two flour barrels (and two beavers). Its monopoly lasted until 1694 when Governor Fletcher annulled the act, reportedly after receiving a £400 bribe. The city's economy promptly collapsed as Upstate merchants immediately jumped back into the flour trade, cutting off supply to New York. City leaders appealed to the king, saying that the colony's bread, biscuit, and flour, which had been "high grade and high price," had become "inferior and cheap," but the Crown upheld the order.[8] Nevertheless, city merchants had one advantage over the flour dealers up the Hudson: they had far better connections to the shipping trade and knowledge of market conditions overseas. Within a few years New York had regained its dominance of the flour trade. Merchants sent agents on buying missions to farmers in New Jersey, Maryland, Virginia, and western New York and sold flour in New England, the West Indies, Spain, and Portugal. Unfortunately competitors were emerging in the colonies next door.

On the west side of the Delaware River, the land known as the Pennsylvania Colony proved excellent for growing wheat. Settlers built first windmills and then watermills along the regions many streams and rivers. In 1698 the Welsh Quaker Gabriel Thomas published a "historical and geographical account" of Pennsylvania to attract settlers and attention to the colony. The region's rich soils were planted with grain crops such as wheat, buckwheat, rye, barley, oats, and Indian corn. The wheat, he reported, "is very White and clear from Tares [a noxious weed], making as good and white Bread as any in Europe." Credit for its quality went to a millwright named Peter Deal, or Daile, who built the flour mills: "The Water-mills far exceed those in England, both for quickness and grinding good Meal, their [*sic*] being great choice of good timber, and earlier Corn than in the aforesaid Place, they are made by one Peter Deal, a Famous and Ingenious Workman, especially for inventing such like Inventions."[9]

By 1750 the region on the west side of the Delaware River had become the Thirteen Colonies' largest flour producer and exporter. Nearly every river and creek heading down to the main stream was lined with mills incorporating many labor-saving innovations. Their grindstones could come from local quarries or from near Kingston, New York, but the best were purchased from France. A French traveler reported on the workings of one Pennsylvania mill: "There were three sets of stones destined to the making of flour of degrees of fineness. They employ only the stones of France for the first quality flour. They are exported from Bourdeaux and Rouen. In these mills they have multiplied the machinery, to spare hand-labour in all the operations; such as, hoisting the wheat, cleansing it, raising the flour to the place where it is to be spread, collecting it again into the chamber, where it is to be put in barrels."[10]

The most radical improvements in flour mill design came from the mind of Oliver Evans, one of the greatest inventors in the early United States. He grew up on a farm on Red Clay Creek in northern Delaware, right in the heart of mill country. Evans believed that the traditional method of milling flour entailed too much human effort, too much waste, and too many impurities entering the flour during the process:

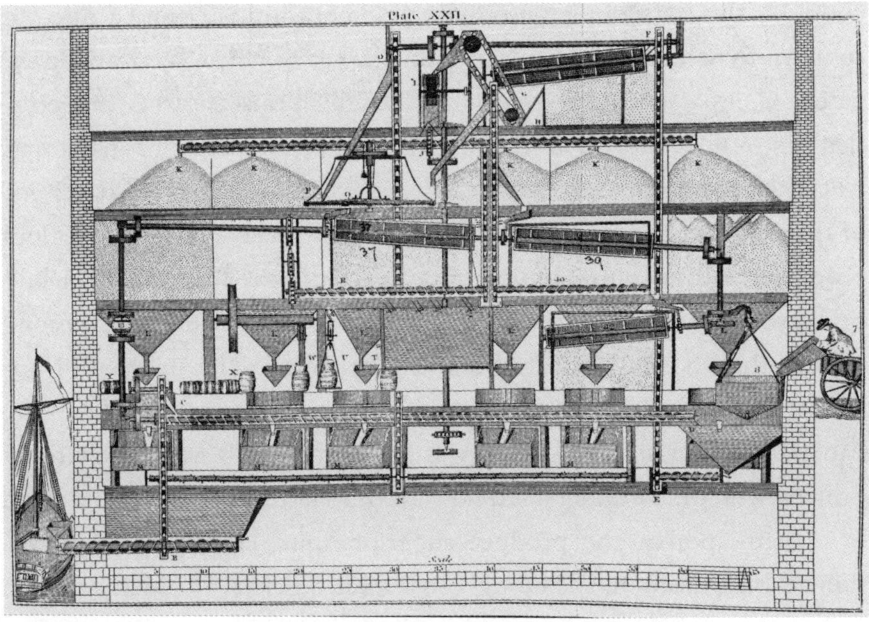

Figure 6. Fully automatic flour mill designed by Oliver Evans. The grain is poured into the mill from a wagon on the right, while the finished flour is loaded onto a boat on the left. *Source*: Oliver Evans, *The Young Mill-Wright and Miller's Guide* (1795).

"which with the great quantity of dirt constantly mixing with the meal from the dirty feet of every one who trampled in it, trailing it over the whole Mill and wasting much, caused great part to be condemned, for people did not even then like to eat dirt, if they could see it."[11] In the 1780s he designed and built the world's first water-powered, fully automatic flour mill that operated without human labor. The heart of this machine was a conveyor belt grain elevator that carried the wheat up to the highest level of the mill. From there the grain passed down through all the stages of processing, each set in motion by a complicated web of leather straps, wheels, and long Archimedean screws carrying the energy from the waterwheel.

Evans publicized his designs through books and broadsides that included elaborate cutaway views of his mill's machinery. In them the only human being visible is a man pouring grain from a wagon down a chute on the outside of the building: "The grain is emptied into the spout A, by which it descends into the garner B; when, by drawing the gate at C, it passes into the elevator CD, which raised it to D, and empties it into the Crane-Spout E, which is so fixed on gudgeons that it may be turned to any surrounding granaries."[12] And so on. At the other end of the mill a boat sits in the river waiting to receive its cargo of flour produced with minimal human intervention. In reality, human laborers were required to fill the sacks and barrels with flour—Evans complained that those workmen were usually drunk. The Evans mill was one of the first applications of the continuous production process in American manufacturing, but it was not immediately adopted by other millers, who didn't understand how all this clattering machinery could save them money and produce superior flour. However, a few far-sighted businessmen, including gentleman farmers Thomas Jefferson and George Washington, saw the advantage and invested in Evans's process. By the early nineteenth century, Evans mills had been constructed across the Middle Atlantic states and also in Europe, transforming the nature of both the flour industry and its principal product.

In the seventeenth century most grist mills had been small and family-run. The grain that went into them was all grown locally, either raised by the miller himself, purchased from nearby farmers, or brought to the mill by neighbors to be ground in return for the miller taking a portion of the flour. As the flour export trade grew, the new class of flour merchants began to purchase grain and flour not just in their immediate neighborhood but wherever they could find cheap supply. They would then take it back to New York, Philadelphia, or Baltimore (which in the early nineteenth century became one of the country's most important milling centers), process it, mix it, and pack it into barrels. Their customers were far away; most of the barrels were intended for the export market. When they were unloaded at the docks, the purchasers frequently discovered that the flour was bad—dirty, pest-ridden, rancid, water-logged, and so forth. In response to complaints, state authorities hired inspectors to make sure that mills kept quality high and demanded that merchants stamp their barrels with identifying marks so they could identify who was selling bad flour. Nevertheless, flour became a commodity, an industrial product that had lost contact with its roots—the field and farmer that had produced it—a trend that only increased after high-volume mills such as Evans's came on line.

Despite the progress of the flour and milling industries, baking remained a craft performed by small tradesmen. Large cities such as New York and Philadelphia—with populations in 1776 of twenty thousand and thirty thousand, respectively—contained a few bigger bakeries producing ship's biscuit, crackers, and loaves for the export trade. Most loaf bread bakers, however, were family businesses with the proprietor living above his shop and ovens. As in European bakeries, the heavy work was performed by journeymen and apprentices. Unlike in England and the Netherlands the bakers were not organized into guilds for mutual aid and political power. From the 1779 assize of bread published by the British military, we know that bakers made long loaves of "sweet flour, of the first quality" as well as round loaves of "inferior quality of merchantable flour."[13] These would have been wheat loaves made from either all-white flour or a mix of whole wheat and perhaps wheat meal. (The 1775 bread assize for Philadelphia covered "white bread," "middling bread," and "rye bread.") Presumably New York bakers also produced varieties of sweet and spiced breads, particularly around the holidays. To enforce the assize, the government appointed an inspector named Balthazar Creamer to make the rounds of the bakeries, check the weight and price of the loaves, and fine any baker who violated the ordinance. Although bakers complained regularly and often loudly about the institution of the assize, the practice continued in New York and other cities well into the nineteenth century.

City homemakers either purchased their bread at the local bakery or made their own—if their homes were large enough to fit an oven.

Country folk had to bake it themselves. This was a formidable task for a housewife. Her usual practice was to bake once a week, making sufficient bread to accompany all of her family's meals. In large households with servants, the cook could bake a dozen hefty loaves a week. Her first task was to have enough liquid leaven on hand. While townsfolk still bought ale barm from the local brewer, it was increasingly common for women to make their own yeast. The crucial ingredients for homemade yeast were water, some kind of starch—flour, potatoes, or sliced pumpkin—and a bit of old yeast that could be used to jump-start the mixture. After the starch was boiled, the mixture was boiled, cooled, and the old yeast was stirred in. In a day or so the new batch began to fizz and was ready to use. If the housewife didn't have any old yeast, she could add sugar to speed up the fermentation using natural yeasts (and stray lactic acid bacteria) found in the air. Here's a typical early nineteenth-century recipe:

TO MAKE YEAST OR BARM WHEN VERY SCARCE

Boil one pint of good flour, and a quarter of a pound of brown sugar, and a little salt, in two gallons of water, for an hour, when milk warm cork it close. It will be fit for use in 24 hours. One pint of this will be sufficient for 18 lbs. of bread.[14]

Another common ingredient in homemade yeast was hop flowers, which were also used as a flavor agent in beer. Hops not only contained a lot of naturally occurring yeast but were less likely to go bad due to chemicals in the plant that retarded microbe growth. The drawback was that hops' bitterness—considered a good quality in beer—also became part of the loaf's flavor profile. After it was ready, the liquid yeast was bottled, corked, and kept in a cool place, such as a cellar in summer, until it was ready for use.

The basic method for preparing household bread was essentially unchanged since the Englishman Gervase Markham gave his recipe for manchet, or white bread, in his 1615 cookbook *The English Hus-wife*.

The central piece of equipment was a large wooden kneading trough (that could be converted into a table by putting boards on top). The housewife, or her servant, would first pour fine-ground white flour into the trough and dig a well in the center for the liquid ingredients. For a large household she would use a bushel, making around fourteen four-pound loaves; a home for four or five people would use half that amount, or twenty-eight pounds of bread a week. Detailed instructions were given in *A New System of Domestic Cookery*, written by the Englishwoman Maria Rundell and published in New York in 1814:

> TO MAKE BREAD
>
> Put half a bushel of good flour into a trough, or kneading tub; mix with it between four and five quarts of warm water, and a pint and a half of good yeast, put it into the flour, and stir it well with your hands till it becomes tough. Let it rise about an hour and twenty minutes, or less if it rises fast; then, before it falls, add four quarts more of warm water, and half a pound of salt, and work it well, and cover it with a cloth. Put the fire then into the oven, and by the time it is warm enough, the dough will be ready. Make the loaves about five pounds each; sweep out the oven very clean and quick, and put in the bread; shut it up close, and two hours and a half will bake it.[15]

The process of making the weekly bread took at least half a day of demanding physical labor. For the young housewife seeking instruction on how to bake for her family, Sarah Josepha Hale gave a frank description of the work entailed, and the benefits:

> Only half or three quarters of an hour, devoted to the kneading of the bread, is wanted in active exertion; and this would be one of the most beneficial exercises our young ladies could practise [*sic*]. The exercise of the hands and arms, in such a way as to strengthen all the muscles of the body, is very seldom practised by ladies; and hence much of the debility and languor they undergo. Many kinds of household labour are unpleasant, because they soil the clothes, or render the hands dark, rough and hard. But bread-making (not the heating and cleaning of the oven) is as neat as

cake-making; and kneading the dough will make the fairest hand fairer and softer, the exercise giving that healthy pink glow to palm and nails which is so beautiful.[16]

Aside from the labor, the other downside to making one's own bread was that the result was often bad, what Hale described as: "the hard, heavy, sour, crude stuff now found under the name of 'family bread.'"[17] The complaint was echoed by numerous early nineteenth-century writers, including this Upstate New York journalist: "We venture the assertion that not one family in twenty, in York State, habitually eat that of a first rate quality." He called for every young woman to learn the science of baking bread "that will not only do one's stomach good, but is fit, also, to feast his eyes."[18]

The causes of bad bread were many, beginning with the leaven. If the liquid yeast was sour, rank, or flat, the bread would have an off taste or simply not rise at all. To "correct" a dough, housewives learned to add a bit of saleratus, which the cookbook author Eliza Leslie reported "will remove the acidity, and rather improve the bread in lightness."[19] Further causes of poor loaves came from issues with the flour, which could be old, musty, bug-infested, or ruined by water. In her manuscript cookbook Arriet Van Rensselaer, direct descendant of Kiliaen Van Rensselaer and mistress of the Cherry Hill mansion in Albany, had a cabinet full of chemicals for dealing with damaged flour and helping the loaf to rise:

> If you are obliged to use grown [spoiled by damp and heat] or damaged flour, to one pound mix in 30 or 40 grains of common carbonate of magnesia, or an equal wt. 30 or 40 grains of common whiting will answer the purpose of correcting the flour grown wheat. If that is not at hand 25 grains of pot or pearl ash [potassium carbonate] or a teaspoon full of strong lye made be used. Musty grain should be washed in boiling water.[20]

Further reasons for bad bread were many, and usually due to the hands of the housewife. The dough could be over-risen or under-risen, the oven could be too hot or too cold, the bread could be burnt or pulled too soon from the oven, and on and on. Unpalatable bread was "extremely unwholesome," according to Leslie, and should never be eaten: "These accidents so frequently happen when bread is made at home by careless, unpracticed or incompetent persons, that families who live in cities or towns will generally risk less and save more, by obtaining their bread from a professional baker."[21]

4

GRAHAM BREAD

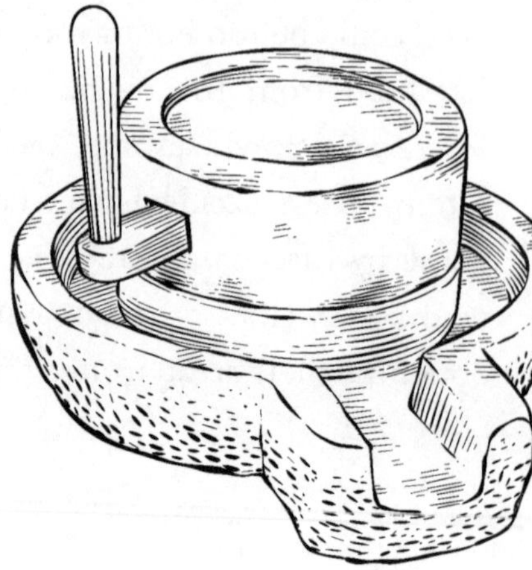

IN 1820 A BOSTON NEWSPAPER published the following extract from a citizen's diary:

> April 5—Got up with increasing stricture over my eyes;—acute pain in the left breast;—sense of weariness;—thought it might be want of food. Breakfasted on strong tea, and dipt toast, and slices of ham. Had the heartburn shockingly;—very uneasy about the breast;—thought I was going to be unwell;—had a great mind to consult a physician;—postpon'd it;—never liked physic, think it don't agreed with me. Had a disagreeable forenoon, business irksome.
>
> Came home to dinner; took a little bitters. Dined upon fried fish, râgout veal, and boiled flour pudding;—avoided all vegetables, but potatoes; drank cider and six glasses of wine. No fruit;—but felt miserably all the afternoon.
>
> Thought I was low spirited, and that if I kept my engagement for the evening, I might be better. I limited myself, at supper, to some fine fat cheese, new bread, and porter. Came

> home no better. Had a most restless night. All the imps of the lower regions seem to have been sent to stare me in the face, the moment I closed my eyes. Began to fear that I have got the *dyspepsia*, and *if* I have, what a villainous disease it is![1]

After three more days enduring debilitating heartburn, stomach pains, flatulence, and nightmares, the diarist finally called in his doctor for confirmation that he was indeed suffering from dyspepsia, the most fashionable disease of early nineteenth-century America.

The dyspepsia epidemic was at its most virulent in the large cities of Philadelphia, New York, and Boston. The *New York Mirror* reported: "The disease called dyspepsia has become so general and obstinate in this city, as to constitute one of the most terrible plagues with which we are afflicted. There is scarcely one in five among persons of sedentary habits, who are not more or less affected by it."[2] Today dyspepsia is defined as chronic stomach upset, most often after eating or drinking, with no obvious cause. Back in the early nineteenth century, those who suffered most from it seemed to be the most idle, such as "those devoted to literary pursuits," including writers and editors. Laborers and farmers and others who lived in the countryside seemed to be immune. Edward Hitchcock, professor of chemistry at Amherst College, wrote an entire book on preventing the disease, calling the epidemic a national crisis: "The premature prostration and early decay of students and professional men in our country, excite a deep interest in the mind of every friend to learning and humanity. Time was, when it was generally thought, that this was but the dismal spectre of melancholy minds: but the fact is no longer doubted. Too many budding hopes have been blasted; too many wrecks are strewed around us, to suffer the reality to be hid any longer."[3]

The question on everyone's minds was how to cure dyspepsia, which seemed to be a particularly stubborn and long-lasting disease. Respected doctors treated their patients with short courses of laxatives and emetics, followed by bloodletting, bowel massage, and doses of chemical tinctures and powders; they also recommended horseback riding and travel. Patent medicine salesmen and other quacks advertised a wide range of pills, panaceas, and elixirs that could alleviate not only dyspepsia but a host of other ailments. Folk remedies also circulated: eating foods such as tomatoes and sandwiches of fat-boiled bacon and drinking water dosed with gin. By about 1830 nearly all studies of the disease seemed to agree that diet was one of the principal causes of dyspepsia and that a change of eating habits could alleviate or even vanquish its symptoms. Hitchcock's rules for a cure included consuming less food at meals, eating less variety of food, vegetarianism, exercise, avoiding all forms of alcohol, and chewing food slowly and deliberately. To replace all that meat, rich gravies, puddings, wine, and brandy, experts recommended a diet based on bread and water. The prescribed bread, however, was not the typical delicate, well-risen white loaf. It was a brown and dense bread made from coarsely ground and unbolted wheat meal and known as "bran bread" or "dyspepsia bread." From 1830 this is a typical recipe:

DYSPEPSIA BREAD

3 quarts unbolted wheat meal, 1 do ["ditto"] soft water, warm, but not hot, 1 gill fresh yeast, 1 do molasses, or not, as may suit the taste, 1 tea spoonful of saleratus.

This will make two loaves, and should remain in the oven at last one hour; and when taken out, placed where they will cool gradually. Dyspepsia crackers can be made with unbolted flour, water, and saleratus, that will be much esteemed, and found very convenient for travelling.[4]

Other recipes for the bread omitted the molasses or added white flour to lighten the loaf.

The purpose of these loaves was to treat "costiveness" (i.e., constipation), which was one of the symptoms of dyspepsia. Intestinal blockage was particularly common among sedentary persons, and most experts agreed that the culprit was white bread: "We have no doubt the princi-

Figure 7. Sylvester Graham, apostle of whole wheat flour. *Source*: Library of Congress.

pal cause of its prevalence is the unwholesome nature of the bread in common use. This, like many other articles of food, has been refined till its nutritious qualities are almost destroyed. For the sake of fineness and whiteness, the coarser, but more nourishing particles, are excluded from its composition: and it is wrought into a tough, dry, and indigestible substance, highly pernicious to the stomach."[5] In dyspepsia breads the coarse grains of bran would have the opposite effect: "It is certain that *bran* has an abstersive [cleansing] virtue: bread therefor which is made of flour not thoroughly cleansed from the bran, *provided it be duly fermented*, seems to be more wholesome, and also more savoury, than that which is made of pure flour."[6] Housewives could make these loaves at home, but in cities they more likely bought them at the local bakery—also purveyor of injurious white breads—usually for the same price as loaves of rye and Rye and Indian.

Hitchcock was just one of the health reformers seeking to save the sedentary portion of the citizenry from the woes of an imbalanced lifestyle. In 1830 a somewhat hapless thirty-four-year-old minister named Sylvester Graham was hired by the Pennsylvania Society for Discouraging the Use of Ardent Spirits. His early life had been marked by tragedy and ill health. His father died when he was two; his mother was declared "in a deranged state of mind." Graham spent most of his childhood bouncing between relatives. Finding refuge in religion, he grew into a pious and priggish young man who shunned liquor and chasing after women and struggled with depression. At age twenty-nine he enrolled in an academy to train as a minister until a nervous breakdown forced him to withdraw. Recovering, Graham roomed with a Rhode Island sea captain's family, whose daughters nursed him back to health and one of whom became his wife. After being tutored by the local pastor, Graham finally earned his license to preach and was hired by a New Jersey church. However, his fervid advocacy of the anti-alcohol cause didn't endear him in the community; he leaped at the job offer from the Pennsylvania Temperance Society. In the summer of 1830, he began to hold temperance meetings around the Philadelphia area and quickly gained a reputation as a thrilling orator, drawing overflow crowds: "The lecture commenced at seven, and continued until half-past ten; during which time the interest of the audience was constantly kept up, and occasionally was excited even to enthusiasm; and when Mr. Graham closed, a unanimous burst of applause broke from the whole audience. . . . His efforts have left an impression on the public mind here, which promises the most auspicious results for the cause of temperance and moral reformation."[7]

Graham was not just speaking about avoiding alcohol when advocating for temperance. For him, intemperance was equivalent to overstimulation, referring to all those practices, both physical and mental, that tended to arouse the mind and body. God, Graham preached, had laid down laws for humankind to follow to achieve health, vigor, and long life. Intemperance violated those laws, inevitably leading to suffering in the form of diseases such as dyspepsia, immorality, and early death. The practices that contributed to physical overstimulation included consuming wine, beer, brandy, coffee, tea, chocolate, tobacco, pepper, oil, vinegar, mustard, horseradish, butter, fat, gravy, meat, fish, and pastry. All of these "unduly stimulate and irritate the nervous system, heat the blood, and early develop a preternatural sensibility and prurience of the genital organs."[8] Other damaging behavior included the "disproportionate exercise of the brain," lack of physical exercise, wearing tight clothing, sleeping on feather beds, hot baths, reading lewd books, obscene conversation, masturbation, and indulging in carnal relations for reasons other than reproduction. All these acts defiled the body, the temple of the soul, causing a "preternatural excitability of the nerves of organic life" and kindling internal fires. Inevitably, Graham believed, the volcano would erupt. To cure this depravity, he preached that following the path of physical reformation via temperance would inevitably lead to moral reformation. The key was a diet based around bread in as close to its "natural state" as possible.

In the first half of the nineteenth century, reformers such as Sylvester Graham believed that the bread eaten by most city dwellers (i.e., bakery-bought bread) was harming its consumers. The problem began with the quality of the flour, which could have been grown as far away as Ohio and transported to the East Coast by boat (via the Erie Canal) or wagon in a journey that likely took weeks. When shipments arrived, flour wholesalers often discovered that the product had been spoiled by water, rot, vermin, and so on. Newspapers regularly carried advertisements for "flour, damaged" being offered at auction. A journalist reported: "Immense quantities of damaged wheat are daily sold—carried to the east and made into flour. Unslaked lime is ground up with it to disguise the smell. Fictitious red brands are put on it, and it turns out the most profitable flour. On this the poor live. What effect will have it on the bowels of the children?"[9]

Like Arriet Van Rensselaer in chapter 3, bakers had a wide array of additives at their disposal that could dilute bad flavors and make loaves white and airier: "potato starch, bean, pea and Indian-corn meal, rye flour, chalk, bone earth (burnt bones), powdered flints, plaster of paris," and so on.[10] Other possible adulterants included alum for whitening flour and blue vitriol (copper sulfate) to help doughs rise. The cookbook writer Sarah Josefa Hale warned of the many deleterious substances that could be lurking in store-bought flour and gave her readers instructions on how to detect them.

In his 1837 book *A Treatise on Bread and Bread-Making*, Graham's argument against public bakers was not just that they tended to use bad flour and chemicals to produce white, puffy, poor-tasting, and unhealthy loaves. He detected a moral element—virtue—in good bread and believed that commercial bakeries could never make the best loaf by the very fact of what they were: "But should the public bakers always use the best of flour, their bread, as a general statement, would still be very inferior to well made domestic bread, in point of sweetness and wholesomeness. Their mode of manufacturing bread—to say the least of it—destroys much of the virtue of the flour or meal; and hence their bread is only palatable."[11] Only a person with a special moral sensibility—and that did not include bakers or even domestic servants—was capable of producing a proper loaf:

> No;—it is the wife, the mother only—she who loves her husband and her children as woman ought to love, and who rightly perceives the relations between the dietetic habits and physical and moral condition of her loved ones, and justly appreciates the importance of good bread to their physical and moral welfare—she alone it is, who will be ever inspired by that cordial and unremitting affection and solicitude which will excite the vigilance, secure the attention, and prompt the action requisite to success, and essen-

> tial to the attainment of that maturity of judgment and skillfulness of operation, which are the indispensable attributes of a perfect bread-maker.[12]

You can hear the cadences of Graham's public oratory in his writing, and his argument about who should make a family's bread impressed his audiences. One journalist commented that this passage combined "in a high degree, homely truth and eloquence."[13]

It's unclear whether Graham ever dug his hands into a trough of dough. We know that his wife made the bread during the family's sojourn in New Jersey, and he also remembered with intense nostalgia the family bread of his first New England home: "There was a natural sweetness and richness in it which made it always desirable; and which we cannot now vividly recollect, without feeling a strong desire to partake again of such bread as our mothers made for us in the days of our childhood."[14] Graham nevertheless had very strong opinions about every stage of the bread-making process, beginning with the ingredients. Although he allowed bread made from rye, corn, barley, and oats, the best and healthiest loaf was made using "unbolted and coarsely ground wheaten meal." This should not be just any wheat but that grown on previously untilled ground, what he called "virgin soil":

> They who have never eaten bread made of wheat, recently produced by a pure virgin soil, have but a very imperfect notion of the deliciousness of good bread; such as is often to be met in the comfortable log houses of our western country. It is probably true that the new soil, in its virgin purity, before it becomes exhausted by tillage, and debauched by the means which man uses to enrich and stimulate it, produces most, if not all kinds of vegetables appropriate for human aliment, in a more perfect and healthy state, than any soil which has been long under cultivation, can be made to do.[15]

Graham claimed that flour raised on fields fertilized with stable manure had a markedly different smell than flour grown in "new and undepraved soil."

Given the dangers of finely ground and bolted commercial flour, Graham recommended that housewives either grow their own wheat or purchase it from a reputable supplier of grains "produced by proper tillage from good soil." They should wash the wheat in two or three rinses of water to remove impurities, dry the grains, and then grind the wheat themselves using a "modern patent hand-mill, constructed after the plan of a coffee-mill." With the flour ready, the next question he considered was whether to leaven the bread or not. Looking back at culinary history, he declared that "the coarse unleavened bread of early times, when of proper age, was one of the least removes from the natural state of food,—one of the simplest and most wholesome forms of artificial preparations . . . and therefore best adapted to sustain the most vigorous and healthy state of the alimentary organs."[16] He nevertheless believed that a leavened loaf could be made "in accordance with the vital laws and interests of our bodies" and also be "light, and sweet, and well baked."[17]

Brewer's yeast, Graham warned, was likely contaminated by the "impure and poisonous substances" with which beer makers adulterated their product. It was far better for a housewife to make her own "good lively sweet yeast, or leaven." He favored a recipe mixing water in which hops had been boiled, enough wheat flour to make a thick batter, and a pint of yeast from the previous batch. Only if the housewife was pressed for time or her yeast turned bad would Graham allow chemical leavening such as saleratus or whiting. After the dough was kneaded, allowed to rise, and baked in the normal manner, the loaves were placed on a "clean and sweet shelf" (any hint of uncleanliness was a sign of "reprehensible carelessness, not to say sluttishness") in the pantry for twenty-four hours before it was ready to cut. It then "becomes perfectly matured, and so changed in character, that it is, if properly made, one of the most wholesome characters entering into the diet of man."[18]

In the summer of 1832, Sylvester Graham's renown extended beyond temperance circles amid the panic that accompanied the first outbreak

Figure 8. "Here is the staff of life!" Satirical engraving of a Sylvester Graham lecture. *Source*: Joel R. Peabody, *World of Wonders* (Robert S. Peabody, 1838).

of cholera in the United States. This disease, which we now know is caused by the bacterium *Vibrio cholerae* (often found in fecally contaminated drinking water), began to sicken and kill city dwellers, particularly poor slum dwellers. The public was desperate for a cure; with typical assurance, Graham claimed he knew the cause. He rejected the widely recommended preventive diet of meat, meat-based soup, wine, and no fruits or vegetables, contending that the answer was "an entire abstinence from flesh-meat and flesh soups, and from all alcoholic and narcotic liquors and substances, and from every kind of purely stimulating substances."[19] Graham gave his "Lecture on Cholera" in New York, Albany, and across southern New England. The origin of the disease, he said, was found not in some external source but in the individual's actions, specifically indulgence in dietary and sexual stimulation. The best deterrent for cholera was shunning doctors' medicines and adopting the Graham System, based on a diet of bran bread and water.

The presumption of Graham's claims outraged the medical profession. A doctor named Caleb Ticknor accused him of "ill-timed money-making quackery" and stated: "If any man, in possession of his health and senses, prefers bread made of unbolted flour to any other, he runs no risk of being injured by indulgence in such a luxury—to the invalid I only have to say, follow the claims of no mountebank, but consult a physician."[20] Another doctor listed multiple cases of men and women who were driven to insanity by following the Graham System. Critics dubbed Sylvester Graham "Bran-Bread Graham," and a New York bakery advertised its Brown Bread, assuring customers that it was not "that dry, insipid, straw-chopped stuff, denominated *Graham Bread*."[21] A supposed seeress named Mrs. Matilda Fox psychically visited a Graham lecture in Boston to give this report:

> After watching the violent, shoulder-dislocating, seesawings of the person whom she verily believed had just escaped from a madhouse, and wondering who he could be, and what he was saying to keep so many lank, pale-faced, toothless old maids fast in the seats three hours at a sitting, with an air of exultation, his light grey eyes protruding like sprouts on a chenango potato, the man in the pulpit finally held up a loaf of bread, which was whirled over and over, that all its surfaces might be seen, with as much activity as a juggler would play with a tumerous ball. With a fixed look of earnestness, a terribleness which nothing but a portrait of his own face can express, the broad top of the loaf was turned to the audience, with an assurance of manner which seemed to say, "Here is the staff of life; here

> is longevity; here are concentrated the laws of vitality; here is anti-indigestion; anti-all things; the elements of famine in the shape of a loaf," and she read the stamped letters on the branny upper crust, as the clear gas-light fell upon it, "Graham.—Admittance four pence!"[22]

One writer even accused Graham and his fellow reformers of trying to ruin Thanksgiving: "It is a matter of duty—nay of piety—to eat their turkeys with joy, and drink their wine with a merry heart. They are commanded to do so—they are commanded by the book of books—and how dare they do otherwise? How dare any man, in face of such authority, quote Graham, or any other of the sour-faced fraternity? How dare they interpose, between the hungry and the smoking sirloin, a loaf of their infernal bran bread?"[23]

Despite the calumny, Graham's true believers remained faithful to the orator. Grahamites in New York and Boston opened boardinghouses where like-minded citizens could enjoy the benefits of their mentor's recommendations about diet, sleeping, bathing, and exercise. One journalist expected to find the boardinghouse filled with skeletal inmates surviving on dry and insipid rations but was pleasantly surprised:

> The first article of food which attracted my attention, was a plate of wheat bread. On tasting it, I found the quality to be excellent. I had eaten what passed for good bread, in the by gone days of *rye and indian*, and what was denominated first rate in this more refined age of wheat flour; but neither of them was to be comparable to this. Here was no smell of that fashionable corrective, saleratus, insinuating itself into the nose like camphor, nor taste of musty yeast, or half neutralized sour milk so offensive to the purified palate; but the real flavor of the wheat, unadulterated by unnatural processes. When received into the mouth, the gustatory powers seemed to greet it with a hearty welcome. . . . The cooking was plain and simple, giving you the natural taste of every article.[24]

Contrary to rumor, the Graham house's boarders "appeared to be in fine health and spirits, except one young man who, I imagined, came there to be cured." The proprietor of the Boston house, David Cambell, also founded *The Graham Journal of Health and Longevity* to propagate the "Graham System of Living," each issue replete with testimonials from Grahamites whose lives had been saved by bran bread and cold baths. When that publication closed, Cambell moved to Oberlin, Ohio, where the country's first coeducational college had been founded. Fearing that the presence of men and women together in classrooms would be overstimulating, Oberlin College's president hired Cambell to oversee the school dining halls and apply Graham's principles to the food. This lasted only a few years until parents complained that their children were starving, forcing Cambell's ouster.

In 1839, Sylvester Graham bought a house in Northampton, Massachusetts, and, tired of the brickbats, jeers, and false accusations he faced in public life, largely retired from the lecture circuit. He occupied himself writing long letters to editors and attending town meetings. Unfortunately he tended to be argumentative and long-winded, making him, an obituary writer later said, "not a popular man in the town which he lived."[25] As Graham entered his fifties, the gastric problems that had plagued him all his life worsened. Clearly failing, he sought the advice of a physician who put him on a diet of meat and wine and administered an opium enema. This treatment apparently had little effect, and Graham died in 1851 at the age of fifty-nine. Graham had expected that after his death his home would become a pilgrimage destination for a thankful, healthful citizenry and that Northampton would erect a monument in his honor. That did not happen—although his house eventually did become an un-Grahamite restaurant called Sylvester's.

After his retirement and death, Sylvester Graham and his precepts were slowly forgotten by the American public. If they heard his name, it was only because it was attached to unbolted "Graham flour," which was used to make "Graham bread" and "Graham muffins." For the small but devoted coterie of American health reformers, however, Sylvester Graham and his principles remained central to their views of how to achieve good health away from the doctrines of conventional medicine. In the second half of the nineteenth century, they followed a hodgepodge of doctrines, including phrenology, herbalism, homeopathy, hydrotherapy, and animal magnetism, aimed at curing their physical and moral afflictions. Whether they believed in the guiding influence of the shape of one's skull or the efficacy of sitz baths, their systems all recommended that practitioners adhere to a vegetarian diet, with bran bread as the staple, washed down with water. Although Graham believed that the best possible bread was made from unbolted and unleavened wheat flour, he had allowed loaves made with yeast or baking soda. The new generation was less tolerant of "deviations from the straight line of physiological health," deciding that all forms of leavening were harmful.

In the first half of the nineteenth century, American bakers were still unclear about what triggered the fermentation of bread dough. The work of Louis Pasteur showing that yeast was a living microorganism that caused ferment in beer and wine would not be published until 1858. Health reformers knew that the fermentation produced alcohol and carbonic acid gas (CO_2) but ascribed it to the same process that caused decay in flesh: "We are aware that the nerves of those who have been affected by leaven may be slightly shocked. Nevertheless, the truth, the whole truth, and nothing but the truth will in the end do us only good. The fact has been long known, that leaven is living rottenness; and that if fermentation should be allowed to proceed, the dough would all be destroyed."[26] Russell T. Trall, a leading practitioner of hydropathy and phrenology, wrote that there existed four types of fermentation: "panary" in bread doughs, "vinous" in fruit juices, "acetous" in doughs that overferment and sour, and finally "putrefactive," when fermentation is allowed to progress too long. For William Alcott, the era's most prominent vegetarian, the problem with leavening was that it "not only induces fermentation, and thus introduces a loss of nutritious substance, but that fermentation is, practically and really, the first stage of decomposition or putrefaction; so that he who eats raised or fermented bread, eats putrefied or rotten bread. At least, it is partly rotten, and can never be so well adapted to the wants or a normal stomach as that which is pure."[27] The answer was unfermented bread.

For Alcott the "true idea of bread" was "coarse or cracked and unbolted meal, formed into a mass of dough by means of water, and immediately baked in loaves of greater or lesser thickness, according to the fancy."[28] The addition of any other ingredient—including salt, baking soda, and milk—was "a departure." Salt made bread hard and less digestible; baking soda was a poison; and the inclusion of milk made a loaf "too nutritious" and thus bad for the stomach. In his vegetarian cookbook Alcott divided breads into three "orders," beginning with the best, or first order:

> BREAD OF THE FIRST ORDER
>
> Take a sufficient quantity of good, recent wheat meal; wet it well, but not too soft, with pure water; form it into thin cakes, and bake it as hard as the teeth will bear. Remember, however, that the saliva aids the teeth greatly, especially when you masticate your food slowly. The cakes should be very thin—the thinner the better. Many, however, prefer them an inch thick, or even more.[29]

Second-order bread was made the same way but from two types of grains. (Normally Alcott was against the mixing of foods in any dish but in this case thought it wouldn't be dangerous.) The third order, which he included even while condemning, covered all loaves raised with chemicals or yeast. Trall called his version of a first-order loaf "Premium Bread": "Mix unbolted wheat-meal (Graham flour) with pure cold water—the colder, the better—to a stiff dough; knead thoroughly for ten or fifteen minutes, or until the dough becomes elastic or spongy, and does not require the bread-board longer to be dusted with flour to prevent sticking as it is rolled out."[30] The dough could then be cut into any shape the housewife preferred and then well baked to produce what some called loaves but others dubbed "Graham crackers."

Health reformers' notions about the evils of fermented bread were adopted to a small extent in the larger culture, as bakeries sprang up offering Graham bread that had been "certified by hundreds of our most prominent physicians." In most major cookbooks, however, Graham loaves were included as just another bread, eaten to treat dyspepsia or constipation. Reformers' ideas were far more influential in circles around the centers of hydropathic and phrenological thought in Upstate New York and New England. James Caleb Jackson operated the "Our Home on the Hillside" hydrotherapy spa in western New York State, feeding his patients food "prepared in obedience to the laws of life and health"—and a Graham flour cereal he had devised called "Granula." One avid reader of Jackson's pamphlets was Ellen G. White, the prophet and founder of Seventh Day Adventism. She had a vision of God's plan for her and her followers: "to come out against intemperance of every kind,—intemperance in working, in eating, in drinking, and in drugging."[31]

White's vision was confirmed after one of her sons contracted pneumonia, and she successfully treated him with hydropathic baths rather than conventional medicine (i.e., "drugging"). The family adopted the Graham System of "plain food, twice a day" and never felt better. White published a series of pamphlets called "Health: or How to Live" that included Adventists' recipe for Graham bread and whole wheat "gems." Cooked in pans that resembled shallow muffin tins, the little loaves called gems were one of the fad foods of health reform world, found on the dining tables of every sanitarium. After White's visit to Our Home on the Hillside, she returned to the Adventist center at Battle Creek, Michigan, determined to build her own sanitarium on the same plan. Called the Western Health Reform Institute, the spa struggled until 1875, when John Harvey Kellogg, one of the few Adventists then with a medical degree, was hired as its manager. Kellogg determined to operate the sanitarium along health reform principles blended with modern medical science. Renamed the Battle Creek Sanitarium, the spa's diet plan wasn't too different from that of a Graham boardinghouse thirty years earlier, only updated with certain technological innovations made by Kellogg and his wife Ella. Like Sylvester Graham, Kellogg believed that bread was the most important food and that "wheat-meal or Graham bread is incomparably sweeter, richer, cheaper, and healthier than that made of the superfine, bolted, impoverished article."[32]

The problem was that unleavened Graham loaves were harder to chew than the raised variety. Although full mastication "insures more thorough mixing with that important digestive agent, saliva," some guests at the sanitarium still complained that it made their teeth hurt. Copying James Caleb Jackson, the Kelloggs invented a line of grain "health foods" that were easy to eat, including Graham crackers and a new cereal called "Granola." (Jackson sued for copyright infringement but lost.) By 1890, Kellogg had incorporated the Battle Creek Sanitarium Health Food Company to manufacture and sell these substitutes for Graham bread in grocery stores nationwide.

Kellogg's cracker business caught the attention of a sprawling new baking conglomerate called the National Biscuit Company. In 1898 the giant ovens of its factories began to produce a new Graham cracker that was "so different from the common Graham crackers you buy in a paper bag. Different in baking—different in flavor—different in packing. Made of the purest Graham flour, baked in a manner only the National Biscuit Company knows."[33] It was also "entirely different from the old coarse kind made by Dr. Graham." Nabisco Graham Crackers were made from unbolted wheat flour and water but also white flour, wheat meal, lard, sugar, molasses, salt, baking soda, ammonium bicarbonate, and malt powder. Advertised as "sanitary," they were never touched human hands from the time they left the oven until they were wrapped in their "In-Er-Seal Patent Package." The company advised consumers to "keep Graham crackers on the table as well as bread and the staff of life can be eaten in either form that particularly appeals to taste."[34] More than sixty years after Sylvester Graham issued his plea for homemade bread made with unbolted wheat flour grown on virgin soils, his life-giving loaf had been transformed into an industrial product manufactured in some of the largest bakeries developed to date.

During the twentieth century a small but devoted band of health food advocates managed to keep the Graham flame alive. I go more deeply into this, and particularly the blossoming of the whole grain bread movement during the 1960s and 1970s, in chapter 12 on "hippie bread." More recently, a number of bakeries across the country have attempted to adapt the Graham ethos to modern culinary trends by making a whole wheat bread called the "Approachable Loaf." The concept came from Dr. Stephen Jones, director of the Bread Lab at Washington State University. He wanted to make a 100 percent whole wheat loaf that was both healthy and looked and tasted like something the average American would eat. In other words it had to be soft, presliced, inexpensive, and come in a plastic bag just like the loaves in the supermarket. The only other requirements were that it could contain no more than seven ingredients, none of them "nonfood," and that it retail for less than six dollars. The recipe below for the Approachable Loaf, making two loaves, was formulated by Jeff Yankellow of King Arthur Flour:

APPROACHABLE LOAF

773 grams unsifted (whole wheat) flour

710 grams water

45 grams honey

45 grams oil

7 grams instant yeast

273 grams sourdough starter

20 grams salt

In a medium-sized bowl, gently hand mix flour, water, honey, and oil. (You may find it easier to whisk together water, honey, and oil before adding liquids to the flour.) Cover and let sit 30–40 minutes. Add instant yeast

> and starter to the flour mixture. Now, use your hands to work the mixture until yeast and starter are well incorporated into the dough. Add salt. Continue to hand work the dough until it is formed into a smooth and cohesive mass. This can be done in the bowl or by removing the dough from the bowl and working on a flat surface or countertop. Place the dough back into the bowl, cover, and let sit for 45 minutes. Fold the dough. Cover and let sit for another 45 minutes. Now cut the dough in half and use the dough knife to pre-shape on a flat surface. Oil two loaf pans. Let sit 30–40 minutes. Shape and place in dough pan. Now, proof at room temperature until dough rises to the edge of the loaf pan (usually about 1 1/2 to 2 1/2 hours). Preheat oven to 425°F. Load and turn oven down to 375°F. Bake for 45 minutes.[35]

The honey gives it the slight sweetness favored by American palates; the oil softens the crumb; and the sourdough levain helps temper the whole wheat flavor. By 2020 dozens of bakeries across the country were selling their own versions of the Approachable Loaf, a small beachhead against the wall of industrial loaves sold in every supermarket.

5

SOURDOUGH BREAD

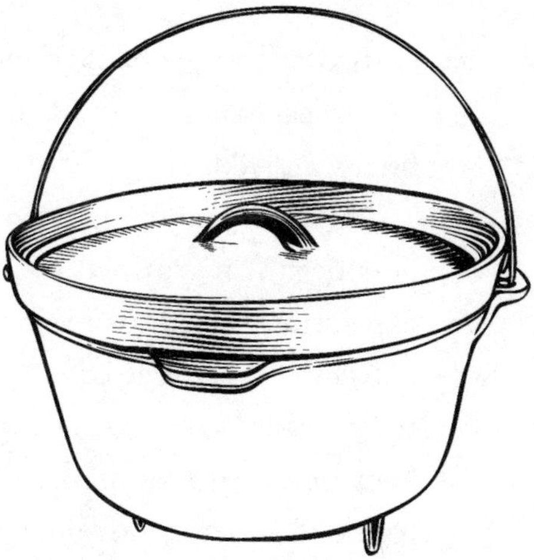

AFTER THE END OF THE AMERICAN REVOLUTION the citizens of the United States embarked on a second period of exploration and colonization. They headed west from the Atlantic Coast, first winding through the steep hills of the Appalachians and following the rivers that eventually found outlet in the Mississippi River, the nation's western border. All of this land was territory of various Indigenous tribes. Like the first English and Dutch colonists, settlers faced the challenge of maintaining their old way of life, including foodways, while living days or weeks from the nearest town. They found that the most practical way to sustain themselves was by following the "hog and hominy" diet of the earliest colonial era: cornmeal mush and pone and pork (mostly in the form of bacon), supplemented by wild game such as deer and turkeys. Wheat bread was a luxury. Unlike corn, wheat required properly tilled fields to produce an adequate crop, and then there was the knotty problem of leavening the bread, particularly in the harsh environment of the frontier. When they could finally eat wheat bread every day, they knew that "civilization" had finally arrived.

The most ambitious attempt to forge a path into the western wilderness began in 1803, led by US Army Captain Meriwether Lewis. His expedition would, in its own way, be as daring as the voyage of the *Mayflower.* That year United States had acquired a huge tract of territory from France comprising more than five hundred million acres from New Orleans to Montana. The Louisiana Purchase was one step closer to President Jefferson's goal of extending the United States to the Pacific Ocean and transforming North American into one vast "Empire of Liberty." First, however, Jefferson had to find out if it was even possible to travel overland or, even better, by some water route from the Mississippi River to the Pacific. To lead this expedition, Jefferson chose Meriwether Lewis, a dashing young army officer who knew the frontier well and happened to be Jefferson's private secretary. Lewis asked William Clark, who had served under him, to be co-leader, and the two began procuring the necessary equipment and provisions to support a party of about forty men on a two-year journey into the wilderness. They knew that their biggest challenge was obtaining food, including bread, that could sustain them as they traveled into unknown lands.

Along the way Lewis and Clark expected to hunt game for food and barter with any tribes they met for corn, meat, fish, and so on. However, they also wanted to bring along as much of their accustomed rations as they could carry. Saint Louis grocers were used to outfitting trapping parties and were happy to supply this large expedition flush with federal funds. Lewis and Clark purchased more than eight tons of food and alcohol: salt, sugar, coffee, peas, beans, lard, salt pork, "grees" (probably buffalo tallow), whiskey, and "portable soup" (made from stock that had been boiled down into hard gelatin and then dried). More than five tons of that weight was made up of wheat flour, corn, and "biscuit" (i.e., hardtack). The provisions were packed into wooden barrels that were loaded onto three boats that they had built for the trip—a fifty-five-foot keelboat and two long rowboats called pirogues. On May 21 the party, dubbed the Corps of Discovery Expedition, set out up the Missouri River on its four-thousand-mile journey to the Pacific Coast.

To simplify work, Lewis and Clark divided their men into three squads or "messes" that would share living and eating. Sergeant Ordway, the expedition's quartermaster, distributed rations to each mess on a three-day rotation: "The day after tomorrow lyed corn [hominy] and grece [bear tallow] will be issued to the party, the next day poark and flour, and the day following indian meal and poark; and in conformity to that ratiene provisions will be continue to be issued to untill further orders."[1] From the cornmeal they probably made pone, and they also learned from Native American tribes how to mix ground meal with wild berries and fat to make a kind of pemmican. It was much more problematic to produce risen bread. The expedition journals make no mention of leavens such as baking soda or yeast. Unfortunately the flour ran out halfway through the expedition, so the only "bread" that they ate for many months was made from either Indian corn or wild roots that had been pounded and dried into a kind of flour. Secretly their interpreter, Sacagawea, stashed a last chunk of wheat bread in her belongings and one day generously offered it to Clark: "The Squar [Sacagawea] gave me a piece of bread made of flour that she had reserved for her child and carefully kept untill this time, which has unfortunately got wet, and a little sour—this bread I eate with great satisfaction, it being the only mouthfull I had tasted for several months past."[2]

Lewis and Clark returned to Washington, DC, with botanical and zoological specimens, Indigenous artifacts, and journals that documented every stage of the journey to the Pacific and back. Nevertheless, their two-year trek did not lead to an immediate rush of settlers to the Far West. To Jefferson's dismay, the Corps of Discovery had found that there was no water route that crossed the continent. Instead, they had to climb over forbidding mountains through territory that was still firmly in control of Native American tribes. For the next three decades those settlers brave enough to head west from the original Thirteen Colonies found huge tracts of good farmland far closer in Ohio, Indiana, Illinois, and Kentucky. Wherever they could, they planted wheat, a grain crop that boomed after the opening of the Erie Canal in the 1820s. The settlers pushed further west, first into Missouri, Iowa, Wisconsin, and Minnesota, and then, in the 1840s, all the way to Oregon and California. As they traveled, they carried wheat flour to make into their daily bread.

The settlers that followed Lewis and Clark found various means to solve the problem of leavening their breads. The usual method of making liquid yeast out of potatoes, flour, or hops apparently didn't work in the extremes of heat and cold faced by travelers on the trail. Luckily the women who grew up on the frontier were nothing if not ingenious. During the late eighteenth century, rural housewives in central Appalachia had invented a method of leavening bread called "salt-rising." Using only flour, water, baking soda or saleratus, and heat, they could make delicious bread while enduring the rugged trail west. In 1839 nineteen-year-old Keturah Penton Belknap and her husband packed their possessions into a covered wagon and departed their Ohio farm: "We had heard of the prairie land of Illinois but we had never seen anything but heavy timber land so we set our face westward." Every night she made their meal by the side of the wagon using a Dutch oven and a skillet. When the remnants were cleaned up, she started the bread for the following day: "When I made bread I made 'salt raising.' When we camped I made rising and set it on the warm ground and it would be up about midnight. I'd get up and put it to sponge and in the morning the first thing I did was to mix the dough and put it in the oven and by time we had breakfast it would be ready to bake. . . . By the time I got things washed up and packed up and the horses were ready the bread would be done and we would go on our way rejoicing."[3]

Salt-rising was probably invented out of some measure of desperation. Somehow, frontier women discovered that starters left too close to the fire for too long would begin to foam and release a strong aroma. It has been called putrid and likened to, among other things, rank sneakers and dirty diapers. (One baker claimed that the worse the starter smells, the better the bread tastes.) Maybe a woman in city or town would simply have thrown away the starter and started again. Yet frontier women discovered that if you mixed that starter into a dough with flour and salt and baked it, it would turn into a fine-grained loaf with a distinct—but not disagreeable—cheesy flavor. The activating agents in salt-rising bread are bacteria of the Clostridium family, particularly *Clostridium perfringens*, along with some lactic acid bacteria. Occurring naturally in the environment, *C. perfringens* thrives in flour-and-water solutions heated for a few hours to between 104 and 110 degrees. Unlike CO2-producing yeast and sourdough starters, this bacteria primarily generates (smelly) hydrogen gas. Many Clostridium species, such as *C. difficile*, can be pathogenic to humans. However, scientists believe that baking kills the bacteria—and in any case there have been no reports of illness after eating salt-rising bread. The disadvantage of salt rising is that the starters are finicky and frequently refuse to "take." The advantage is that it's a one-stage, overnight process—perfect for families like Keturah Belknap's that were on the trail west.

At first the method for making salt-rising bread was undoubtedly transmitted orally, from mother to daughter. It's not known when the name "salt-rising" (also "salt-raisin" and "salt-risin'") was attached to it, but this 1789 recipe makes the loaf in all but name:

TO MAKE EXCELLENT BREAD WITHOUT YEAST

Scald about a double-handful of Indian meal, into which put a little salt, and as much cold water as will make it rather warmer than new milk; then stir in wheat flour, till it is as thick as family pudding, and set it down by the fire to rise. In about half an hour, it generally grows thin; you may sprinkle a little fresh flour on the top, and mind to turn the pot round, that it may not bake to the side of it. In three or four hours, if you mind the above directions, it will rise and ferment as if you had set it with top yeast; when it does make it up in a soft dough; flour a pan, put in your bread, set it before the fire, covered up, turn it around to make it equally warm, and in about half an hour it will be light enough to bake. It suits best to bake at home in a Dutch oven, as it should be put into the oven as soon as it is light.[4]

This recipe was reprinted frequently (and without attribution) over the next half century, most notably in Lydia Maria Child's *The American Frugal Housewife*. Many salt-rising recipes begin with a cornmeal-flour-water starter. However, some housewives had better luck with adding milk.

HOW TO MAKE HOME-MADE BREAD

Take half a pint of new milk; add one teaspoonful of salt; pour on one pint boiling water; when cold, so as not to scald, stir in flour enough to make a batter; set the vessel in a kettle of blood-warm water until it rises well, which should be in about five hours. When the rising has come, warm enough water, or milk (which is better), to make up the dough; add to the water or milk a teaspoonful of soda; then make up the dough—working it well; put into the pan, keep warm until the loaf is up, then bake about one hour. This quantity of milk, salt and soda should make three or four common sized loaves of bread.[5]

Salt-rising breads never caught on in the cities along the East Coast; they were a staple of families living on inland farms and in small towns. In the second half of the nineteenth century, nearly every local fair from West Virginia to Oregon and California had a category for "best salt-rising bread." In 1889 the judge's decision at the West Union, Ohio, fair to award the blue ribbon to one entry was so controversial that it caused fights and shouts that the judge "did not know anything about bread, no how."[6]

In the mid-1840s the small stream of settlers heading to the Pacific turned into a river as wagon routes were opened from the Missouri River to Oregon and then to California. Travelers started their journey at one of several towns along the Missouri River, where provision merchants and trail bosses made big business out of gathering and outfitting the wagon caravans heading west. They could also buy guidebooks for migrants that gave detailed lists of what to bring on the four-month-long journey: "The following is deemed requisite, viz.: 150 lbs of flour, or its equivalent in hard bread; 25 lbs of bacon or pork, and enough fresh beef to be driven on the hoof to make up the meat component of the ration; 15 lbs of coffee, and 25 lbs of sugar; also a quantity of saleratus or yeast powders for making bread and salt and pepper."[7] That was enough to feed one man for the trip, a diet supplemented with wild game and whatever could be bought or bartered for along the way. Wheat flour made up the largest portion of the provisions, because "good bread is the most important and best food to be had on the journey"—if travelers knew how to make it: "That made by most of the emigrants was a vile compound of bad flour, hog grease, and saleratus. Such bread, with the free use of bacon and the neglect of the bath, produced camp-fever. Every person who starts on this journey should know how to make good bread. It should not contain a particle of grease—it should be mixed with its own leaven or yeast cake, and well kneaded. It is quickly baked in thin loaves, or in the form of biscuit, in a portable sheet iron bake-pan."[8]

The "yeast cake" mentioned above was made from monocalcium phosphate (an acid) and sodium bicarbonate (an alkali) and sold as a leavening agent similar to baking powder. However, saleratus was far more commonly used by wagon train cooks. The chemical's great advantage was that it was quick-acting. Women merely had to mix it with flour and water, shape the dough into biscuits, rolls, or small loaves, put them into a Dutch oven to rise, and then plop it down directly on the coals. Within half an hour or so, the family would have bread. If their supply of saleratus ran out, they could replenish the mineral at various natural outcroppings found along the trail. The most famous of these was at the famous Soda Springs along the Bear River in southern Idaho. In 1838, Sarah White was part of a missionary wagon train that arrived at these springs: "The water is bubbling & foaming like boiling water. . . . We find it excellent for making bread, no preparation of the water is necessary, take it from the fountain & the bread is as light as any prepared with yeast."[9] Nearby were dry ponds thick with saleratus sediment that travelers could collect for the journey onward. However, there were drawbacks to breads made with saleratus—that is, their look, smell, and flavor. As the cookbook writer Mrs. Cornelius delicately put it: "There are tables where the effluvia of this article, and the deep yellow color of the bread, offend the senses before it is tasted."[10] The loaves may have been light and airy, but they tasted bitter. When settlers arrived at their ultimate destination along the Pacific coast, it was a relief to have the time and ingredients to make yeast bread again.

Around the mid-nineteenth century, American colonists in the West found a use for a leavening method long known by bakers but until then rarely used. In his 1836 guide to trades and professions, Edward Hazen wrote that bakeries used three methods of making bread: "1st. by mixing meal, or flour, with water, or with water and milk; 2d. by adding to the foregoing materials a small quantity of sour dough, or leaven, to serve as a fermenting agent; and, 3d. by using yeast, to produce the same general effect."[11] In England and on the Continent the sourdough method was commonly used by bakers; in Central Europe and Scandinavia the vast majority of breads were sourdoughs. The English writer Maria Rundell believed that "bread made with leaven is preferable for general use to that made with yeast, for the sour quality of leaven is more agreeable to the ferment of the stomach than yeast, is easier of digestion, and more cleansing."[12]

Most American cookbook writers disputed that assertion, maintaining that the best loaf is "light and sweet" and that sourness indicates that bread is "injured," indigestible, and disagreeable. If they mentioned sourdough, it was as a condition to be corrected, usually by adding baking soda, rather than a desirable breadmaking process. In rural parts of the country, however, sourdough was one more leavening process, like salt-rising, that housewives used instead of liquid yeast or chemicals. The scientist William Henry Brewer was born and raised in Upstate New York and gave a description of baking during his youth in his 1880 book *Fermentation in Its Household Relations*:

> If dough is allowed to stand, in a longer or shorter time it begins to ferment, and after an uncertain length of time sours without the use of yeast. This sour dough is called *leaven*, which added to fresh dough starts that into fermentation; and this was the method used from the earliest time down to the last, and even extensively into the present century. . . . Families still resort to it in back settlements where there is difficulty getting yeast. . . . I remember, when a very small lad, it was used in some families in a pioneer population, but now the method has so completely passed away, in making bread, that many of the younger generation have never seen it.[13]

In 1896 a newspaper reported that descendants of a Pennsylvania farmer named McThomas had been using the same starter for 103 years: "On the morning of March 17, 1792, the wife of McThomas prepared a jar of 'rising,' or as it is better known among housewives, 'emptings.' This she used for a decade or more, adding thereto at each baking."[14] From her it passed down through the women in the family until a century later it was being used regularly by the great-granddaughter of Farmer McThomas. Most sourdoughs were kept in ceramic jars, which were easily transportable if the family ever decided to join the westward migration.

In January 1848 the trickle of travelers to the Pacific Coast turned to a flood after a workman for John Sutter discovered gold in the hills east of Sacramento. Four months later, California officially became

United States territory, ceded by Mexico at the end of the Mexican-American War. By August, eastern newspapers blared headlines like "Gold Fever in California" and reported that miners could pan a hundred dollars' worth of gold a day from rivers near Sutter's Mill. The California Gold Rush set off a stampede of adventurers, nicknamed Forty-niners, from all over the world heading to the diggings. Those who could afford the passage embarked on crowded ships that sailed for San Francisco; the rest headed to Missouri, where they could find space on the wagon trains. When they finally arrived in California, they found that the frenzy for gold had sent prices soaring, so that in San Francisco a barrel of flour (imported from Chile) cost $50 and a pair of boots $16. One restaurant listed a plate of bread and butter at $1.50 and found eager buyers. Undeterred, the Forty-niners bought all the supplies they could afford and headed into the hills intending to make their fortunes.

When miners arrived at the diggings, they were so intent on gold that they ignored creature comforts. They lived on hardtack for bread, "slapjacks" made from flour, grease, and water, and pork and coffee. However, the longer they stayed up at the diggings, the more they missed their old standard of living, particularly regarding food. In their old lives their meals had been prepared by mothers, sisters, or wives, but now they were thrown back upon their own devices and craving real bread:

> We now determined to follow the example of all around us, and, like good housewives, bake our own bread. Our first experiments were not very encouraging. The saleratus and citric acid we used instead of yeast produced but a slight effervescence, and our loaves were nowise remarkable for lightness. . . . But in process of time we abandoned this imperfect method, and first allowing our dough to sour, neutralized the acid with a due proportion of saleratus, and thus succeeded in producing loaves which, as Dr. B. pertinently remarked, may have been surpassed but never been equaled.[15]

Figure 9. Cowboys eat at the chuckwagon, Texas, 1900. *Source*: Library of Congress.

In the early days of the Western gold rush, miners raised their doughs with saleratus or baking soda, but these chemicals were expensive and rumored to be unhealthy. They soon learned to appreciate the natural flavor of sourdough bread, a taste they carried with them as further mines were opened in territories such as Colorado, Nevada, Idaho, and Montana.

All across the West, people found that sourdough bread was a perfect food for lives on the move. Oliver Nelson was an Indiana farm boy who journeyed to Kansas to make his fortune in the cattle business. He decided to start the trade as a camp cook, learning the rudiments on a small ranch: "We had breakfast at daybreak: coffee, sow bosom, sour dough bread minus soda, flour gravy, and sorghum. Sour dough is made by mixing flour and water, and letting it stand until it ferments; or one can start with yeast—it's not needed but it starts quicker. Use half the batter to make your biscuits; then refill the container with water and flour, add sugar if you like, mix well, and let stand for next time."[16] The cowboys that Nelson fed were always in motion, either on their home ranges or driving herds of cattle north to the nearest railheads in Missouri. The ranch cook followed the herd in a mobile kitchen called a chuckwagon containing all the supplies that he would need to make the cowhands' meals. Sacks of flour were carried on the bed of the wagon; on its back was the "chuck box" in which were stored salt, coffee, beans, sugar, and so on. The cook's most precious possession was his sourdough starter, usually contained in a five-gallon keg. On cold nights he wrapped it in a blanket and slept with it to keep it warm. From the outside it was not the most attractive object: "No matter how particular its cleaning at the start, only a few weeks passed before the inside was coated with an inch or so of hardened dough and the outside streaked and spattered with dry batter. This caused the keg to look anything but sanitary, but most cooks claimed that this coating made the sourdough better."[17]

Cattle ranch cooks usually began their day when the sky was still black outside. Their first task was to mix the dough:

> The cook poured flour into a large pan until it was about two-thirds full, made a deep impression in the center, and poured in the proper amount of sourdough batter. Added to this was a teaspoon of soda dissolved in a little warm water. A small amount of salt and lard was next. Bacon grease could be used with equal success. Some cooks added a little sugar to make a browner crust. As he stirred this batter, the cook gradually worked the dry flour from the sides, being careful that the soda and shortening were distributed thoroughly. As soon as all was worked into a mass of dough, he drenched his work table with flour and proceeded to knead the batch until it was thoroughly mixed.[18]

"Cookie" also had to start a fire on which he would cook the beans, bacon, and coffee for the cowboys' breakfast. When he had a good bed of coals, he would swirl some grease around in his Dutch oven and form the dough into rolls or loaves that fit into the bottom of the pot. He would place it near the fire to rise for half an hour or so; he then put it onto the coals and piled more coals on the Dutch oven's lid. When the top of the bread was browned, it was pulled off the fire, tipped out of the Dutch oven, and distributed on the plates. If there wasn't time to prepare bread, Cookie could also use the starter to make flapjacks that he'd serve with sorghum syrup.

As the West was settled, the sourdough tradition slowly dwindled, replaced by the yeast, Graham, brown, and corn loaves of civilized society—what cowboys scorned as light and insipid "women's bread." The exception was the far Northwest—the "last" frontier. In 1896 prospectors discovered gold along the Klondike River in Canada's Yukon Territory. This sent off a gold rush in the Yukon and Alaska rivalling 1849. This time, however, the motherlode was far more remote than in California. Each prospector was required to carry in a year's worth of supplies, including four hundred pounds of flour per person. Due to the rugged terrain and frigid climate, the only way to traverse most of the route was on foot. Once again, the men were so intent on gold that they couldn't be bothered to worry about the quality of their food. One of them was a young Jack London, who reported: "'Just so long as it's grub,' they say, coming in off the trail, gaunt and ravenous, 'grub, and piping hot.'" Sourdough bread was again the miners' staple:

> The pride of the Klondike cook in his bread is something which passes understanding. The highest commendatory degree which can be passed upon a man in that country, and the one which distinguishes him from a tenderfoot, is that of being a "sour-dough boy." Never was a college graduate prouder of his "sheepskin" than the old-timer of his appellation. There is a certain distinction about it, from which the new-comer is invidiously excluded. A tenderfoot with his baking-powder is an inferior creature, a freshman; but a sour-dough is a man of stability, a post-graduate in that art of arts—bread-making.[19]

This designation became formalized, so that recent arrivals to Alaska were called "Cheechakos" (from Chinook Jargon), but if you lived there more than a year, you became a real Alaskan, proudly bearing the title "Sourdough."

Many of the big Yukon and Alaskan gold mines were tapped out by 1910, after which the crowds of miners evaporated. Those that stayed retained the tradition of hanging a crock of sourdough starter by the fireplace to keep it warm. Part of this was tradition, but it was also due to the fact that Alaska remained a frontier territory well into the twentieth century. Supplies only arrived irregularly and were expensive. It made more sense to use the familiar sourdough starter than rely on store-bought soda, baking powder, or yeast. This 1947 recipe gave instructions for both in town and in the bush.

HOW TO START A SOURDOUGH POT

Take a gallon crock or cookie jar and put in

2 cups flour

1 teaspoon salt

3 tablespoons sugar

1/2 teaspoon yeast (Use Maca dry yeast or Fleischmann's dry)

2 cups lukewarm water

Stir till mixture is a thin smooth paste. Put on a lid and set in a warm place to sour. Stir it several times a day. In two or three days your sourdough will be ready. If you are out in "The Woods" and have no yeast add four tablespoons sugar and one 1/2 tsp. salt to the start and it will sour the same, only it takes about five days.

Once the sourdough began bubbling, you could make the bread:

1 quart sourdough

1 quart lukewarm water

3/4 cup or 1 cup sugar (if you like sweeter bread use 1 cup sugar)

2 tablespoons salt

6 tablespoons shortening

12 cups of flour

Mix in the order given, adding flour last, using enough of the flour to make dough that can be handled; knead until smooth and elastic. Place in greased bowl and let rise. It will take longer than yeast bread. Knead it down and let it rise again. Mold into loaves and let rise and bake like ordinary bread. It is not a real light bread but good for a change. Makes four loaves of bread.[20]

For outsiders Alaska's sourdough habit was one of the territory's quaint customs, a relic of a past, more colorful age. At the 1934 Chicago World's Fair, a star attraction of the Alaska exhibit was a champion "dog-musher" named "Slim" Williams, who told a reporter: "Sure, I make sour-dough bread when I'm out on the trail but I make yeast bread when I'm at home. . . . And sour-dough hot cakes are a regular thing with me. Baking powder gets wet, you see, so we make sourdough. You start it with yeast and it hangs in a wooden kettle. Some men have kept sour-dough for 10 years. When traveling, you just mix up a little hard ball of it the size of your thumb and take that along."[21] In an era when most people bought their sanitary, presliced, paper-wrapped loaves at the grocery store, Slim's bread-baking routine seemed almost primitive.

American cookbooks of the mid-twentieth century emphasized speed and convenience in their bread recipes. Sourdough was not in their repertoire. Nevertheless, in 1953 an Alaska businessmen sensed a market for "authentic" Alaskan sourdough starter in the Lower 48. Jack Mabee had obtained some fifty-year-old starter that he figured out how to dehydrate and turn into a powder. He took out ads promising "1,000,000 Flapjacks! For $1.00 By Using ALASKA SOURDOUGH STARTER."[22] Lured by Mabee's canny marketing, people from around the country were soon sending their dollars to P.O. Box 667, Fairbanks,

Alaska, in return for packets of "Sourdough Jack's" starter. He barnstormed around the country appearing at dinners in a big fur coat and hat to prepare his famous flapjacks and hawk his sourdough. Mabee also wrote a series of sourdough cookbooks, some of which were sold with packets of dehydrated Alaska sourdough attached. Competing Alaska cookbook writers condemned him as a sourdough "huckster," but Mabee laughed all the way to the bank.

6

VIENNA BREAD

THE LATE NINETEENTH CENTURY was the era of world's fairs, when nations were eager to display their agricultural, technological and artistic achievements for a global audience. They participated not just out of pride but to drum up trade for their leading industries, many of which went to huge expense to present everything from delicate jewelry to entire train engines for potential customers. In 1873 it was the turn of Vienna, the seat of Franz Joseph I, Emperor of the Austro-Hungarian Monarchy. Centered on its two-thousand-foot long Industrial Hall, with its enormous Rotunda in the middle, the Vienna International Exposition drew more than seven million visitors, including tourists, locals, and representatives of nations eager to learn from the latest advances in technology. The United States had been preparing for this event for two years. The administration of President Ulysses S. Grant wanted to boost American industries and gain insight about organizing and building its own world's fair in advance of the 1876 United States Centennial Exposition in Philadelphia.

Early in 1873, thirty leading experts in their fields were appointed to be the nation's eyes and ears in Vienna, tasked with studying everything from church art to battleships. Among them was a retired Harvard professor named Eben Norton Horsford who would focus his attention on Viennese bread. During this era many travelers to Europe believed that Vienna's bakeries produced the world's best loaves. Thurlow Weed, an American politician visiting the city in 1852, reported:

> We could learn one lesson from Austria with great advantage to our people. This is the art of making good bread, which, being as it is here, universal, is really a great national blessing. . . . Nor is it a luxury for the rich alone. The same light, sweet bread is in all the bake shops at prices which enable all classes to purchase. . . . A Vienna baker who should go to the city of New York and vend such bread as we get here would be able to ride in his coach and reside on 5th avenue in two years.[1]

Professor Horsford agreed, noting that this was in distinct contrast to the majority of American loaves, both commercial and homemade, which were "sometimes good, more frequently indifferent, and oftentimes positively bad."[2] The pride of Viennese bakeries was the Kaiser Semmel, or "Emperor Roll": "Foreigners visiting the Austrian capital find at every hotel and restaurant the Kaiser-Semmel, a smooth, irregularly-rounded, small, wheaten loaf, or roll, of uniform weight, and always fresh, but not warm. It presents a rich, reddish brown crust, and a delicately-shaded, yellowish, almost white, interior. It is always light, even porous, free from acidity in taste, faintly sweet without any addition of saccharine matter, slightly and pleasantly fragrant, palatable without butter or any form of condiment, and never cloying upon the appetite."[3] If anyone could bring back the secret to making Viennese bread, it was Horsford, at the time considered America's foremost scientific authority on bread baking and fermentation.

Horsford was born into a farm family in the town of Moscow (now Leicester) in upstate New York. He was one of the most promising young men in the region; local businessmen paid his way to the Rensselaer Institute, forerunner of Rensselaer Polytechnic, in Troy, New York, for an engineering degree. In 1844 his patrons collected another fund to send him to Germany to study under Justus von Liebig, the greatest chemist of his era. Horsford spent two years in Liebig's laboratory, learning the most advanced techniques to study the chemistry of agricultural products, foodstuffs, and other substances. At the end of Horsford's stay, Liebig recommended his student for the Rumford professorship at Harvard, which was named after Benjamin Thompson, Count Rumford, the famed British-American scientist and inventor.

In his Cambridge, Massachusetts, laboratory Horsford was always more interested in practical chemistry than theoretical, conducting experiments on a wide range of subjects but particularly fertilizers and food. Like Liebig, Horsford believed that phosphates were just as important to human growth as they were to healthy crops. In 1854 he and a partner began to experiment with a yeast substitute to replace such chemicals as baking soda and cream of tartar, which were thought to cause stomach problems. Their aim was to help bread rise and increase its nutritional content by adding phosphates, and to make their fortunes. In 1858 they began to sell the product that became "Rumford Yeast Powder," with active ingredients calcium phosphate and sodium bicarbonate, "for those who would avoid the trouble and uncertainty of hop yeast." By 1861 the Rumford blend was so successful that Horsford decided to scale back his Harvard teaching so he could devote more time to the baking powder business.

Horsford continued to study bread science, keeping up with the latest advances from Europe and continuing his experiments with wheat and leavens. Following the work of Liebig and other researchers, Horsford now knew that yeast was a fungus. That was a problem, because scientific research told him that fungi in food were often bad and potentially poisonous. Scientists of that era could not yet differentiate between good bread yeast (i.e., *Saccharomyces cerevisiae*) and the bad yeasts and bacteria that could spoil a dough. To Horsford, other downsides to yeast included its "fitfulness, inconsistency, and untrustworthiness" and his belief that it lowered the nutritional content of the flour. In his booklet *The Theory and Art of Bread-Making*, he examined the principal methods for making bread and concluded that only by avoiding fermentation can the best bread be made. If you used a phosphate baking powder (i.e., the Rumford brand), you could produce a consistent, healthy, nutritionally rich bread in less than an hour. This baking powder loaf from a Rumford cookbook takes only ten minutes to mix and forty-five minutes to bake.

RUMFORD WHOLE WHEAT BREAD

2 cups fine whole wheat flour

4 level teaspoons Rumford Baking Powder

Milk or milk and water to mix to a light, soft dough (about 1 cup)

2 level teaspoons sugar (if desired)

1 level teaspoon salt

Sift together twice the dry ingredients twice; place in a large bowl and mix to a dough with the milk or milk and water, mixing with either a spoon or knife. When smooth turn into a greased pan inverted, unless the double round sandwich pan is used, in which case fill the lower section of pan. Let the bread stand five or ten minutes, then bake in a steady oven, not too hot, about forty-five minutes.[4]

The Rumford loaf rises consistently, but its density and chewy crust make it more like an Irish soda bread than a light and puffy yeast bread. Horsford's promotion of his baking powder for homemade loaves apparently did not convince housewives of the era. Most late nineteenth-century cookbooks used baking powder for biscuits, muffins, and cakes, but for straight bread they continued to recommend the old standby: fickle homemade liquid yeast.

The administration of President Grant appointed Professor Horsford as commissioner to the Vienna exhibition with the task of studying "food as products of industry." There were thousands of foodstuffs on display along the massive hallways of the fairgrounds, everything from Indian chutneys to German sausages, Neapolitan macaroni to dried Chinese shark's fins. However, Horsford ignored all those products and went straight to the "Viennese Bake House," a freestanding café on the exposition grounds. It was operated by Roman Uhl, court baker to the Austrian emperor, whose Kaiser Semmel was regarded as the premier example of Viennese bread. Behind Uhl's cafe stood a spacious modern bakery where his workers made the Kaiser rolls and also *kipfeln* (or *kipferln*)—crescent rolls—and a variety of pretzels. Admiring Uhl's bread, Horsford asked the baker his secret. "We have none," Uhl replied. "We use Hungarian flour and press-yeast, and these constituents are manipulated with cleanliness, care and intelligence."[5]

For deeper investigation into these topics, Horsford only had to stroll into the Industrial Hall, where Austria-Hungary had the largest space, and interview representatives of the country's flour, milling, and yeast industries. Hungarian flour was then considered the world's best, thanks to soil and climate that produced a particularly hard, white wheat. After harvest the grain was shipped to Budapest, where highly sophisticated mills first removed every trace of impurity from the wheat and then sent it to be ground. On display in the hall were examples of the various machines used by the Hungarian companies. Most of them used what was called the "high-milling" process, employing slow-turning grindstones that were carefully graduated so that they would remove the bran and other coarse parts without overheating the grain or pulverizing it into bits—as did "low-milling" American grindstones. The most sophisticated Hungarian millers used newly invented metal rollers that could be kept cool and precisely separate the grain. The result was flour that was "cleaner, whiter, and purer" than any other in the world.

The next crucial element to the baking process was the use of "compressed yeast," an invention that revolutionized the bread-making industry. In the early nineteenth century, Viennese bakers had largely relied on brewer's yeast to produce their white breads. However, they were frustrated by the erratic quality of the product, which was also becoming increasingly hard to get. Viennese breweries were turning from the old top-fermentation process of making beer, which produced brewer's yeast (*Saccharomyces cerevisiae*), to making lager beer using bottom-fermentation, which yielded *Saccharomyces pastorianus* that was unsuitable for bread. In 1845 the Viennese Bakers' Guild offered a reward to the first person who could produce commercial quantities of a consistent, stable baking yeast. In 1850 a brewer named Adolf Ignaz Mautner claimed the prize with a special fermentation process that used a mash of corn, rye, and malt and produced large quantities of yeast-rich froth. This foam was scooped from the vat, washed, and pressed into blocks of fresh yeast that could last for days or even a couple of weeks in cold weather. This compressed yeast consistently produced light, fluffy, and sweet breads. The distilling process also yielded alcohol that the company could turn into all kinds of spirits. Another advantage of Hungarian compressed yeast was that it was nearly pure bread yeast, *Saccharomyces cerevisiae*. It didn't have the bitter off-flavors of brewer's yeast or homemade yeast made with hops. As long it was fresh, it could always be counted to raise a sweet and fluffy dough.

In Uhl's bakery Horsford watched the workers transform pressed-yeast and "first quality" Hungarian flour into the famous Kaiser Semmel. Herr Uhl, who apparently did not believe in trade secrets, freely gave the proportions of the dough's ingredients:

VIENNA BREAD

8 pounds of flour;

3 quarts of mixed milk and water in equal proportions;

3 1/2 ounces of press-yeast;

1 ounce of salt[6]

The process began with workmen pouring lukewarm milk and water into troughs, adding enough flour to make a "thin emulsion," and crumbling the yeast and salt into the liquid. This sat for forty-five minutes until the workers dumped in the rest of the flour and began to knead the mixture into a dough using their bare hands and arms. The dough was allowed to rise for two-and-a-half hours, after which it was fed into a divider—the only mechanical part of the process—that cut and pressed the dough into discs, each weighing about an ounce and a half. Then teams of workers, fingers flying with practiced motions, made five pleats around the edges of the discs, so they looked like pentagonal wheels with five spokes. They were allowed to double in size and then fed into a 500-degree oven for fifteen minutes. Once the rolls had cooled, they were carted through the door to be sold to visitors who needed a coffee and a delicious morsel of bread after taking in the wonders of the fair.

Horsford's 122-page *Report on Vienna Bread* was published in 1875 by the Government Printing Office in Washington, DC. He ends it by asking the question: "Can we have Vienna bread in America?" His answer? Maybe. The first necessity was acquiring "sound, pure wheat" and milling it into a flour that contains only the cleanest, whitest portion of the grain. That depended on the ability of American farmers and millers to produce the best product. Given the mediocre showing of American flours at the exposition, that was a big if. The next requirement was using compressed yeast. That, stated Horsford, was not a problem: "Press-yeast is now produced in this country."[7] Thanks to the immigration of two Hungarian brothers to the United States, a factory in Cincinnati, Ohio, was already producing packages of fresh pressed-yeast and distributing it all over the Midwest.

Charles and Max Fleischmann were born into a large Jewish family in the Austro-Hungarian town of Jägerndorf, now known as Krnov in the Czech Republic. Like their father, the brothers went into the distilling trade, learning the latest methods in Budapest and Vienna.

However, they and their five siblings saw their future in the United States, which was emerging from the strife and chaos of the Civil War. Charles and Max immigrated around 1866, landing in New York City and finding work at a "Hungarian process" distillery. Like many immigrants, they soon moved west, settling in Cincinnati, home to a large Central European Jewish population. James Gaff, an influential local businessman and liquor manufacturer, saw the Fleischmann brothers' drive and technical skills and offered them a partnership in his distillery. From their factory in the Riverside district of Cincinnati, Gaff, Fleischmann & Company began to produce various kinds of alcohol and "compressed yeast," the same kind of leaven used by the top Vienna bakeries. The only problem was finding a market for their product.

Fleischmann Yeast faced a number of challenges entering the American marketplace. In the age before widespread refrigeration, each tinfoil-wrapped cake had a short shelf life, five to seven days in summer and ten to fourteen days in winter. The Fleischmann brothers were master distillers, but they also had to become experts at shipping and marketing. This was the great era of railway building, when every city and large town was being linked by steel rails. The Fleischmanns developed a system to pack their yeast in sawdust-filled boxes for insulation and ship it to their agents in communities around the Midwest. To cover the last mile, salesmen drove elegant little wagons emblazoned with the "Fleischmann" logo as they delivered to every corner store and market. As the business expanded, they looked to other markets, building a large distillery near New York City so they could cover the East Coast. Their other problem was selling bakeries and housewives on this new product. The company took out ads in every newspaper boasting about their yeast's excellence and belittling their competitors. Fleischmann marketing teams also displayed their product at trade fairs, such as an exposition in Cincinnati where they advertised a "Grand Doughnut Jubilee" and offered a "practical demonstration of the quickness and reliability of our celebrated Compressed Yeast."[8]

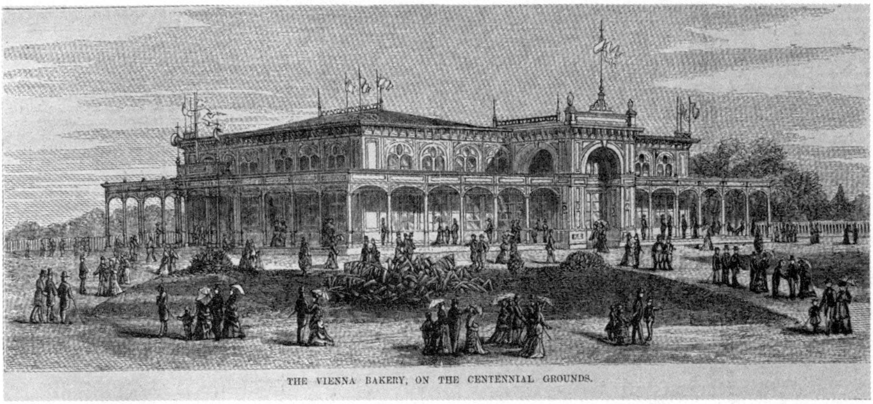

Figure 10. Engraving of the "Vienna Model Bakery," Philadelphia Centennial Exposition, 1876. *Source*: Andrew Coe Collection.

By far the largest of these events was the 1876 Centennial Exposition in Philadelphia. On the east side of the fairground, the Fleischmanns erected the "Vienna Model Bakery," a copy of Roman Uhl's establishment at the 1873 Vienna exposition. Under the management of Charles's and Max's younger brother Louis Fleischmann, the bakery sold Kaiser rolls and Viennese-style coffee. As they sipped and ate, customers could watch through glass windows the process of making the rolls using Fleischmann's yeast and white flour. The famous travel writer Bayard Taylor reported that the coffee was like in Vienna—far better than the "insipid slops poured out to him in so many hotels." The crisp rolls were "equally genuine, and the favor which they have already won among our people shows that a whole generation of 'saleratus biscuits' cannot entirely destroy the taste for honest bread."[9] The Vienna Model Bakery was so successful that Louis Fleischmann made plans to open similar bakeries in downtown Philadelphia, New York, Cincinnati, Saint Louis, and other cities. The flagship was "Fleischmann's Vienna Model Bakery" in New York at Broadway and Tenth Street, where elegant diners could enjoy the same Viennese breads and drinks as at the exposition. Its other claim to fame was the midnight "bread line," started by Louis Fleischmann, at which bakers handed out chunks of free bread to hungry men. This became a New York institution, drawing the unemployed and homeless and also tourists eager to observe the spectacle.

Leaping on the trend, bakeries selling "authentic" Vienna bread spread to nearly every city across the country. If they lived too far from a bakery, housewives made the loaf at home, following a reduced quantity version of the recipe Horsford learned back in Vienna.

VIENNA BREAD

The proportions of an ordinary family baking are four pounds of flour, three pints of milk and water, half an ounce of salt, and one and three-quarters ounces of very fresh compressed yeast. The process of making is as follows: Place the flour in the bread bowl, and in it put the milk, water, and salt; mix with the liquid enough of the flour to make a very thin batter; next rub the yeast to powder between the hands, and mix it into the batter; cover the bowl closely, and let it stand for three-quarters of an hour. At the end of that time mix in the rest of the flour smoothly, and let the dough thus made stand again closely covered for two hours and a half, until it is light and elastic; then cut into pound pieces, and each pound into twelve equal parts; flatten these small pieces of dough in squares three-quarters of an inch thick, fold their corners to the center, pinch them down to hold them, and turn the little rolls thus made over on board covered with cloth; let them stand for about ten minutes, turn them up again on a baking sheet, and put them into a hot oven to bake quickly for about fifteen minutes, when half done brush them with milk, return them to the oven and finish baking them. This process seems to imply a little trouble to the bread-maker, but the delicious quality of the bread thus produced well repays the extra pains taken in making it; and a little practice will enable any person to accomplish the result successful always [*sic*].[10]

Housewives could also use homemade potato or hops yeast make their Vienna rolls, but compressed yeast was easier to use and produced better results. As the noted cookbook writer Maria Parloa noted: "When it is convenient to get fresh cakes of Fleischmann's compressed yeast, it will be much better and cheaper to use them than to make your own. This yeast is wholly free of injurious substance, and with it good bread can always be made, provided the flour is good and the rules are followed."[11] (The Fleischmann company liked this quote so much that they used it in their advertising copy.) The question was whether housewives could find the right flour to make white and fluffy Vienna loaves.

For much of the nineteenth century, American flour mills emphasized quantity over the quality of their product. Following the tradition of Oliver Evans, they eagerly adopted new technologies, such as high-speed grindstones and mechanical purifiers that separated the bran from the rest of the wheat grain, allowing them to process more wheat in less time. (An unfortunate side effect of these new machines was that they kicked up lots of highly combustible flour dust inside the mills. Flour mill explosions became more common and more deadly as the plants increased in size.) In Europe there was a market for every grade of flour from dark and coarse to white and fine. American consumers preferred white bread, so flour mills threw out all their darker flours—or fed them back into the mill to be ground again—and mostly produced just one inexpensive, mediocre, "white" flour that was often actually gray and mottled with impurities. By 1875 the center of the milling industry had moved from the East Coast to Minneapolis, Minnesota, which lay in the middle of the highly productive wheat-growing region of the Upper Midwest. Minneapolis millers were aware of the new technologies being used in Europe, and particularly Hungary, and were eager to install any machines that would allow them to produce whiter flour at less expense.

On May 2, 1878, a massive explosion caused by a spark igniting flour dust leveled Minneapolis's Washburn Crosby Mill, the largest flour mill in the country if not the world. Eighteen workers were killed. The mill's owner, Cadwallader C. Washburn, rushed to the scene and immediately announced that he would rebuild: "In the new structure I shall adopt the Hungarian system using rollers, and shall dispense with a great amount of machinery heretofore used."[12] The new mill used porcelain-coated metal rollers just like those used by the big Budapest mills but employed American ingenuity to organize them in a complicated system to gradually reduce the grain and separate out the various products, including the best quality white "patent" flour for bread baking. (Hard or soft "patent" flour is the commercial white all-purpose, bread, pastry, and cake flour that we use today.) The "Hungarian craze" took over all the other big Minneapolis mills, and by 1890 rollers had replaced millstones in virtually every large American mill.

Midwestern millers installed European rollers not only because they increased production. The technology also allowed them to process new kinds of wheat that were being grown on the fields of Kansas, Nebraska, Minnesota, and the Dakotas. Before 1880 the vast majority of American wheat was soft winter wheat, which was easy to mill using traditional grindstones and could be used to make everything from bread to cakes. However, that type of grain did not grow well on the Great Plains or the Northern Prairies, where the climate was drier and suffered from greater extremes of heat and cold. The farmers who settled Minnesota and the Dakotas began to plant a hard red wheat called Red Fife, which had been developed in Canada from seed originating in Eastern Europe. In the 1870s large numbers of German-speaking Mennonites from southwestern Russia migrated to Kansas and Nebraska, where the land reminded them of southern Ukraine. They brought with them a hard red wheat they called "Turkey wheat" and began to plant it across thousands of acres. Soon these wheat fields were yielding tons of hard wheat that they offered to Minneapolis millers. This grain had two advantages: it was cheap and it produced a high-gluten flour excellent for making into bread. On the downside the grain was too hard to be effectively processed by traditional low-milling or even the new high-milling process, which left too many impurities in the flour. However, steel rollers proved excellent at the gradual reduction of hard red wheat into its component parts. The Minneapolis

Figure 11. "America's Greatest Flour," advertisement for Washburn-Crosby's Gold Medal Flour, from Minneapolis, one of the country's biggest selling white flours. *Source*: Andrew Coe Collection.

mills began to churn out huge quantities of flour—five million pounds in 1886—perfect for making into white bread. Now all they needed was a market.

At the end of the nineteenth century three-quarters of all bread consumed was made at home. This was decades before real supermarkets existed; housewives bought their flour at the local grocery store. In larger towns and cities they could also buy loaves at a nearby bread bakery, which usually had fewer than five employees and distributed its product only locally. In the large cities there existed only a few dozen bread bakeries employing more than one hundred workers (unlike biscuit and cracker makers, who had the advantage of a less perishable product and were building huge plants with many hundreds of workers). To reach this diffuse market, the big Minneapolis flour brands, such as Pillsbury's Best and Washburn-Crosby's Gold Medal, had to build huge marketing machines to reach consumers. Their flour was delivered to stores in brightly painted wagons that let consumers know that a quality product was inside. Their home economics departments published and distributed tens of thousands of pamphlet cookbooks giving housewives dozens of new ideas for preparing their products. They were also looking at social and economic trends to try and figure out how they would affect their business. One fact was evident to every miller: Housewives judged the quality of the flour they bought at the corner grocery and the loaves they purchased at the bakery by the color. They believed that the whiter the product, the higher its quality.

The modern steel roller mills produced the whitest flour ever seen in the United States. However, even the highest-quality patent flours still retained an off-white, slightly yellowish cast. This was caused by carotenoids, which are nutritionally valuable pigments occurring naturally in wheat grains. Millers had long known that if they stored the flour for a few months, oxidation would cause these pigments to dissipate, leaving it a purer white. They dreamed of a method that would speed up this process, both so they could ship their product sooner and, more important, "improve" darker, lower-quality flour and sell it for higher prices. In 1904 a Kentucky engineer named James Nathaniel Alsop patented an invention that could "purify" flour without harming its nutritive properties, revolutionizing the milling industry. Alsop's machine worked by first shooting an arc of electricity through air to produce nitrogen dioxide gas (a potentially toxic compound that also contributes to the brownish haze of pollution in the sky on smoggy days). This is injected into a container where the flour is agitated and speeds up the oxidation process through a chemical reaction, whitening the flour. Within a year more than five hundred mills had adopted the Alsop process to whiten their flour "with pure air modified by electricity." The general public, however, did not embrace bleached flour with the same enthusiasm.

The early years of the twentieth century were marked by a series of scandals involving the foods and drugs that Americans put into their bodies. Patent medicines were revealed to be filled with opium, alcohol, and large amounts of such toxic chemicals as formaldehyde used as preservatives. Muckraking journalists like Upton Sinclair exposed the practices of the big meat-packers who sold sausages and other products filled with rotten beef and pork dosed with chemicals to remove the smell. The collective outcry over these scandals led to the passage of the 1906 Pure Food and Drug Act, which banned any food "mixed and packed . . . so as to reduce or lower or injuriously affect its quality or strength" and with "any added poisonous or other added deleterious ingredient which may render such article injurious to health." Dozens of chemists across the country began to study bleached flour to see if it was somehow dangerous to human health. The results were inconclusive. Nevertheless, three states banned it outright, and a number of others allowed its sale but with restrictions. Alsop was also forced to remove his claim that his process improved flour's nutritional benefits. In 1920 the US Supreme Court finally allowed the sale of bleached flour nationwide, as long as it could be shown safe to eat and the bags were clearly marked "bleached." Today, although it's illegal in most European nations, the bulk of flour sold in the United States has been bleached, most often by the addition of benzoyl peroxide.

The abundant supply of white flour—and the easy access to compressed yeast such as Fleischmann's—gave American bakers the ability to produce fine rolls and loaves nearly the same as Roman Uhl had made at the Vienna Exposition. They did not, however, have the same reverence for the Viennese bread tradition. By the early 1900s "Vienna bread" had become nearly indistinguishable, at least as far as ingredients, from other commercially produced white breads. Uhl made his famous Kaiser rolls from just white flour, water, milk, salt, and compressed yeast. American bakers removed the milk and added sugar or malt extract (for sweetness and a better rise) and a shortening, most often lard. They then shaped their "Vienna" breads into long, free-form loaves that were baked until they were brown with a crisp crust. Inside, the crumb was moist and fluffy, with few large holes, a bit sweet, and spongy in the mouth. The only difference between them and pan-baked white bread was the shape.

7

FRENCH BREAD

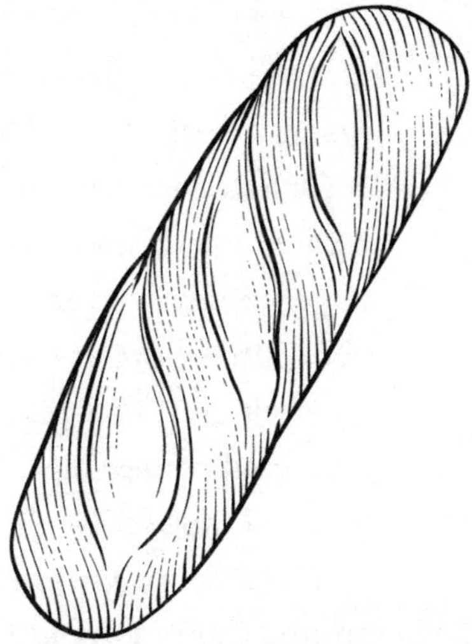

IN NOVEMBER OF 1848 A PARIS NEWSPAPER ran a brief notice reporting that a "multitude" of American citizens were emigrating to the newly acquired territory of California. The writer had learned that the lure was the prospect of sudden wealth: "It seems that mineral deposits of great value have been discovered; everyone speaks of gold mines, of fabulous riches awaiting only the hands of the miners to be picked up. Whether true or false, exaggerated or not, these rumors seem to have powerfully aroused public imagination."[1] The news sparked Parisian interest but was overwhelmed by turmoil closer to home. France was then in the second year of a severe economic depression. Just months before, revolutionary workers and students, backed by many in the middle class, had ousted King Louis Phillippe and formed a provisional government. Protests, often under the banner of "Bread or Death," nevertheless continued, and in June the new government cracked down, killing thousands of radicals and injuring many more. That December, Prince Napoleon Bonaparte (nephew of Napoleon I) was elected the new president of the French Republic, but he could do little at first to calm political fighting. Meanwhile, headlines about "L'Or de la Californie" grew larger and larger in nearly every French newspaper. Amid chaos and hardship at home, the allure of California, of adventure and wealth, became overwhelming. At first one by one and then in organized expeditions that chartered whole ships, Frenchmen—and a few French women—sailed for San Francisco.

The arduous voyage took half a year if the ship took the long route around Cape Horn at the southern tip of South America. For a quicker journey boats sailed for Chagres on the Caribbean coast of Panama. Passengers disembarked and traveled via riverboat and muleback over jungle trails, braving crocodiles, snakes, and mosquitoes, to Panama City on the Pacific, where they picked up a second ship to take them to California. When they finally sailed into San Francisco Bay, passengers found a forest of masts and hundreds of empty boats deserted by crews who had rushed to the gold fields to make their fortunes. The French "Argonauts" (as gold seekers were known) were among the peoples from all over the world, including Chinese, Hawaiians, Peruvians, Chileans, British, German, and Americans, crowding into the city. Beyond the docks piled high with crates and sacks stuffed with supplies, the muddy San Francisco streets were lined with canvas tents and ramshackle wooden buildings often made of ship timber. The French contingent included a wide range of professions and social classes, from doctors and lawyers to artisans and radicals who had been exiled by their country. Some immediately began making plans to head to the diggings in the hills east of Sacramento. Others decided they could find better opportunities in San Francisco, Sacramento, and other large settlements that didn't require one to do actual digging.

A Scottish journalist named J. D. Borthwick visiting California during Gold Rush days admired "this enviable facility, which the Frenchmen appeared to possess in such a high degree, of bringing somewhat of the comforts of civilized life along with them."[2] Their first trade, which some began the day they set foot in San Francisco, was selling the goods they had brought from home at the inflated local prices—French wine and liquor were particularly popular. Others opened gambling houses, theaters, and restaurants with French waiters and chefs. Borthwick reported:

> The immigration of Frenchmen had been so large that some parts of the city were completely French in appearance; the shops, restaurants, and estaminets [small cafés], being painted to the French taste, and exhibiting French signs, the very letters of which had a French look about them. The names of some of the restaurants were rather ambitious—as the Trois Frères, the Café de Paris, and suchlike; but these were second and third-rate places; those which courted the patronage of the upper classes of all nations, assumed names more calculated to tickle the American ear,—such as the Jackson House and the Lafayette. They were presided over by elegantly dressed *dames du comptoir*, and all the arrangements were in Parisian style.[3]

To supply these businesses French immigrants also opened wine and liquor shops, butchers, grocers, laundries, and bakeries. In Gold Rush California men far outnumbered women. With few wives to cook and bake, it was rare to get good homemade bread like back east. If there was one profession France had a surplus of it was bakers. Making bread was an obvious opportunity.

In the eighteenth and nineteenth centuries bread was the principal staple of countries across Europe. In France, however, it was the object of particularly intense scrutiny, not only as a necessity but as a symbol of national pride. The French believed that "France is the country of Europe where the best bread is prepared."[4] For the vast majority of its citizens, the ability to acquire bread meant the difference between life and death. It was the king's responsibility to provide affordable loaves, and if he failed to do so, as in the case of Louis XVI in 1789, it could mean revolution. Consumers also demanded that bakers provide bread at the proper weight and price. And not just any loaves but "good" bread, the whiter the better. From the lowliest street beggar to the aristocracy, the residents of Paris largely refused to eat anything but wheat bread—rye and barley were for rural peasants—fresh from the bakery and with a light crumb.

It was a matter of constant debate among government officials, scientists, farmers, millers, and bakers how to make that bread. French loaves were traditionally prepared using sourdough leaven, but experts such as Antoine-Augustin Parmentier promoted using brewer's yeast to lower costs and increase production. At the beginning of the eighteenth century, the most common loaf was a round wheat bread with a relatively dense crumb. By the 1750s tastes had changed, at least in Paris and other cities, with citizens preferring longer, crustier loaves, culminating in the "flute," ancestor of the baguette. Whenever the French ventured to other parts of the world, they attempted to re-create the bread culture of home, with varying results depending on climate and access to raw materials such as flour.

San Francisco wasn't the first North American city to have a French bakery. At the end of the seventeenth century, when French colonists began to settle along the northern shores of the Gulf of Mexico, one of their first tasks was to build ovens to produce their staple bread. About 1720 a man named François Lemesle, or Lemelle, opened a French bakery a few steps away from the church in the new settlement of New Orleans. The flour used originally came from France, but by the early nineteenth century this had been replaced by North American grain, either shipped from New York or Charleston, South Carolina, or carried down the Mississippi River on rafts. Much of the heavy work in New Orleans bakeries was performed by enslaved Africans. Lemesle would have mostly baked round loaves from coarse wheat flour in weights of one, two, and four pounds. Only the wealthy would have been able to afford his white bread. As in France, the leaven would have been a piece of dough left over from last bake rather than English-style ale yeast. The French tradition continued in New Orleans after the Louisiana Purchase of 1803. By 1820 the city had sixty bakeries, the vast majority of them owned by Frenchmen, and other Gulf cities such as Mobile, Alabama, also had French bakeries. As the nineteenth century progressed, however, the loaves they produced gradually Americanized. Bakers discarded their sourdoughs and just used straight yeast doughs that they made into long loaves with crispy crusts and a soft crumb inside. They proved a perfect base for the early twentieth-century invention of "po'boy" sandwiches stuffed with fried seafood or meat.

In California, French bakers clung to their traditions far more successfully. The most important was the use of sourdough leavening, which, according to legend, at least a few bakers brought from France. However, any knowledgeable baker would also have known how to build a sourdough starter from scratch. The sourdough gave loaves a slight tang that set them apart from the usual English and American-style breads—and from the typical Western camp and trail sourdough that was made with baking soda to cut the sourness. In 1850 one of the favorite dining spots on the outskirts of San Francisco was MacClaren's Hotel, where patrons could feast on cold meats, good butter, and Stilton cheese served on slices from a "great, crisp, brown, home-made English loaf." For American Argonauts this was real bread, not like what you got in other city eateries—the "sour French bread or stereotyped German loaf."[5]

A market existed for "sour French bread," because by 1856 there were at least ten French-operated bakeries in San Francisco, including one owned by Isidore Boudin (whose firm still operates today), and others in nearly every large settlement in the state. They usually operated out of basements, where workers toiled in the heat stripped to the waist just as in France. In 1883 an official toured the bakeries to make a check of working conditions: "Almost without exception the establishments visited were found to be squalid, dark and badly ventilated cellars and basements, the sanitary conditions being the poorest, cleanliness at a discount, and the workmen being a pale, haggard and worn-out looking body of men, who have no time for recreation and are strangers to sunlight. . . . In some of the French bakeries the men were found at work perfectly naked, barring a loin-cloth."[6]

By the early twentieth century, Californians had begun to recognize that there was something special about their city's bread: "These French breads are very tough, are filled with large holes, and are, so far as I can find, confined to San Francisco. I've offered 50 cents for a loaf of it in New York and it can't be got. It's not made in Seattle, in Portland nor in Tacoma. There may be a stray baker of it in Los Angeles or Sacramento, but that's all. It's San Francisco and only San Francisco."[7] Aside from the loaves' texture and holes, their defining characteristic was sourness. Somehow Californians had developed a taste for sourness in bread—a quality that most Americans had long rejected and American bakers did their best to eliminate. The bakery community was glad to accommodate (even though their output was noticeably more sour than loaves back in France). Newspaper bakery ads proclaimed "Do You Like Genuine Sour French Bread? Ours is Superior to Any Other in our Vicinity" and boasted of their "Extra Sour French Bread. A Real Treat."[8] The French-owned Taix Bakery in Los Angeles trumpeted: "For That Real, Sour Dough French Bread, That's Taix."[9] Despite the arrival of rival Italian, German, and American industrial bakeries, the loaf helped French bakers thrive in the baking trade. The 1920 *Guide Franco-Americain* to Northern California identified twenty-six boulangeries in San Francisco, four in San Jose, two in Oakland, and more in Alameda, Stockton, Sacramento, and other cities.

San Francisco sourdough remained a strictly regional product until the decades after World War II. Its profile was lifted by the rise in jet travel, mass tourism, and the savvy marketing of the biggest San Francisco bakeries. In 1960 the *New York Times* reported that an Upper East

Side gourmet shop was flying "sour French bread" from San Francisco to New York: "Sour dough is normally associated with tough old prospectors of Alaskan gold rush days, but it has its sophisticated side too. Sour French bread apparently also figures prominently in the lives of San Franciscans. In fact, it is said that it is as indigenous to San Francisco as the Golden Gate."[10] Tourists discovered the joys of San Francisco bread in the city's restaurants and also at outposts of bakeries such as Larraburu, Parisian, and Boudin along Fisherman's Wharf, the Bay Area's premier tourist attraction. When it came time to leave, those same bakeries had shops at the airport selling loaves for visitors to bring home. Thanks to the bread's denseness and sourdough content, they lasted days longer than, say, a baguette. By the end of the 1960s many big East Coast markets and department stores were receiving regular shipments of the San Francisco specialty, and it even appeared in the bread basket at New York's Four Seasons restaurant.

As the fame of San Francisco sourdough spread, so did the legends around it. Bakers claimed that it could be made only with their special sourdough starters, which dated back to Gold Rush days, and only in the cool, foggy climate of the Bay Area. Rumors circulated that the Larraburu bakery's walls were imbued with the special mold that infused the dough, but when the health department visited, they found the bakery spotless. After Larraburu remodeled its production space, scavengers liberated its old wall boards from the scrap pile in hope that they teemed with the necessary "bugs." Inspired by these accounts, researchers at the USDA lab in nearby Albany, California, decided to study the San Francisco starter to determine what, if anything, made its microbiology unique. The scientists collected starters from five city bakeries and propagated them in their lab. They tested the samples for two types of organisms, yeasts and bacteria, and discovered that two species dominated. The main yeast was *Saccharomyces exiguus*, the most common sourdough yeast (as opposed to *S. cerevisiae*, or baker's yeast). The mystery was the dominant lactic acid bacterium, heretofore unknown, which they could see through the microscope as little rods of short to medium length. It fed predominately on maltose and produced high levels of lactic and acetic acids (as well as carbon dioxide). In fact, the starters were so acidic that *S. exiguus* was one of the few yeasts that could tolerate the environment. In honor of the sourdough's origin, the researchers decided to dub the bacterium *Lactobacillus sanfrancisco* (now known as *L. sanfranciscensis*).

The USDA team reported: "Virtually everyone who has had occasion to visit San Francisco recalls with pleasure their encounter with sour dough French bread, and expresses regret that this product is not manufactured in their own locality."[11] To make it possible to manufacture it efficiently, economically, and in any location regardless of climate and topography, they received a nonexclusive patent for a process for making the loaves. All it needed was an inoculation of the correct starter containing *S. exiguus* and *L. sanfranciscensis*. That was difficult if you didn't live in the Bay Area near a bakery willing to share its starter, so in 1975 the scientists developed methods for producing freeze-dried and frozen concentrate San Francisco starter cultures that soon went into commercial production. For industrial baking operations, using these products simplified production because they didn't have to keep feeding a starter three times a day seven days a week but could go from scratch to finished sourdough loaves in less than forty-eight hours.

The new technology allowed bakeries in other parts of the country to make their own "San Francisco sourdough" bread and rolls. In the Bay Area, meanwhile, bakeries such as Boudin's were coping with a slow but seismic shift in local customer tastes. In 1983 the *Los Angeles Times* reported: "San Francisco's legendary sourdough bread is being challenged for the hearts and palates of discriminating diners by a cadre of sweet continental contenders—French bread, French rolls, even (gulp!) French croissants." A new crop of French nouvelle cuisine restaurants were opening whose chefs, from France, wanted "real" French bread, not the sour local product. At the same time, artisan bakeries were opening around the Bay Area making loaves following French and Italian baking tradition. In response to this competition, Louis Gallaudo, head of Boudin Bakery, declared that "no one is going to run the sourdough bread industry out of San Francisco."[12] Boudin Bakery remains open but is now more a tourist attraction than a bakery for locals. Bakeries making European-style artisan breads (explored in chapter 13) have supplanted the sourdough factories as the pride of San Francisco.

After San Francisco and New Orleans the third city that fostered a rich French baking tradition was New York. French immigrants had been living in New York since the seventeenth century, most prominently the Huguenots who settled in both New Amsterdam and north along the Hudson River. A small number of émigrés arrived in New York after the 1848 Revolution, but the largest driver of French immigration to East Coast cities was France's loss of the 1870–71 Franco-Prussian War and the crushing of the Paris Commune. The refugees, many of them left-wing radicals, settled in the blocks south of Washington Square, next to Germans and Irish immigrants and one of New York's largest African American neighborhoods. They had arrived at a time when New York City was particularly receptive to French culture and the skills that French immigrants had brought with them.

In the 1870s and 1880s the city was home to a group of self-styled "Bohemians," mostly artists, writers, actors, and journalists, who were fascinated by the immigrants then flowing into Manhattan from all parts of the world. In the "Quartier Français," they found:

> The people are nearly all French. French, too, is the language of the signs over the doors and in the windows; and the population is of the lowest and poorest class. The Commune has its emissaries and exiles here. There are swarthy faces which have gladdened in mad grimace over the flames of the Hôtel de Ville and become the hue of copper bronze under the sun of New Caledonia [then a French penal colony]. There are secret meetings in obscure little *cáfes*, into which strangers seldom enter; where the last

Figure 12. The French Bakery on Greene Street, New York City. *Source*: "The French Quarter of New York," *Scribner's Monthly*, November 1879.

> movements of the Nihilists are discussed, and the would-be regicide is commended over draughts of absinthe and more innocent beer. . . . Here is Triquet, *le charcutier*; Roux, *le boittier*; Malvaison, *le marchand de vin*; Givac, *le charcutier Alsacien*, and innumerable basement restaurants, where dinner, *vin compris*, may be had for the veriest trifle.[13]

The district's main restaurants were the Taverne Alsacienne and the Restaurant du Grand Vatel, where one could sup on a bowl of soup, a dish of beef, and a hunk of bread for ten cents. Café au lait was five cents extra. The best source of *pain français* was the boulangerie at 159 Greene Street, owned by one Charles J. Medicus, who boasted of being "from the city of Paris," presumably to show his revolutionary credentials. The Bohemians were enchanted by the romantic, slightly dingy, and dangerous atmosphere of the French Quarter. Other New Yorkers were more interested in the immigrants for their culinary skills.

In the decades after the Civil War, New York became a magnet for the nouveau riche. These families had made piles of money in industries such as iron, steel, shipping, and petroleum and now wanted the finer things in life: Fifth Avenue mansions, servants, elegant carriages, fine jewelry, clothing in the latest fashion, and French food on their table. When dining out, they patronized Delmonico's, the temple of haute cuisine, at Fifth Avenue and Fourteenth Street (and later just north of Madison Square), and imitators such as Maison Dorée. Upper-class men belonged to exclusive clubs, such as the Union and the Manhattan Clubs, where the dining rooms served only French cuisine. At home it became de rigueur for wealthy families to hire a French chef to command the kitchen. If the wives of the rich didn't already speak French, they had to learn it to give their chef his daily instructions. Of course, the French chef preferred to have trusted (French) sources of kitchen staff, meat, fish, vegetables, knives, toques, wine, and bread. A small universe of French immigrant purveyors sprang up to serve the chefs who ruled New York's most important restaurant, hotel, club, and home kitchens.

For the uninitiated, French bread was described as "all crust" and baked into long "staves" (i.e., baguettes) and little "twists" or rolls. An 1873 article reported:

> The French is white and wholesome, but it is manufactured solely by French bakers, has a limited sale, and is known only to the wealthy and French workmen. . . . It is fashioned in thin lengths and in rings, simply to make it as nearly all crust as practicable, the French being wisely of the opinion that the crumb of the bread is by no means so digestible. The twists are small, and perhaps the most perfect bread to be found in the world. They are, therefore monopolized by the wealthy, and by hotels and restaurants of the first-class.[14]

In 1889, New York's *Guide Franco-Americain* listed eight boulangeries selling loaves both wholesale and retail—and some offering brioche every Sunday. The 1911 edition of the same guide included thirty-one boulangeries, the largest of them, including the Ycre French Bakery Company and the Marseillaise French Baking Company, specializing in *petits pains* for clubs and hotels. The baking consultant Paul Richards recognized their distinctive qualities: "The original French bread is an all-water bread. The bread is not as white as the American breads—more of a yellowish color. The body of the bread is light and moist, and of a slight sourish taste, but good to eat."[15] That yellow color was due to the fact that, as in France, New York's French bakers used flour that had not been ground and sifted so much that every last vestige of color (and flavor) had been removed from it.

French bread's elite status and reputation for excellence motivated more New York bakeries—and home cooks—to try to produce their own French loaves. For housewives the most common recipes used the same dough they mixed up for their regular white flour household breads only shaped into either long loaves with a furrow down the middle or small rolls. The latter were a favorite of the prolific cookbook author Marion Harland, who boasted of her own recipe: "Having seen these rolls, smoking, light, and delicious, upon my own table, at least twice a week for ten years, with scarcely a failure in the mixing or baking, I can confidently recommend the receipt and the product." After letting the dough rise, Harland suggested cutting across the center with a sharp knife: "This will make the cleft rolls, so familiar to us in French restaurants."[16] Her little loaves may have looked like restaurant rolls, but in addition to flour, water, salt, and yeast, Harland added milk, egg, butter, and baking soda to give them the slight sweetness and soft mouthfeel that American palates expected. The baking soda would have eliminated any trace of sour.

By 1900 many of the large industrial bakeries were also selling what they called "French bread." Paul Richards admitted: "It is usage in many bakeries to make French, Vienna, and the ordinary pan breads all out of one dough, the only difference in the breads being in the name and shape."[17] Even in bakeries that used separate doughs, their "French" recipe was not that different from their mainstay white pan loaves. The Ward Bread Company (which later grew into the conglomerate that produced Wonder Bread) used a French bread formula that began with a "sour," or preferment, of flour, water, and yeast. After three hours of fermentation, this was mixed into the main dough of flour, milk, salt, sugar, and lard. This was essentially the same list of ingredients as Ward's popular "Tip Top" pan loaf, which was a "straight dough" bread that didn't use a preferment. The loaves were shaped into something like elongated footballs with a crisp exterior and a white, bland, cotton-wool textured crumb inside. This style of French bread was the pride of Philadelphia's Freihofer's Bakery, which boasted:

> Freihofer's French Loaf is the kind of bread that is so chockfull of rich, tasty "goodies" it virtually melts in your mouth. . . . The crisp, nicely brown crust is so deliciously appetizing you eat every bit of it. Unlike in other breads, there's no waste in FREIHOFER'S FRENCH BREAD. Every particle is eaten. That makes it the real economy loaf. . . . Youngsters like FREIHOFER'S FRENCH BREAD. So do the grown-ups. A generous slice, spread with butter or jam—oh boy! It can't be equaled. It tastes even better than cake.[18]

After World War I, the number of French-operated bakeries in New York City slowly dwindled. Prohibition led to the closure of many haute cuisine restaurants dependent on wine and liquor sales for their profitability. Then immigration restrictions and the economic collapse of the Great Depression made it harder for businesses reliant on sales of low-margin fancy rolls to survive. Among those that endured were Trio French Bakery and Zampieri Brothers (French despite the name), both situated on the same Greenwich Village blocks as the French Quarter of the previous century. During the 1950s and 1960s these bakeries found a new market with the resurgence of pricey French restaurants such as Le Pavillon, La Côte Basque, and La Caravelle. At the same time, the boom in American tourism to France allowed us to taste the real thing fresh from the oven. The question was, did the "French bread" produced by American bakeries measure up? Apparently many New York chefs believed it did not.

In 1971 a French baking machinery company opened a big bakery in Manhattan under the name "Interbaco." The French chefs tasted its product and immediately made Interbaco the sole supplier of their loaves. Roger Fessaguet, owner of La Caravelle, claimed: "This bread is the best French bread I have found in 22 years in this country. It's crusty and as good as any bread you find in France."[19] The following year, John L. Hess, a veteran journalist who had reported for years from Paris, was named restaurant critic for the *New York Times*. On his new beat he visited New York's most renowned French restaurants and found that the bread they served was hit or miss—sometimes good (Le Perigord) but too often "poor" (Lafayette). In fact, Hess found that in general many of the city's best known restaurants served "plasticized, tasteless breads," often delivered frozen to their kitchens and then reheated. The food writer Mimi Sheraton, who became the *Times*'s restaurant critic in 1976, agreed with Hess's exacting critique. She located the city's best bread in its ethnic bakeries, which she celebrated in an article called "A Toast to Ethnic Bakeries, and Noble Loaves of Splendor." Included in her round-up were Italian, Eastern European, Jewish, German, Scandinavian, Greek, Middle Eastern, and Puerto Rican bakeries—but not French. "If no French bread appears here," Sheraton said, "it is because no decent French bread was found."[20] Luckily a revolution was in the making.

8

RYE BREAD

ON AUGUST 1, 1855, the New York State government opened an immigration depot at the southern tip of Manhattan Island. It was housed in Castle Garden, a vast theater capable of seating at least six thousand people that had been built inside an old military fort. In earlier years Castle Garden had hosted operas, theatricals, political rallies, lectures, and performances, including an evening with the famous Swedish soprano Jenny Lind. Now the state found more pressing uses for the space: as a place to process the tens of thousands of European immigrants landing in the city every year, guarding against the spread of any contagious disease they might be carrying and protecting them from predators seeking to plunder them once they came ashore. The neighborhoods nearest the Lower Manhattan docks then teemed with people and businesses, including boardinghouses, money changers, railroad ticket agents, and employment agencies, all bent on fleecing the "greenhorns" down to their last penny. Under Castle Garden's domed roof, inspectors registered each immigrant, then sent them to the medical office for a health exam. At the next desk officials gave them advice on how to reach their destination and, if necessary, sold them railway tickets to places like Illinois, Michigan, Ohio, and Wisconsin eager for settlers. In 1867 authorities opened the Castle Gardens Labor Exchange to help new arrivals learn about job opportunities in the rapidly growing city, where employers were desperate for able-bodied workers.

In 1857, 183,773 European immigrants were processed through Castle Garden. Of those, the largest portion—80,976—were Germans, mostly Christian but also many German Jews. A few of them were political refugees fleeing political repression across German-speaking states following the failed Revolution of 1848. Many more were economic refugees, their livelihoods as artisans and farmers upended by industrialization, crop failures, and rising land prices. According to F. W. Bogen, a German immigrant pastor, his countrymen sailed to the United States because they wanted to be "free and happy," and in no country did they have a better prospect of achieving this goal than in America:

> Every one can travel, free and untrammeled, whither he will, and settle where he pleases. No passport is demanded, no police mingles in his affairs and hinders his movements. Before him lies the country, exhaustless in its resources, with its fruitful soil, its productive mines, its immense products, both of the vegetable and animal kingdom, a portion of which he has never seen; its countless cities and villages, where flourish industry, commerce, and wealth.[1]

However, warned Bogen, it was essential that the immigrant find "as soon as possible, an occupation adapted to his powers and abilities."[2] If he decided to stay in New York City, which was then by far the country's largest city and the trade and finance hub for the Western Hemisphere, he was usually lucky enough to get hired "just off the boat."

Although German immigration to the United States first peaked in the mid-1850s, German speakers had been settling in North America since the days of Jamestown and New Amsterdam. The largest concentration was found in Pennsylvania, where members of religious sects such as the Amish and the Mennonites facing persecution in the old country found refuge. In New York City so many Germans had arrived in the early nineteenth century that by the 1840s a section of the Lower East Side had earned the name "Kleindeutschland," or Little Germany. Here German immigrants opened groceries, taverns, boardinghouses, tobacconists, workshops, breweries, and bakeries, all of which needed workers, preferably fellow countrymen willing to work hard for low wages. In 1855 more than half the employees in city bakeries were German-born, a proportion that remained steady for most of the century. German bakeries were at first small, family-owned businesses, usually housed in the basements of tenement buildings employing no more than four or five workers. The owners earned a profit by paying their workers abysmally—eight to twelve dollars a week—and working them as many as sixteen or even twenty hours a day. A bakery union leader called his members the "worst treated men of any trade practiced in the civilized world." Strikes were common, but they did little to change working conditions, hours, or pay.

As the number of German immigrants swelled, New Yorkers began to notice some distinctive characteristics of their new neighbors. They had a strong organizational impulse, gathering in German labor unions and clubs devoted to singing, gymnastics, shooting sports, and the like, and they loved to go to parks for mass picnics with their countrymen. In 1855 the *New York Daily Times* reported on an excursion of more than five thousand Germans up to Manhattan's Elm Park (near Eighty-Fifth Street on today's Upper West Side) for a day to enjoy singing, drinking beer, and eating: "The tables groaned with cold boiled and roast meats, sausages, rye bread, cakes of most uncouth shapes and strange construction, and the inevitable lager bier keg."[3] Their love of rye bread was one of the Germans' distinguishing traits. In the mid-nineteenth century some New York bakeries were still producing rye loaves, particularly New England–style brown bread, but the taste for it was dying out. An advertisement asked: "Who Uses Rye Bread When Wheat Can be Had?" An 1871 survey of New York's bakeries discovered that it was immigrants on the Lower East Side who kept the taste alive: "The Germans consume most of the rye bread made. This is of two kinds. The sweet rye bread is made in the ordinary way of making fermented bread. The sour rye bread is allowed to pass through acetous fermentation before baking. It generally contains caraway seed."[4]

Central European immigrants were able to enjoy rye bread in their new home, because American farms were still growing sufficient rye grain to supply urban bakeries. These included farmers in New England, where locals still relied on Rye and Indian and Boston brown bread as staples, and rural Pennsylvania, home of the Pennsylvania "Dutch" (or "Deutsch," meaning "German"). The latter had been settling in south-central Pennsylvania since the seventeenth century and still preferred dark rye sourdough breads over wheat. As further waves of European immigrants arrived after 1850, they moved west to clear farmland and plant rye as well as wheat and corn. Rye had the advantage that it did well on poor and sandy soils and was more pest-resistant than wheat. In Madison, Wisconsin, the German immigrant Edward Gunkel opened a bakery whose "wheat and rye bread [was] known throughout the city for its excellence and flavor."[5] Larger farms sold their rye grain to millers, who turned it into flour or meal, packed it in barrels, and sent it by wagon and boat to the New York docks, where the big flour wholesalers sold it to city bakeries and grocery stores.

Not all rye bread eaten by New York City's German community was produced by commercial bakeries. Many German immigrant housewives had access to a book that was nearly as common as the Bible on their shelves: the *Praktisches Kochbuch für die gewöhnliche und feinere*

Küche ("Practical cookbook for everyday and fine dining"). Its author was Henriette Davidis, a Lutheran minister's daughter from the Ruhr region whose cookbook held a similar position in nineteenth-century Germany as *The Joy of Cooking* in twentieth-century America. Davidis's book went through dozens of editions, including its first American printing in 1879, three years after her death. Although they were frequently revised and augmented, all of the editions include her recipe for Sour Rye Bread.

SOUR RYE BREAD

To 1 quart of water add 5 pounds of rye flour and some sour dough (leavening) the size of an apple.

The evening before baking warm the water and mix the leavening with part of the flour into a thin dough, dust with flour and set aside to raise until the next morning. Then knead in the salt and the remaining flour, make into a long loaf, set to raise again and bake in a hot oven for 2 hours.

If the dough should not have raised enough, work in a little yeast when kneading; if buttermilk is used instead of water, the bread will be nicer; then use only half of the leavening.[6]

Seeing Davidis's success, German American publishers and authors rushed to produce competing cookbooks, most importantly *Aunt Babette's Cookbook*, issued in 1889 by Bloch Publishers of Cincinnati. "Aunt Babette" was the pseudonym for Bertha Kramer, a German-Jewish housewife living in Cincinnati, who gave her own version of Davidis's sour rye recipe:

RYE BREAD

Get a piece of sour dough from a baker, about as large as an apple; mix the dough in a pan, say about four pounds of flour and one quart of lukewarm water (buttermilk is better, if you can get it), a handful of salt and some caraway seed. Make a soft sponge and let it rise all night. In the morning work in the rest of the flour and make a pretty stiff dough. You may use a little wheat flour on your baking board in kneading it in the morning.

> Work the mass of dough into a ball, your hands having been well floured; knead hard, always toward the center of the ball, which should be repeatedly turned over and around that every portion may be manipulated. The longer you knead the finer the pores of your bread. No matter if you do feel fatigued, the exercise is beneficial to your arms and chest. Now work the dough into shapely loaves and let it rise again for an hour, then wet, or rather brush, the top of the loaves with water and bake slowly for almost two hours. Break off a piece of dough and keep for next baking; and if you find at any time that your dough has not risen properly, add some yeast in the morning.[7]

To make these loaves, you needed either a German bakery nearby that could provide the sourdough or the knowledge on how to propagate your own sourdough leaven. The vast majority of American housewives evidently did not, because I could find only one sourdough rye recipe published outside German immigrant communities between 1850 and 1920. In 1925 the *Chicago Tribune* food columnist Jane Eddington surmised: "Perhaps the tradition grew up that rye breads were too strong of flavor for American tastes because of the sour rye breads made with a starter of sour dough and a darker flour than the sweet rye breads which seem popular today."[8]

In the decades after the Civil War, German immigrants in New York prospered as the city grew. A few rose to become noted bankers, merchants, publishers, and civic leaders. Their new wealth allowed them to move out of Kleindeutschland and up to newer and more spacious buildings, particularly in the Yorkville neighborhood of the Upper East Side. The Lower East Side, meanwhile, filled up with a new immigrant population: tens of thousands of East European Jews. These were mostly poor, Yiddish-speaking Jews from the shtetls, or predominantly Jewish villages, of what is today Belarus, Hungary, Lithuania, Poland, Russia, and Ukraine. They moved into tiny tenement apartments, established synagogues, and found jobs in neighborhood businesses, including German-owned basement bakeries. Like the Germans, the new Jewish immigrants had a taste for rye loaves, preferably baked following recipes they knew from their homelands. Because of their poverty, their staple was coarse and dark rye bread. Their typical weekday diet involved a hunk of rye with a cup of weak tea or coffee for breakfast, bread and a bit of farmer's cheese for lunch, and a dinner of bread and soup. Bakers sold their wares by the pound, cutting off chunks from big, brown loaves decorated with a paper stamp with the bakery logo weighing five pounds or more. The cheapest loaves of all were sold from pushcarts that lined the neighborhood shopping streets:

> On a street stand in Essex Street was a pile of bread which resembled varnished black walnut. Though very unsightly, it seemed very popular. In a half an hour no less than forty loaves were sold to the poor Russians and Slovaks who populate that district. The proprietor of the little establishment, a short, wiry, black bearded son of Wallachia, said: "It doesn't look very good, but it is very strengthening. It is made out of yellow corn meal, rye, salt, molasses and yeast. The two meals should be cheap, coarse and a little sour, or spoiled. When they are soured they make better bread and are much cheaper. The bread is very solid, being more than twice as heavy as the white breads you Americans make from wheat flour. Its price is two, two and a half, and three cents a pound. One pound a half a workman eats, and its keeps him in good health and strength. Most of my customers use two types in their daily diet, the one plain and the other flavored with anise seed or caraway seed. Generally they use skim milk cheese with it. The people here are too poor to use anything else."[9]

Actually it's doubtful that this bread contained any cornmeal; the baker probably just dusted the bottom of the loaf with meal to keep it from sticking to the pan. Nevertheless, these heavy, dark, rye loaves that he described remained staples of New York Jewish bakeries into the twentieth century.

In 1900 the United States Census counted 2,498 bakeries in New York City. The majority were owned by immigrants, mostly Germans but

Figure 13. Residents of a cellar bakery: a baker and his cat, who liked to sleep on loaves of bread warm from the oven. *Source*: Factory Investigating Commission, *Preliminary Report of the Factory Investigating Commission*, vol. 1 (Argus Company, 1912).

also East European Jews, French, Swedes, Irish, and Italians. Nearly all of them were housed in basements in the same neighborhoods where immigrants lived. Around 1892 the German bakery–dominated workers' unions began to agitate to ban the "cellar bakeries," calling them "foul," "filthy," and "disease-laden." The ceilings of their work rooms averaged only seven to eight feet tall, with no windows, no ventilation, and no access to the outside world except a narrow flight of steps up to the street. Bakeries' refuse-strewn wood or dirt floors were often damp; sewage pipes from the tenement above leaked; and flies, roaches, and rats infested the cellar. To keep pests under control, bakers kept cats, which often slept on warm loaves of bread cooling from the oven. Some owners even raised pigs, rabbits, and chickens in the same space as their bakeries. In this "stale and foul" environment, bakers toiled mostly nights, for low pay twelve or more hours a day seven days a week. Only Jewish bakers got a day off for Shabbat. With little money and exhausted from work, they often ended up sleeping in the bakery. Many suffered from occupational diseases such as bronchitis and tuberculosis, with few able to work past age forty-five. One journalist described the eerie appearance of bakery workers emerging during hot summer nights: "Out of the mouths of those unwholesome cellar bakeries now attracting unfriendly criticism there come in the small hours of night ghostly figures that sit on the stone steps at street level or lie flat upon one of the inclined doors. These are the flour-dust and dough-bedaubed journeymen come up from their little hell below stair to breath the comparatively cool air of the semi-tropical summer night in the street."[10]

Newspaper articles under headlines like "Disease Laden Bakeries" outraged the public and spurred progressive politicians to try to pass laws to clean up bakeries and improve working conditions for the journeymen. Similar anti–cellar bakery campaigns occurred in cities with large immigrant populations, including Baltimore, Chicago, Milwaukee, Philadelphia, and Saint Louis. They were vigorously resisted by associations of bakery owners. In 1895, New York's governor signed the Bakeshop Act, limiting workers to sixty-hour weeks, mandating sanitary conditions, and banning animals. Conrad Moll, a Lower East Side bakery owner and leader of the city's Boss Bakers' Association, was indignant:

> This bill is outrageous and unconstitutional. It says a man shall work only sixty hours a week. What right has the Legislature to forbid a man working as many hours as he pleases? The journeymen bakers all want to be bosses, and they think they can run our shops, but they'll find themselves mistaken. Their wages will be reduced and they'll be sorry they meddled in our business. As for animals in our bakeshops, what nonsense! Can you help it if your dogs follow you into the bakeroom? Cats are good to catch rats, and there's no harm having rabbits around. They eat the waste flour, and it makes them healthy.[11]

Unfortunately, enforcement of the new laws was ineffectual, mainly due to corruption and inefficiency in the new corps of bakery inspectors.

Then, in 1899, Joseph Lochner, a German immigrant who owned a Utica, New York, bakery, was charged with working his men over the sixty-hour limit. After his conviction (which led to a fifty-dollar fine), Lochner appealed and, with the support of the New York State bakers association, brought the case all the way up to the US Supreme Court. In a controversial 1905 decision (that remains contentious today) the majority held for Lochner, stating that the state could not interfere in a contract between an employer and his workers. Following the deadly Triangle Shirtwaist Factory fire in 1911, New York State began a new round of investigations into all kinds of workplaces, including bakeries. They found conditions in cellar bakeries largely unchanged from two decades earlier. Lawmakers were unable to close the bakeries or reduce workers' hours, but they did strengthen the sanitary inspection system and forbid the establishment of new cellar bakeries. Today New York City's cellar bakeries have disappeared, closed by owners who retired, changes in the neighborhood population, and health codes banning coal-fired ovens in residential buildings. One of the last was Orwasher's on the Upper East Side, which was opened by a Hungarian immigrant in 1916. The Orwasher family sold their business in 2007; the breads, many still made with the original recipes, are now baked in a modern, aboveground facility in the South Bronx.

As urban bakeries moved by fits and starts into the modern era, their customers retained their taste for rye breads. Exactly which variety depended on the neighborhood, wealth, and place of origin of the consumer. The loaves could range from dark, 100 percent rye loaves made with sourdough leaven to light, yeast-risen white rye breads, with many gradations in between. The darkest and densest was Westphalian pumpernickel, a sourdough that was at first only favored by German immigrants. Then American medical authorities noticed its high fiber content and recommended it for dyspeptics, and hostesses discovered they could slice it thin and use it for little sandwiches—perfect finger food for parties. You could buy pumpernickel loaves imported from

Westphalia (it kept well thanks to its density) or from German bakeries that used formulas like this: "584 lbs coarse rye flour (unbolted); 33 gal. water, 15 lbs leaven, adding sufficient salt. The dough so prepared rests two to three hours, is moulded, rested again one hour, then put into the oven."[12] For customers who wanted a lighter loaf, bakeries would make a sourdough "Bohemian rye" with fine rye flour or a "Half Rye" with a fifty-fifty mix of rye and wheat flour. You could buy them either seasoned with caraway seeds or plain. Jewish bakeries developed an even softer loaf called "Russian pumpernickel" that replaced most of the rye with wheat flour and added some colorant, usually coffee, molasses, or burnt sugar, to give it the proper dark brown color. Raisin-dotted Russian pumpernickel rolls became a staple of breadbaskets at Jewish dairy restaurants such as Ratner's on Delancey Street.

In the first half of the twentieth century, Central and Eastern European immigrants and their descendants moved out of the tenement districts into the suburbs. Bakeries followed them. Their customers now had more money in their pockets and wanted a wider range of products for their tables. Bakers' display cases were no longer dominated by rows of big, dark, round rye loaves. Shoppers desired rolls both seeded and kaiser, white and whole wheat loaves, challahs, and, in the rye department, everything from pumpernickels to light ryes. Bakeries marketed their dark ryes, and particularly pumpernickel, as "Necessary to Good Health," extending their market beyond immigrants into the larger population. The light ryes came in football-shaped loaves so they could easily be sliced for sandwiches. This was the "streamlined" era of American eating, when housewives were urged to shop for speed and convenience. Rather than spend hours over a hot stove, they preferred to go to the neighborhood delicatessen and buy some sliced meat, potato salad, pickles, and a loaf of bread to make the family dinner.

The demographic changes stimulated a boom in the sales of rye loaves, and even the largest bakeries added them to their production lines. Seeing the market, big millers such as Washburn-Crosby, producer of the Gold Medal brand, and Pillsbury opened high-volume mills to produce rye flours. Their timing was excellent, because when the United States entered World War I, Herbert Hoover's US Food Administration launched a nationwide campaign to convince housewives to cut down on wheat flour so the grain could be sent to feed our soldiers and foreign allies. Instead, they were shown how to make tasty loaves out of rye, oats, barley, corn, and other grains. Of course, many Americans were not fans of 100 percent rye loaves, so millers sold "rye blend" flours made of 30 percent rye and 70 percent wheat. Rye flour sales peaked at 2.5 million barrels in 1919 but then dropped after the "wheatless" campaign ended. Except in cities with large immigrant populations, bakers were no longer taught how to propagate a sourdough. One professional manual suggested that students interested in making sourdough bread use starter "taken from a Jewish shop"—that is, a Jewish bakery where the process hadn't been forgotten.[13] Rather than bother with the time-consuming—and therefore more expensive—sourdough process, you could buy "sour" flavoring, often made with vinegar, from a bakery supply company to give your loaves a little tang.

One bakery that attempted to navigate these changes in the marketplace was Levy's Bakery in Brooklyn. In 1888, Henry S. Levy, a Russian Jewish immigrant, opened his bakery specializing in sour rye loaves in a Williamsburg storefront. During the 1920s he moved its operations out of the old storefront into a Bushwick factory building, which he began to outfit with all the latest machines. Determined to reach a wider customer base, Levy's descendant owners began to reduce the sour flavor of their traditional breads and introduce new, more "American" loaves. In 1949 the *New York Times*'s Clementine Paddleford was invited to tour the spotless baking rooms: "We saw the bread mixed, an automatic operation. Each ingredient was mixed exactly to formula, unbleached flour for the white bread, no softening agents, whole milk

Figure 14. This ad for Levy's bread, featuring an unlikely fan of "real Jewish rye," became a counterculture icon during the 1960s and hung on many dorm room walls. *Source*: Library of Congress.

powder (not the skim milk), honey the sweetening, yeast of course. The bread goes through all the usual processes, and finally to the hopper, the cutter, the rounder, the proofer, the moulder, it's racked for rising and into the oven."[14] The occasion was the introduction of Levy's new "oven-crust" white bread, formulated with the assistance of baking experts from General Mills and the Fleischmann's Yeast Company.

Nevertheless, it was Levy's rye loaves that remained the bakery's biggest seller. To market it, Levy's hired Bill Bernbach of the upstart ad agency Doyle Dane Bernbach to oversee an eye-catching advertising campaign. Levy's wanted to sell more to Jewish customers, but after tasting the—to him—lackluster loaves, Bernbach supposedly told the company's president: "Mr. Rubin, no Jew would eat your bread. If you want more business, we have to advertise to goyim."[15]

Counterintuitively Bernbach did that by emphasizing the Jewish character of its products. Levy's "Real Rye Bread" became "Real Jewish Rye," presumably because customers would be attracted by the deep "ethnic" flavor of the loaves. A 1954 ad shows a slim, WASPy looking woman grabbing the shirt of her grocer and putting her face angrily in his. "All right, all right," he concedes, "tomorrow I'll have it for you!" The copy asks: "Why are people all over New York insisting on Levy's Jewish rye bread? This is *real* rye . . . with a satisfying richness, a tang and texture Grandma would have been proud to serve."[16] In the early 1960s Doyle Dane Bernbach launched one of the most famous campaigns in advertising history. The text, written by copywriter Judy Protas, merely stated "You Don't Have to Be Jewish to Love Levy's Real Jewish Rye." Those words framed big photographs of distinctly un-Jewish figures—a Native American, a Catholic choirboy, an Irish cop, and so on—happily chewing a slice of Levy's bread. The ads first appeared on posters hung in every subway station and then in newspapers. Their directness, humor, and incongruity made them a symbol of the societal upheaval of the era. Some college students would tear down the ad featuring the Native American and hang it in their dorm rooms. The DDB campaign continued until 1979, when Connecticut's Arnold Bakers bought the Levy's name, bread formulas, and sourdough starter and closed the Brooklyn factory. The Levy's brand has changed hands several times since then. Today's yeast-risen Levy's "Real Jewish Rye"—which gets its tang from grain vinegar not sourdough—is produced by Bimbo Bakeries, a branch of Mexico's Grupo

Bimbo, the conglomerate with the largest share of the world's baking industry.

Rye bread had become sandwich bread, a vehicle to enclose slices of ham or bologna smeared with mustard or mayo. Consumers bought it at the supermarket, first squeezing the plastic-wrapped loaves to make sure they were soft, a sign that they were fresh. For rye purists who remembered the old days of corner bakeries, this was blasphemy. "A good piece of bread, you can step on it, and it'll come back," claimed a Philadelphia baker named "Nookie" Rosen. "Today the rye bread's not worth nothing. Did you ever squeeze the middle? . . . chewing gum. It's raw dough. . . . They got no crusts, no bottoms and no tops."[17]

For rye bread aficionados, however, there remained one loaf that symbolized all the best that rye could offer, scrumptious enough to eat with just a smear of good butter. It was called in Yiddish *Kornbroyt*, literally "corn bread" or more commonly "corn rye." In this case, "korn" didn't mean "maize" but, as in German, "grain." Corn ryes were only available in old-school Jewish bakeries like Nookie Rosen's North Philadelphia bakery. It was a rye sourdough made with about one-third rye flour and two-thirds a wheat flour grade called "first clear." This was the flour that remained after the milling process removed all the "patent," or high-grade white flour from the "middlings" (what was left after all the bran and other coarse parts had been removed). First clear flour had a grayish color, a high protein content but relatively low gluten. Jewish bakers liked it because it made loaves denser than white flour, giving it a chewier texture, and because it was cheaper. To make corn rye loaves, they mixed the flours in big troughs along with sourdough starter, yeast, salt, and more hydration, or water content, than regular ryes so that it had the texture of a very damp sponge. In about an hour the dough was sufficiently risen. Bakers reached into the trough with both hands and pulled out big floppy balls of dough that they plopped onto a baking sheet strewn with cornmeal. After roughly shaping them, they pricked the tops to keep them from splitting and immediately slid them into the ovens. Afterward, they brushed the hot loaves with a cornstarch and water glaze and moved them to the bakery shelves. Those customers who were in the know showed up just at the right time to buy loaves warm from the oven to rush home and eat.

As the mom-and-pop Jewish bakeries began to close down and the loaf became harder to find, home bakers determined to learn the secrets of what they called "Jewish corn bread" and make it themselves. Their goal was a heavy loaf with a cornmeal-crusted bottom, chewy crust, dense grayish crumb, and a faint nutty aroma of blended rye and wheat. It could be flavored with caraway seeds or not. The journey was long, and lined with missteps. The first problem was the word "corn" in "corn rye," which led them to assume, wrongly, that it must have cornmeal in the crumb. They found a recipe from Rita Leinwand, food editor of *Bon Appetit* magazine, who included cornmeal and mashed potatoes in the rye-wheat dough but no sourdough starter. It would have made a dense loaf but not a classic corn rye.

Then in 1979, Helen Witty and Elizabeth Schneider Colchie published their remarkable cookbook *Better Than Store-Bought*, which dared consumers to make at home foods that they were used to buying at the supermarket—everything from liverwurst to tofu, bagels to "Jewish 'Corn' Bread." The authors weren't sure why it was called "corn bread," but they knew that cornmeal wasn't in the Jewish bakery loaf. They told readers how to make their own rye sourdough starter, which they added to the corn rye dough along with all-purpose flour, "gluten flour" (now known as high-gluten flour), salt, yeast, a tiny bit of sugar, and water. They instructed home bakers to hand-knead the dough and let it rise before putting in the oven sprinkled with caraway or nigella seeds. This was much closer to a bakery loaf, though it was a bit lighter in texture and had less sourdough flavor due to a short fermentation time.

Decades later, a couple of Jewish bakers peeled back the veil and allowed us to understand how they really made corn rye. The books were *Secrets of a Jewish Baker* (1993) by George Greenstein and *Inside the Jewish Bakery* (2011) by Stanley Ginsberg and Norman Berg. The latter book in particular, which was based on professional baker Berg's formulas and decades of experience, gives the most authoritative recipe for corn rye, including two-stage overnight fermentation and high hydration. After Berg's death his coauthor Ginsberg followed up with *The Rye Baker*, a cookbook of recipes for not only corn rye but rye loaves from all over Europe from west to east. Through it, a home baker can trace the history of rye in the United States, from Boston brown bread and New York–style deli rye back to almost-black Baltic loaves and the Westphalian pumpernickel that helped launch European-style rye in this country.

9

ITALIAN BREAD

DURING THE 1880S JOURNALISTS liked to go down to the immigration station at Castle Garden, located at the southern tip of Manhattan, to observe the spectacle of just-landed immigrants piling into the great hall to be examined and sorted. A new group had joined the English, Irish, Germans, Scandinavians, Hungarians, Russians, and East European Jews who crowded the vast space: Italians, largely from the southern provinces of Campania, Puglia, Basilicata, Calabria, and Sicily. Reporters at first noticed their vivid dress: "In the next corner a group of Italians nervously fidgeted about, keeping up an endless chatter. The women wore brightly colored dresses of cheap material and with ugly rings dangling from their ears."[1] The men "were generally dirty, with unshaven faces and unkempt hair and soiled clothing."[2] The reporters pegged the Italians as "paupers" and likely to become burdens upon the city government. Soon, however, the newspapers learned that most immigrants from southern Italy were men who had been lured overseas by a *padrone*, a kind of labor broker. The *padrone* paid for their steamship tickets and, after their arrival in the United States, found work for them as unskilled laborers, taking their pay and giving them a pittance to live on. Most of these contract workers were sojourners, planning to work for a few years, save a small nest egg, and return to their families back in Italy. Until then, they intended to live as they always had, including basing their diet around chunks cut from big, round, dark-baked loaves of Italian bread.

These Italian immigrants were largely peasants escaping the grinding poverty of their lives in the fields and villages of southern Italy. For generations they and their families had toiled as sharecroppers on vast estates owned by absentee landlords who had little interest in modern farming techniques or improving the lot of their workers. Their lands were wracked by erosion and drought, their crops undersold by cheap grain from the United States and Canada. While the men sweated in the fields, the women tended the home. These were usually simple, one-room stone houses situated in small villages; the family often shared their living quarters with a mule or other livestock. There was no running water, so the women had to draw their drinking, cooking, and cleaning water at the village well and carry it home in clay jars. Their tasks also included washing, taking care of children, sewing, and preparing the family's food. Meals were based around bread, beans, cheese, olive oil, onions, garlic, and whatever greens the women could forage in the nearby hills. Most of their calories came from bread.

Women baked once a week, usually on Saturday or Monday. They would take some of their family's store of wheat to the village miller to be ground. Wheat was the preferred grain, but in the poorest areas they would also add rye, chestnuts, and beans to fill out the dough. They would mix the flour with water, salt, and as leaven a piece of old dough left over from the previous week's bake. Each region had its preferred styles and shapes of loaf, particularly for feast days, but the basic

Figure 15. Italian bread peddlers on Mulberry Street, New York, 1900. *Source*: Library of Congress.

bread was a big round loaf weighing from two to five pounds. Depending on the size of her family, the housewife could make as many as a half dozen of them at a time. Only wealthier families had their own ovens; usually women had to take their risen loaves to the neighborhood communal oven to bake. As she slid them onto the hot stones, the housewife said a prayer over the loaves to ensure success. Further superstitions followed the finished bread. Before it was cut, the knife had to be kissed and the loaf blessed. "Food" meant "bread," and they believed that without this gift from God they would starve.

In the United States, Italians found jobs in New York and other big cities like Boston, Philadelphia, and Baltimore; in the textile mills of Lawrence, Massachusetts, and Paterson, New Jersey; and in coal mines, stone quarries, railway construction projects, and farms all over the East. In each of these places one of the first things they did was acquire a source of their accustomed loaves. In New York they largely settled in the East Side neighborhood that became known as Little Italy and in East Harlem, where Italian bakeries opened to serve immigrants. Bakers both sold their own loaves and rented their ovens to housewives who couldn't bake in tiny American stoves.

> At the hour when the baker has his oven heated just right all patrons of that bakery are on hand. They form in line behind him. At one side of the oven is the white garbed, energetic baker. Two long lines of women are there with immense pans of bread poised on their heads. All are carefully covered with tablecloths. The Italian bread may not suit American palates; but the women are careful in guarding it from dirt before it is baked. When Giorgio gives the signal flop goes the first woman's pan. An immense loaf a foot and a half in diameter is turned on the bread paddle. With a quick thrust Giorgio sends it back into the rear of the oven. Another and another follow, as quickly as the women can empty them onto the paddle and Giorgio can arrange them, until, in the orange white light of the oven, there rest so many white fat cushions of dough, and Giorgio shuts the doors. The oven is full. Four or five hours later the women will come again. Some bring small boys to bear big loaves home upon their backs. Some with the loaf wrapped in cloth will walk home with overgrown crowns on their heads.[3]

Most Italian immigrants, however, were men who had left their bread-baking wives back in their villages. They had to either buy their loaves from the baker or, if desperate, purchase the stale product returned by grocery stores: "The bread that used to be thrown away is now taken back by the big bakeries from the retail houses, and is collected by men, who sell it to the women; the latter retail it at one to three cents a loaf from the curbstone. . . . The economical, however, still purchase the black bread of their youth . . . at three cents a pound."[4]

Away from the cities, Italian workers had to fend for themselves to find bread. If they were lucky, a nearby town had an Italian bakery to supply them. In Maine, Italian railway workers either had a baker in their camp or had to import it from the nearest city. While waiting at a rural station, one journalist saw a large sack "which had come up from Bangor that morning consigned to a camp on the line . . . and it contained one hundred loaves of Italian bread."[5] The railway's chief engineer explained that, to his workers, the bread was a necessity for life. Italian farm workers led more settled lives and often were able to bring their wives over. In places like southern New Jersey or the Mississippi Delta, they built small homes with large vegetable gardens and in the yard, an oven: "At a short distance from each house is the typical Italian oven, built of stones and bricks, covered with cement. In these ovens the Italians bake their bread once a week."[6] In Hammonton, New Jersey, an investigator reported: "Bread is made from the best white flour, usually baked into hard, round loaves, in the characteristic ovens. Sometimes one oven is used by several families."[7] To outsiders, these ovens seemed primitive, like something unearthed at Pompeii, but to immigrants they were easy to build, inexpensive to heat (often with scavenged wood), and good at baking the familiar loaves at the center of their diet.

As they had back in Italy, the residents of these Italian communities saw bread as much more than a starch to accompany their meals. In his memoir of growing up in a Rochester, New York, Italian neighborhood, Jerre Mangione remembers:

> My relatives, like all Sicilians, had a deep-seated reverence for bread, and they transferred it to their children to such an extent that none of us, even to this day, can eat food without bread and not feel guilty. It was considered sinful to waste bread, or to permit a loaf to sit upside down, or to eat meat without eating bread. . . . Aside from its traditional association with the body of Christ, bread to my relatives was a daily reminder of the hardships they and their ancestors had endured to survive, a symbol of man's humbleness. They regarded it as some God-bequeathed friend who would keep their bodies and souls together when nothing else would.[8]

For a loaf to be worthy of that respect, however, it had to resemble the breads that they used to eat back in the Old Country—the big, dark loaves of Puglia or the fine-grained semolina breads sprinkled with sesame like they made in Sicily—and not the soft, puffy pan loaves sold in American bakeries.

Immigrants from southern Italy faced far more racial prejudice than the French or Germans during this period. They were seen as backward, uneducated, and prone to violence, and their cuisine as primitive, revolving around tomatoes, olive oil, rank cheese, foraged greens, macaroni, and of course bread. In his authoritative *The Baker's Book* (1901), the German-born baking expert Emil Braun stated:

> That the Italian bread is made the worst in the world, with the possible exception of that of Greece, is fairly well known, and it has kept up its reputation well; dark in color, made in the shape of large buns about a foot in diameter, it is about as uninviting as it could possibly be made, yet, notwithstanding this, the natives want it so badly that in many towns rioting and looting of the bakers' shops for this bread that would not be eaten in the United States is of frequent occurrence.[9]

Consequently it was decades before most Americans dared to taste Italian bread. In 1912, one who dared was this New Yorker who frequented Little Italy:

> I worked for a time in a place on Broome Street, and one Easter I took home a loaf of bread for a joke. It was all covered with dough flowers and curlicues and it looked funny, but it tasted good and the family wanted more. Since then I've had to take all the bread home, for my wife insists that it is better than other baker's bread and she never has a touch of her old indigestion unless she changes to old American bread. The bread is baked more thoroughly and even the freshest bread is never heavy and pasty. It keeps in condition for a week or more and so it's economical as well.[10]

Others discovered Italian bread because of the growing fad for eating at Italian restaurants, the kind catering to the "Bohemian" set of artists and writers looking for romance amid checked tablecloths, candles flickering in old Chianti bottles, and plates heaped with spaghetti and meatballs.

And one night Alberta and I took dinner
At a place near Fourteenth Street where the music
Was like the sun on a breeze-swept lake
When every wave is a patine of fire
And I thought of you not at all
Looking at Alberta and watching her white teeth
Bite off bits of Italian bread,
And watching her smile and the wide pupils
Of her eyes, electrified by wine
And music and the touch of our hands
Now and then across the table
We went to her house at last.[11]

What many city dwellers didn't know was that they were likely already buying loaves crafted in the ovens of Italian bakeries. During the Gold Rush immigrants from northern Italy hurried to California to find their fortunes, some opening businesses like the Genoa Bakery in San Francisco. They were adept at adjusting their techniques to customers' tastes, so that they produced Italian bread but also French sourdough loaves, American white bread, Boston brown bread, and so on. On the East Coast this process of acculturation took longer due to the larger number and concentration of southern Italians in immigrant ghettos like Little Italy. The bakers had all the business they needed producing loaves for their countrymen. In the early twentieth century, however, they and their children began to move out of the inner city into more comfortable homes in the outer boroughs and suburbs. They opened bakeries and found that they faced different market pressures than in the old neighborhood.

Around 1907 an immigrant from Puglia started a bakery in Italian Harlem. His grandson, the political scientist Michael Parenti, told the tale:

> The bread he made was the same bread that had been made in Gravina, Italy for generations. After two days standing it was as fresh as ever, the crust having grown hard and crisp while the inside remained soft, solid, moist and tasty. People used to say that our bread was a meal unto itself. The secret of the bread had been brought by my grandfather all the way from the Mediterranean to Manhattan, down into the tenement basement where he had installed wooden vats and tables. The bakers were two dark wiry men, *paisani da Gravina*, who rhythmically and endlessly pounded their powdery white hands into the dough, molding the bread with finesse and strength. My grandfather, and then my father after him, used time and care in preparing their bread, letting it sit and rise twice in one night, using no chemicals and only the best quality flour. The bread was baked slowly and perfectly in an old brick oven built into the basement wall by my grandfather in 1907, an oven that had secrets of its own.[12]

After Parenti's grandfather died, his father inherited the business, expanding its distribution to the Bronx, first to newer Italian neighborhoods, "where the appreciation of good bread was one of the satisfactions of our labor." Over time, the bakery also began to sell to restaurants, grocery stores, and supermarkets. Then, however, the manager of the Jerome Avenue Supermarket told him that one of the big factory bakeries was going into the Italian line and wanted to give their first 500 loaves for free to the supermarket. Mr. Parenti grudgingly made a deal, offering 300 loaves for free (but later got some of his profit back by sending them 550 loaves in the weekly order instead of 575—they never counted). The next challenge came when the health department demanded that the bakery wrap each loaf in a plastic bag: "Now it looked and *tasted* like modern bread because the bags kept the moisture in, and the loaves would get gummy in their own humidity inside their antiseptic plastic skins instead of forming a crisp, tasty crust in the open air."[13] Mr. Parenti finally gave up, closing his bakery and finding work driving a New York City taxi. Other Italian bakeries, however, aggressively competed for market share and supermarket space by cutting prices, preslicing and bagging their loaves, and adding products like French bread and challah to their line. Their loaves no longer looked and tasted like they had back in the Old Country, but it mattered less because fewer and fewer customers remembered.

The competition from the big factory bakeries began during the 1920s, when their owners decided to try to re-create Italian bread in their massive steel ovens. White American loaves were their principal product, but, with advantages of scale and efficiency, they also made many varieties of rye, Graham, French, Vienna, and Boston brown breads to cater to every taste—and undercut smaller competitors. Why not Italian too? The trade journal *Bakers' Helper* told them: "Italian breads are more of the French Bread type, an all water bread—no milk, no shortening, sponge bread without sugar, some American bakers no doubt using a little malt but plenty of salt."[14] For leavening, they mainly used dough left over from the previous bake. Unfortunately the "old dough" method was too complicated for big bakeries; they preferred quicker straight yeast "Italian" breads made without sugar or shortening. In fact, their "Italian" formulas weren't too different from the "French." As one baking manual stated: "These categories are diffuse." The only way consumers shopping at an average grocery store could tell the difference between industrially produced French and Italian loaves was that the French were longer, while Italian bread sometimes came sprinkled with sesame seeds.

Another issue was the quality of the crust, which in traditional Italian bakeries was always substantial, forming a protective shell that kept the crumb moist for days. The big bakeries, however, decided that the crust did not matter: "In fact, it appears that the average consumer does not really appreciate a classical crisp crust. Tough crusts, as found on many of the health, sourdough, or hearth breads generally owe their toughness to their thickness, and are often sought for and appreciated by the brown bread and buttermilk crowd. . . . This is difficult to achieve in US distribution systems, since the crispness is lost in a few hours due to moisture transfer into the crust from the atmosphere and from the crumb."[15] The crisp Italian crust disappeared, as big commercial bakeries valued long shelf-life over all other characteristics. By the late twentieth century, the "ethnic" breads sold by big supermarket chains lost any resemblance to the loaves that had arrived with European immigrants. Many bakeries used just one all-purpose formula for "American-style French/Italian/Vienna bread." The only way you could tell the difference between them was the name on the plastic bag in the supermarket.

Luckily, discerning eaters still could find old-school Italian loaves—if they lived near an Italian-American community large enough to support a traditional bakery. In 1944 a reader who was "a housewife, an excellent cook" told the *New York Herald Tribune* food writer Clementine Paddleford about the Zampieri Brothers Bakery down in Greenwich Village where you could buy "well crusted" loaves. It turned out that the Zampieris made both Italian bread and French rolls for high-end restaurants. A few years later, Jane Nickerson of the *New York Times* had great "crusty" bread at a Little Italy restaurant and asked the owner where it came from. He bought it from the Parisi family's Villa Roma bakery at 198 Mott Street: "The whole wheat bread that comes in both round and long loaves is so good that it is a mystery that a loaf like it is not more generally available. How anyone could prefer to such a product the white paste that goes by the name of bread in the average grocery is unexplainable."[16] Sally Dorst's 1973 *The New York Food Book* listed a dozen Italian bakeries in Manhattan and Brooklyn where you could get loaves that could transport you, at least in the imagination, to southern Italy.

Unless you were brought up in an Italian immigrant bread-making family, it was much harder to re-create those loaves at home, because recipes were nearly nonexistent. One of the earliest appears in Maria Lo Pinto's 1963 *The Art of Italian Regional Cooking*. Her recipe for "Italian Bread" is made from flour, water, yeast, salt, oil, and honey or sugar—not too different from an American white bread—but formed into a round or oblong loaf and sprinkled with sesame seeds before baking. It wasn't until 1985, and the publication of the groundbreaking *The Italian Baker* by Carol Field, that home bakers—and many professionals—could finally learn about the richness and variety of *pane Italiano*. She begins with an in-depth exposition of the country's baking history, emphasizing the fact that there isn't one "Italian bread" but in reality hundreds or even thousands of regional and local baking traditions. Field opens the book with a chapter on *pani regionali e rustici*: "These are the traditional regional breads of Italy, made only with flour, water, yeast, and salt. Most get their taste from a starter that has been allowed to mature and grow slightly sour, so that the loaves will have the deep mellow taste of the grain itself."[17]

In Italy that starter is called the *biga*, a preferment of flour, water, and yeast made at least the day before the bread. The *biga* is the key ingredient to her *pane pugliese*, which is the direct descendant of the massive loaves made by immigrants a century earlier:

PANE PUGLIESE

1 1/4 teaspoons active dry yeast or 1/2 small cake (9 grams) fresh yeast

1/4 cup warm water

3 cups water, room temperature

4/5 cup (200 grams) *biga*

7 1/2 cups (1000 grams) unbleached all-purpose flour

1 tablespoon plus 1 teaspoon (20 grams) salt

Stir the yeast into the warm water in a large mixing bowl; let stand until creamy, about 10 minutes. Add 3 cups water and the starter and mix with the paddle until well blended. Add the flour and salt and mix until the dough comes together and pulls away from the side of the bowl, 1 to 2 minutes. You may need to add another 1 to 2 tablespoons flour. Change to the dough hook and knead at medium speed for 3 to 5 minutes. The dough will be very soft and elastic but will never pull entirely away from the bottom of the bowl. If you want, finish kneading by hand on a floured surface with floured hands until the dough loses its stickiness and is soft and velvety, about 1 minute.

First Rise. Place the dough in a lightly oiled large bowl or plastic tub, cover tightly with plastic wrap, and let rise until tripled, about 3 hours.

Shaping and Second Rise. Flour your work surface generously, flour a dough scraper, and have a mound of flour nearby for your hands. Pour the dough out of the bowl, flour the top, and cut into 2 or 3 equal pieces, depending on how many loaves you are planning. Flatten each piece of dough and roll up lengthwise, using your thumbs as a guide for how tight the rolls should be. Turn the dough 90 degrees, pat it flat, then roll up again still using your thumbs as a guide. Shape each piece into a ball by rolling the dough between your cupped hand and using the surface of the work table to generate tension and pull the dough taut across the skin of the dough. Place the loaves on floured parchment paper set on baking sheets or peels, cover with a heavy towel or cloth, and let rise until doubled, about 1 hour.

Baking. Thirty minutes before baking, heat the oven with baking stones in it to 450°. Five to ten minutes before baking, flour the tops of the loaves and dimple them all over with your fingertips. The imprints will disappear but will keep the dough from rising crazily in the oven. Let stand 5 to 10 minutes. The loaves will feel soft as a baby's bottom when ready to bake, though you will notice a bit of resistance in the dough. Sprinkle the stones with cornmeal. Italian bakers turn the doughs over into the oven very carefully with a swooping motion that scoops up some of the flour on the peel. You may prefer to slide the loaves onto the baking stones without turning them over, or, if they are on baking sheets, the loaves can be baked directly on the pans. Bake until golden brown and crusty, about 50 to 60 minutes for the larger loaves, 30 to 35 minutes for the smaller ones. Check by knocking on the bottom of each loaf and listening for the hollow ring that indicates it is cooked through, but, if you're in doubt, bake for the longer time indicated. Cool on racks.[18]

Field's meticulous instructions would have helped home cooks, who did not have the benefit of the oral tradition passed down from Italian mothers to daughters or the training of an Italian baker's apprentice, to approximate the massive, crusty loaves that were increasingly hard to find in what remained of the immigrant Italian communities.

Over the past forty years, many Italian storefront bakeries have closed their doors. Neighborhoods changed, families moved out, and the younger generation had less interest in such an arduous, low-profit-margin profession. Of those bakeries included in the Dorst book, only Parisi survives. In April 2026, a broken oven and the reluctance of the younger generation to take up the baking trade led to the closure of Caputo's in Brooklyn. The story of East Harlem's Morrone & Sons bakery illustrates some of the pressures on these family businesses. Rosa Morrone and her husband, immigrants from a little town outside of Naples, opened their bakery in 1956. Mr. Morrone eventually died, and his wife Rosa kept the bakery alive with the help of her son Anthony, the only one of her seven children who wanted to enter the business. But over the years the grueling work injured Anthony's back, and in 2007 the family was forced to shut down the bakery. A few days before closing the door, they posted a sign:

> To our friends and customers:
>
> For over 50 years, the Morrone Family has been providing you with the finest breads baked the Old World way, all natural and of course without preservatives. Along the way, our customers became our friends. Our neighborhood wasn't just a place to do business in, it was our home. Not a day doesn't go by when someone doesn't stop in to say "Hi Rosa" and shoot the breeze. Our neighborhood will still be our home. It is with great regret, that we must now say goodbye to our customers and friends, as we close our bakery.
>
> We wish to thank you, our friends and customers, for your support and loyalty all these years.
>
> Sincerely, the Morrone Family[19]

Other bakeries shuttered down due to rising rents or the loss of their customer base. Today Parisi is the last Italian bread bakery left in Little Italy, a neighborhood that has been swallowed by Chinatown from the south and gentrification from the north. It's easier to find Italian bread in the outer boroughs, at places like Il Fornaretto in Bensonhurst, Brooklyn, and Madonia Bakery on the Bronx's Arthur Avenue, but even those bakeries are facing pressure from changing demographics and the difficulty of passing on their business to new generations.

10

BAGELS

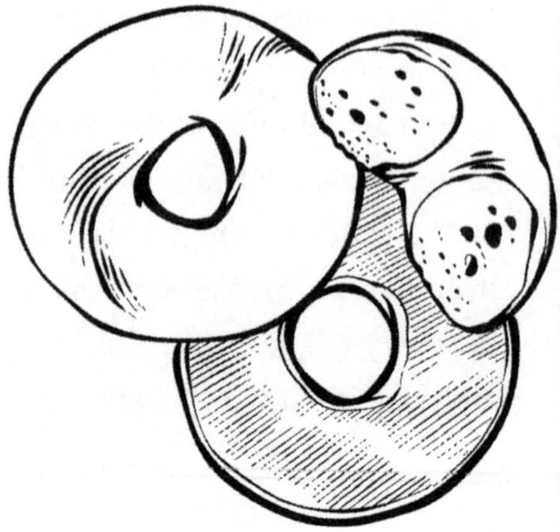

DURING THE NINETEENTH CENTURY the Jews of Eastern Europe lived in cities, towns, and villages stretching from Lodz and Warsaw in today's Poland to Odessa on the Black Sea and north to the Baltic Republics. Each of those communities had their own bread traditions, kinds and shapes of loaves that made them distinct from the those eaten in the next town down the river. Nevertheless, nearly all of them ate some kind of rye bread as their staple at breakfast, lunch, and dinner. On the sabbath it was the housewives' duty to make the ritual challah, a braided loaf made of fine wheat flour and often enriched with eggs, oil, and sugar. They also had a bread for when people were away from home—shopping at the weekly market, stopping by the tavern for a drink, or rushing out of religious school looking for a snack.

The *beigel*, or bagel, was one of the class of ring loaves found from Western Europe all the way into Central Asia.

The first time they're mentioned in a Jewish context was 1610, when the Jewish council of Krakow, Poland, announced that it was permissible to give bagels to women in childbirth, presumably because circular objects were supposed to bring good luck. Eastern European bagels were generally smaller and thinner than American bagels, but not always. In the town of Bobruisk (Babrusky, now in Belarus), the bagels were puffy, probably resembling smaller versions of today's American bagel. When a young man from there moved to the more cosmopolitan Vilna (Vilnius, Lithuania), he found everything new and different including the bagels:

> In the morning, the woman gave me a breakfast that consisted of two bagels with strong yellow butter, like an egg yolk. . . . The bagels were very strange to me, very different from the Bobruisker bagels. The Bobruisker bagels were thick around, swollen and with a small hole in the middle. In general, the Vilna baked goods made an impression on me. . . . I felt something new in life, that I was in a new city, in Vilna and that a new world was beginning for me.[1]

Bagels were made with wheat flour, sometimes with egg yolks added to the dough for richness and color. They were either smooth or twisted and could be plain or sprinkled with salt or poppy seeds. Jews often ate them for breakfast, usually spread with butter, and the best time to bite into them was when they were still warm. One boy looked forward to his grandfather's visits, because he always brought fresh hot bagels, even in winter:

> He crossed the threshold with a cheerful "got helf" [hello], and took off the bundle of sticks he carried over his shoulder. He spoke hastily, wanting the bagels to arrive warm. His beard and mustache were covered with ice and strewn with fluffy snow, and the bagels were indeed still warm, genuine Dzialoshitz bagels, twisted ones, sprinkled with poppy seed, browned to a golden luster, and they crunched gaily between your teeth.[2]

Bagels could be made in a bakery, but men and women also baked them at home to sell on market day or roving the streets as peddlers. The process wasn't particularly difficult: after mixing the dough and shaping it into rings, you let them rise, boiled them for a few minutes to ensure a crisp crust, and then slid them into the oven. (They were often called "water bagels," perhaps due to that boiling process.) One poor rabbi who turned to bagel-making to earn extra money claimed that he had found an easier way: "One takes a hole, surrounds it with dough, and a bagel emerges." Religious school students were particularly ravenous for bagels and were avid customers for the peddlers who showed up at the schoolyard during breaks. Bagels were also portable: they could fit in your pocket, and vendors could carry dozens on a loop of cord over their shoulder. Some peddlers made a good living hawking their bagels on intercity trains. With bagels' capacity for travel, it isn't surprising that they appeared in America shortly after the great wave of Eastern European migration began.

At the end of the nineteenth century, when the journalist Abraham Cahan began to write his essays depicting life on the Lower East Side, bagels were already a staple of that community. After the baker's union went out on strike, he reported that New York's Jews suffered the loss of their staple food: "Like every other foreign colony, the Russian and Polish Jews cling to their own methods and forms in the matter. So they miss their *bagels* (ring-shaped rolls), *challahs* (Sabbath loaves) and loaves of rye bread keenly."[3] By that time bagels had already spread from New York to other cities with Jewish populations, including Hartford, Connecticut:

> There are four Hebrew bakers in Hartford, Katz, Wershafsky, Goldstein and Magazend. They have formed a combine and agreed that all shall sell at the same price, and it is probable that they will raise prices. Many Hebrews call it the "Bagle Trust." A bagle is a kind of bun, shaped like a quoit. They are always found on the Hebrew breakfast table and a good many of them

> are sold by the bakers. The bakers have been running in competition lately, one selling two for a cent, while the regular prices in a penny a piece. This has brought about this combine and hereafter a bagle will cost a penny.[4]

Outsiders were for a long time unsure what exactly was a bagel, which they also spelled "beigel," "beygel," "buegel," "boygel," and so on. Jews tried to explain: "'B-a-g-e-l,' the witness replied. 'It's a hard donut with a hole in the middle.'"[5] In 1933 the *New York Herald Tribune* told readers: "In texture and hardness it resembles a pretzel, mainly because its dough consists only of flour, water and yeast. This mixture produces a pure white compact crumb. The center is soft, however. Because of its hard surface, it is a delicious accompaniment to a cup of hot coffee."[6] By the 1940s hungry New Yorkers had cracked the code on the bagel, figuring out not only how they were cooked but the best way to serve them. The food writer Clementine Paddleford explained:

> Bagels are a bread beloved by Jews and New Yorkers in general once they get the habit. . . . Simonized doughnuts is another pet name, because of their name. Yeast dough is rolled, cut into doughnut shapes, these dropped into boiling salted water and left until the bread floats to the top, and then out to drain well and finish off by browning in the oven. To eat, slice across, spread with cream cheese, lay on the pink slices of the smoke-tinged salmon. Fit on the top half of the bagel, now bring on the coffee.[7]

In the early decades New York's bagels were made in the same kind of Lower East Side bakeries as produced ryes and other Jewish breads, with similarly abysmal conditions. In 1894 the editor of the *Bakers' Journal*, published by the Journeyman Bakers' and Confectionery Workers' International Union of America, wrote to the *New York Press* decrying the horrible sanitation in the cellar bakeries. The *Press*'s reporters investigated, fanning out through the neighborhood and visiting every bakery they could find. One was a small, two-man operation owned by Max Derstenfeld at 183 Allen Street:

> To enter his bake shop a steep flight of eight or ten stone steps must be descended from the sidewalk. At the bottom of this cellar way there is a sort of long, narrow store room, lightened on the night it was visited by the *Press* party only by the rays of the single gas jet that flickered in the shop, proper to the rear. The floor is old, half rotten and mouldy. Barrels and boxes and a great collection of indescribable debris of one kind and another filled the place, with the exception of a narrow passageway. Trays of pretzel biscuit [probably bagels], more or less fresh from the oven, stood upon the barrels.
>
> At first sight the shop itself seemed to the visitor to be not half as bad as bakeshops go. To be sure, the floor was rotten, and bent under the weight of a person in every part; it was broken in some places, and where the bakers' coal had been it was wet, so wet that if a man stepped on that portion the splash of water underneath could clearly be heard. There was also a choice assortment of smells, rank and strong, penetrating and sour, and, at first, not noticeable, but afterward perceived to be all dominant, a singular odor whose quality cannot well be put into words, but which attacked the nostrils with a pertinacity that forced abhorrent recognition.[8]

The reporters declared that they could see "Croton bugs" crawling all over the walls and floors "as though attending a political convention." Derstenfeld replied: "What, the cockroaches? I don't make the cockroaches; I make bread. You want to go for the landlord about the cockroaches, not me."[9] Derstenfeld and his only worker baked twelve hours a day, seven days a week, for which the employee received only a seven-dollar weekly wage and board. For the journeymen bakers' association the only solution was to organize, to fight for better pay and healthier working conditions.

Jewish bakers on the Lower East Side and in Brooklyn and the Bronx participated in major strikes in 1901, 1905, and 1909. They forced bake shops to close, stuffing blankets in chimneys if owners tried to fire their ovens, and blocked scabs from entering the neighborhood. If out-of-town bakeries from Newark and Philadelphia tried to sell their wares in the city, strikers intercepted the wagons and threw the loaves into the muddy streets.

Jewish families suffered a bread drought, only able to eat loaves they baked themselves because "gentile bread" from outside the neighborhood was made with lard for added softness. Nevertheless, the boss bakers—the owners—had time, money, and the police on their side. In 1901 and 1905 their impoverished workers capitulated after a couple of weeks and went back to the shops for the same low pay, long hours, and terrible conditions. When the journeymen bakers' association went on strike on May Day 1909, they were bigger, better organized, and had amassed a war chest to help their men pay their rent and feed their families. They also had the support of the bakers' wives, who were often at the forefront of street fights and attacks on bakeries that stayed open. In face of the strikers' resolve, the boss bakers' association finally capitulated, signing an agreement giving them a twelve-hour, six-day workweek, better pay, and union shops.

On July 2 a five-thousand-strong parade set out from union headquarters at 127 Delancey Street: "In front marched about three hundred children of the bakers, all clad in white. They were followed by a truck on which was carried a loaf twenty feet long and five feet broad, which was decorated with American flags. Then came the bakers in white caps and blouses, kept in step by the music of six bands, and lastly fifty carriages containing the officers of the local unions, their friends, wives and families."[10]

Although bagel makers participated in these strikes, they were actually a breed apart from their union brothers, mainly because, due to custom and union regulations, regular bread and cake bakeries didn't manufacture bagels. Bagel workers had also mastered a unique skill unknown in other bakeries: rolling the dough into rings. The bagel-making process begins with high-gluten flour:

> For 100 pounds of flour, you add a pound and a half of salt, a quart of malt [syrup], 24 quarts of water and a half-pound of yeast. And—in the patois of bagel bakers—you pray "that the dough comes" (that it will rise in the

Figure 16. Bagel baker, Detroit, 1966. *Source: Detroit Free Press.*

kettle later on). Only heart and texture can tell you if the dough is the right texture—this is one of the reasons that there are people who can bake bagels, and people who can only eat them.

Now, when the dough is right, artists such as Frank and Fred pull off strips of the stuff and flip them into bagel shapes. "You clip it with your thumbs and roll it off your fingers," explained Frank. "For larger bagels, you might use four fingers."

The still uncooked bagels are loaded into trays, where they sit for six hours to give the yeast time to take effect. And then comes what is as much a moment of truth as the three-and-two pitch, or the matador sighting along his sword, or the abstract artist coming to grips with his statement. The bagels are tested in a tub of boiling water; if they rise in about 30 seconds they are bagels, if not, they are dead bread. Or as Frank Kralstein said of a bagel that failed to come to the surface, "Hey, look at that one—it's dying a slow death like in 'Sea Hunt.'"

After boiling, the bagels are propelled down a sluiceway, loaded on cedar boards, flavored with salt, onion, sesame, garlic or poppyseed, or left alone in all their natural glory. Then, it's into a 525-degree oven for 15 minutes, and—if providence has been with you—the result is a bagel.[11]

The only part of the process this description misses is that after three to five minutes of baking, the bagels are flipped over and the boards pulled out from the oven. The high-gluten flour and relatively low water content give the bagels their dense, chewy texture, while the malt syrup imparts a mellow, slightly sweet flavor and helps brown the crust.

The key to the success of any bagel bakery was an expert roller. Any journeyman baker could quickly learn the basics of mixing, proofing, boiling, and baking the rolls. He could also figure out how to turn the dough into rings. But when the best bagel men stood in front of the rolling boards, their hands flew, as one journalist described in 1950:

They work with the precision of highly-trained athletes. Operating in teams of two, the twisters exercise of timing and caution against lost motion which would make the most skilled boxer moan with envy.

One member of the team at the floured table slices big chunks from the mixed dough, then rolls it into long, perfectly proportioned strings. In a staccato of jabbing movements, his co-worker whips the strings into circles, snips them off and places them on flat trays.

> Faces immobile, their shoulders dancing a jig tune in faultless rhythm, the adroit unionists who twirl the bagels into shape strive for the highest possible production rate. They are, for the most part, paid by "piece work"—by the number they turn out. But don't be misled by the sparse-sounding name. The fact is that these are some of the highest paid in the baking industry.[12]

With the ability to shape 750 or more rings an hour, no one could replace them, and that is where the bakery unions saw an opportunity. In 1925 they formed the Beigel Bakers Union, a local of the Bakery and Confectionery Workers International Union, and soon leveraged their advantage in collective bargaining with the owners. They evidently didn't need much help from the larger union: "These workers had established an exceptionally high wage standard and other conditions and they asked that they be granted self-autonomy with specially defined jurisdiction in order to protect these established union standards and their branch of the industry."[13]

After World War II their strategy was to strike. There were then thirty to forty bagel bakeries in New York City and the suburbs employing about 250 union workers, organized into Local 338 of the B. & C. They marched out roughly every two years for the next two decades. No one could replace them on the rolling board, and they had the advantage that the bakery drivers' union would also stop work in sympathy strikes, so that the bosses were over a barrel. A union spokesman told a reporter: "Bagel bakers are specialists. They've been training for this job all their lives. Some bakeries tried to turn out their own version of what a bagel should be, but they didn't fool anyone. This isn't a business. It's an art."[14] By 1960 a top man could earn $150 a week ($250 with overtime), enough to give his family a comfortable middle-class lifestyle, with a week or two in the Catskills every summer and Miami Beach every winter. Like masters of some medieval guild, union leaders made it nearly impossible for outsiders to join Local 338; membership was generally open only to family members—sons, nephews, cousins—whose apprenticeship was long and arduous. These good times were not destined to last.

After World War II the bagel-making world was haunted by the "persistent rumor of a bagel machine like the ones used to stamp out doughnuts, which would of course promptly put a number of highly skilled craftsmen out of business."[15] In 1952, Meyer and Daniel Thompson, a California father-son pair of inventors and bagel eaters, received a patent for a machine that could shape dough into a toroid (i.e., doughnut shape). There were already doughnut-making machines on the market, but they could not process "the dough of certain products . . . of such heavy, tough, elastic consistency" as bagels.[16] It apparently didn't work well enough to sell, so the Thompsons went back to their garage workshop, and in 1962 Daniel patented a new device for turning dough into an annulus, or ring-shaped object. Somehow, the Lender family, owners of the New York Bagel Bakery in New Haven, Connecticut, heard word of this new machine. The Lenders employed a dozen or so (union) workers and were eager to expand their business. They were already adding to their doughs shortening, eggs, and sugar to make them softer and last longer; they also packed them in plastic bags and froze them for the supermarket trade. They were limited, however, by the customer base—not enough Jews lived in that part of southern Connecticut—and the fact that their workers could only roll so many bagels. In 1963 they leased a couple of bagel machines from the Thompson Bagel Machine Manufacturing Corporation, and Daniel came east to help start production. On January 5, 1965, they turned on the assembly line that would allow the big new Lender's factory in West Haven to produce up to 120,000 bagels a day.

Within a few years Lender's Bakery had changed the face of bagels across the United States. They were no longer hard rolls available from small bakeries in Jewish enclaves mainly on the East Coast and California. Bagels were now soft and sold presliced and frozen in supermarkets across forty states. They came in a dozen flavors, including—

shockingly to purists—cinnamon raisin and blueberry, and Lender's sold green bagels on St. Patrick's Day and red on Valentine's Day. Murray Lender, the family's chief salesman and marketing whiz, campaigned to "de-ethnicize" the breads: they were no longer a Jewish specialty but "rolls with personality." As sales boomed, Lender's built new Connecticut plants to meet demand, and other bakeries installed the machines to get a cut of the business. One New Jersey company offered franchises for Buddy's Bagel Bakeries, each equipped with a bagel machine and "EVERYTHING YOU NEED TO OPEN YOUR DOORS!," including "BUDDY'S BAGEL MIX. Our own secret formula for perfect bagels! CUT YOURSELF IN ON THE HIGH-PROFIT MULTI-MILLION-DOLLAR BAGEL MARKET! A clean, simple operation—no special skills required—very low overhead—choose your own hours!"[17]

Bagel bakeries proliferated, especially in New York City, and no longer needed specialists in hand-rolling. Seeing the writing on the wall, the members of Local 338 voted to disband, joining a local for regular bakery workers, and advised their children to look for careers outside the bagel industry. By the early 1970s it seemed that the forces of modernity and convenience had won. Newspaper columnists proclaimed that we now would be buying our bagels—machine-rolled, presliced, and frozen—from the supermarket, ready to pop into the toaster oven. But then, in 1973, one food writer dared to say hogwash. In a *New York Magazine* article called "The Bagel Finagle," Mimi Sheraton took stock of the bagel world and did not like what she found. Born and raised in Brooklyn, she judged the ring-shaped rolls on her Platonic ideal:

> Old fashioned bagels (and throughout I refer to them as "water bagels," there being no other true kind) were never more than three inches in diameter and had outside crusts that were both crisp and thick and slightly blistered. When pressed, the fresh ones would give, but would not squash

> down. Once cut, the inside proved to be smoothly finely-textured, and snowy-white in color. If they were not cut, the bagels had to be torn in half, rather than snapped, and after eating one, both jaws and digestive tract knew they had been at work.[18]

For her research Sheraton visited twenty bagel shops across the city but only found eight worth mentioning and only one that really met her standards. At all the rest the bagels were too large, too puffy, filled with additives, and made with bleached and bromated flour instead of unbleached high-gluten flour.[19] At the end of the article she evaluated the various brands of frozen supermarket bagels, with scathing results: "Those baked by Pechter's were crumbly and chokingly dry, as were the bagels produced by the Jersey City Bagel Baking Co.; frozen Lender's and Abel's bagels were mere jokes, containing eggs, and in the former, vegetable shortening, which made them like cake."[20] Murray Lender "hit the roof" when he read Sheraton's article and defensively told the *New York Times*: "We think our bagel is better than most fresh bagels and a fine food product in any case."[21]

If you wanted a better, fresher bagel, one of the answers was to bake your own. Bagel makers were secretive about their formulas, but home cooks soon figured out the crucial step of boiling the rings of dough before putting them in the oven. One of the most influential recipes was supposedly "exacted from a retired baker, who learned the art in Europe and practiced it in one of our large cities for more than forty years." It appeared in Leah Leonard's 1949 *Jewish Cookery*:

> BAGELS (WATER DOUGHNUTS)
>
> 3 cups flour (plus 3 tablespoons for kneading board)
>
> 1 1/2 teaspoon salt
>
> 2 tablespoons sugar
>
> 1 package yeast
>
> 2/3 cup lukewarm water

3 tablespoons salad oil (or shortening)

1 egg

4 quarts boiling water to which add 2 tablespoons sugar

Sift dry ingredients together into a deep mixing bowl. Dissolve yeast in 1/3 of the lukewarm water. Add oil or melted shortening to remainder of warm water and stir in dissolved yeast. Make a well in the center of flour mixture and stir in the liquid, adding slightly beaten egg when half the liquid has been used. Stir briskly to form a ball of dough and knead on a floured board for two minutes. Return dough to mixing bowl, smooth side up, and punch down three times. Cover and let rise at room temperature 15 to 20 minutes, or until the dough had come to the top of the bowl. Knead again on board until smooth and elastic as for rolls. Divide dough into 12 equal portions. Form into lengths not more than 3/4 inch thick, pinching ends together. Place on a floured cookie sheet and slip under boiler flame 3 minutes. Drop each bagel into rapidly boiling water in deep kettle and cook over moderate heat 15 to 20 minutes. Skim out and place on a cookie sheet. Bake at 375° F for 10 minutes then increase heat to 400° F for 5 to 6 minutes or till bagels are golden browned and crisp, approximately 15 minutes.[22]

These bagels will come out a bit sweet and soft—more like Montreal bagels than the New York variety. The length of boiling the dough rings, fifteen to twenty minutes, gives one pause—most professional recipes today call for a two- to three-minute boiling. Leonard's recipe appeared, credited or not, in multiple newspaper recipe columns and Jewish community cookbooks over the next two decades. It wouldn't be until the late 1980s, however, before home bakers finally began to use high-gluten flour, as well as to remove the oil and add malt syrup to their dough, to get that real bagel bakery taste. One of the best recipes comes from *Inside the Jewish Bakery: Recipes and Memories from the Golden Age of Jewish Bakeries* by Stanley Ginsberg and Norman Berg, who was a veteran professional baker:

CLASSIC NEW YORK WATER BAGEL

5 cups	High-gluten flour
1 1/2 cup + 1 Tbs.	Warm (105°F, 40°C) water
1 Tbs.	Diastatic malt (syrup or powder)
2 Tsp.	Salt
3/4 Tsp.	Instant yeast

This is a two-day recipe that takes about 1 hour of actual preparation time, spread out over 16 to 24 hours.

Saturday Afternoon:

1. Dissolve the malt in the water. If you're using active dry yeast, stir it in as well and let stand for 5 to 10 minutes until it foams.

2. Use the mixer paddle attachment at lowest (KA 1) speed, hand whisk or wooden spoon to blend the flour and salt (and instant yeast, if using), then add the liquids. *By hand:* work the dough vigorously for about 10 minutes. *By stand mixer:* continue mixing until the dough is shaggy and well-hydrated, about 1 minute. Switch to dough hook and knead for about 10 minutes. The dough will be ready when it's smooth, silky and stretches when you pull a pinch away from the mass.

3. Turn the dough out onto an unfloured kneading surface, form it into a thick log shape, about 12 in. wide by 4 in. in diameter, and cut it in two the long way. Roll each piece into a log 2 in. in diameter and let them rest, covered, for about 20 minutes to relax the gluten and give the yeasts some time to get frisky.

4. Shape the bagels according to the instructions above. If you can't get enough traction on your work surface, mist it very lightly with water or swab it with a damp paper towel.

5. Arrange the bagels on a cornmeal-dusted or parchment-lined baking sheet, cover well with plastic wrap (or, preferably, put inside a food-grade plastic bag) and refrigerate overnight.

Sunday Morning:

6. Preheat oven to 460° F/240° C. When it reaches temperature, bring 3 to 4 qt. of water, to which 2 Tbs. of malt have been added, to a rolling boil.

7. Take out only as many chilled bagels as you can bake at one time and plunge them into the boiling water until they float.

8. Drain on a rack and sprinkle toppings; bake on boards and flip after 3 minutes, then finish for another 12 to 15 minutes—15 to 18 minutes on parchment if you're not flipping—until they are a rich brown. Let cool for at least 30 minutes and enjoy.[23]

Mimi Sheraton's article may have hurt the Lender family's pride, but they cried all the way to the bank as the frozen bagel business boomed. They bought out Abel's Bagels, their biggest competitor, and built more factory bakeries in Connecticut and New York State. In 1984 they earned their biggest payout when they sold their company to the food conglomerate Kraft Inc. This was a natural match: Lender's and Philadelphia Cream Cheese, another Kraft product, had been working together on marketing promotions for almost twenty years, and the Lenders had a solid working relationship with the Kraft team. The next year, Kraft opened the world's largest bagel bakery in Mattoon, Illinois, giving them the ability to churn out more than a billion bagels annually.

To produce massive quantities, the big factory bakeries decided to eliminate the traditional step of boiling the shaped rolls before baking. Hard to automate, boiling required more manpower and extra plumbing and equipment on the bakery floor. Managers decided instead to simply inject large amounts of steam into the oven for the first three minutes of baking, which would gelatinize the exterior enough to make a crusty-ish finished bagel. One professional manual delicately noted that this shortcut "has a negative effect on the ultimate quality of the product" and that "there is much debate about the quality of bagels made in this manner."[24] To help smaller bakeries compete with the factory-made product, bakery supply companies such as Puratos began to sell "bagel blends" or "bagel improvers" containing enzymes and other chemicals that helped the dough rise, softened the bagel, and delayed staling. The old crusty New York bagel was forgotten. The public seemed to like their new soft and puffy bagels, and sales continued to climb.

Lender's success attracted other corporate bakeries to the bagel business. In 1985, Sara Lee introduced its "Bagel Time" rolls with the aggressive aim of taking over 50 percent of market share. Next, Thomas' (of English muffin fame) and Pepperidge Farms rolled out their own branded bagels, as did a number of regional bakeries. Over the next two decades, Lender's, Thomas', and Sara Lee changed ownership through a series of sales and mergers. Today all three bagel bakeries are owned by Grupo Bimbo, the world's largest baking conglomerate. The biggest seller in the United States is Thomas' Bagels (now also made in the Mattoon, Illinois, plant), with Sara Lee third and Lender's a distant ninth. Flowers Foods, maker of Wonder Bread, recently introduced its line of "light and airy" Wonder Classic Bagels, shamelessly locating them in that niche "where tradition meets taste." In the supermarket aisles, the campaign to "de-ethnicize" the bagel is complete.

Nevertheless, for those who lived in the bagel strongholds, particularly on the East and West Coasts, there remained purists determined to protect the integrity of the traditional bagel. Mimi Sheraton and others fought a rearguard action against bakeries that turned out product that was too big, too puffy, and lacking in the necessary center hole. They sought out, and publicized, those shops, mostly in the outer boroughs, that made bagels the old way, with high-gluten flour and malt syrup, hand-rolling the dough, and giving the rings a boil before the oven. The dichotomy between good and bad bagels was symbolized by the tiny, old-school Bagel Hole in Brooklyn's Park Slope and Manhattan's H&H Bagels producing bloated, machine-made rolls—but would do in a pinch if you couldn't get to Bagel Hole before they ran out in the early afternoon. (Mimi Sheraton claimed that the best use for a mega-bagel was to tear out the puffy dough and use it to clean your wallpaper.)

Another challenge to the traditional bagel was Americans' penchant for playing with their food. In the 1970s West Coast bakeries such as San Francisco's famous House of Bagels began producing sourdough bagels, described as "a savory marriage between the golden-crusted staff of San Francisco life and the tough, ring-shaped rolls of Jewish ancestry."[25] The next innovation, which apparently first appeared on Long Island during the late 1970s, was explained as "for those who can't decide if they want plain, salt, poppy seed, sesame seed, garlic or onion, there's the everything bagel, which is topped with all of them."[26] From there new bagel varieties began to surface that reflected both American's lust for novelty and whatever were the latest food fads, including whole wheat, bran, multigrain, blueberry, chocolate chip, jalapeño cheddar, asiago, gluten-free, olive, gojuchang, miso, za'tar, and so on. Bagel shops also went wild with the cream cheese with which to decorate their variegated wares, offering everything from cream cheese flecked with smoked salmon to chocolate chip cookie dough and pumpkin spice spreads. Novelty bagel mania reached its apotheosis with the 2010 appearance in Williamsburg, Brooklyn, of the "rainbow bagel," each ring a swirl of brightly colored doughs made with liberal doses of food coloring. Perfect products of the Instagram and TikTok age, they are meant to be consumed by the camera, not the mouth, but unfortunately too many people continue to ingest them.

Luckily there are still bakers who respect the bagel and have found ways to innovate without forgetting tradition. Part of this is due to the enduring taste for savory bagel sandwiches, most importantly the classic combination of cream cheese and lox. Somehow, smoked salmon doesn't go well with an Oreo bagel. Today you can find great bagel bakeries not just in Los Angeles, New York, and San Francisco but also in Maine, Vermont, Ohio, Michigan, Tennessee, Kentucky, and Hawaii, where Tali's Bagels & Schmear makes its sandwiches with lox from Acme Smoked Fish in Brooklyn. Some claim to have brought their bagel recipe from Brooklyn, while others state that theirs mixes New

York and Montreal bagel (about which we will not speak) traditions. Some use a sourdough, while others make a traditional yeast bagel. Nearly all of them, however, subscribe to the precepts of El Bagels in Miami: only five ingredients, no preservatives, long fermented, always boiled, and baked fresh.

11

WHITE BREAD

IN THE MID-NINETEENTH CENTURY one of the marvels of New York City was Hecker's Bakery on Rutgers Street, two blocks from the bustling South Street docks. John Hecker, son of German immigrants, opened the bakery in 1835, and a few years later he and his brother George established Hecker's Flour Mills (also known as Croton Mills) around the corner on Cherry Street. Nationally the brothers' best-known product was Hecker's Self-Rising Flour, made from the finest Genesee flour mixed with a chemical leavening agent and salt. All the consumer had to do was mix it with water or milk to make dough that could be turned into bread, biscuits, cake, and so on. In New York City the Hecker name was primarily recognized for the loaves that came out of John Hecker's bakery. By 1858 he had transformed his business from a traditional, manual labor intensive bakery into a fully mechanized bread factory that produced what he called

"Patent Machine Bread." Hecker was proud to show it off to distinguished visitors and journalists:

> We will commence with the making of sponge, the flour for which is drawn from a bin and united with the yeast and water, as they all simultaneously enter the dough mixer. As soon as formed, the mixture is allowed to drop into a vat, where it is permitted to rise. When ripe, it is conveyed to another dough mixer, by which it is combined with additional flour necessary. The dough, when thus produced, is passed from a mixer to a preparer, or set of rollers, by which it is formed into layers, and worked until it becomes perfectly clear and exceedingly fine in texture. It then travels to the cutters, to be formed into squares for one-pound or two-pound loaves, which are perforated at the same time, and its respective weight imprinted on each loaf. After being cut, it is taken up with a wooden shovel and placed into pans, where it remains until after baking. The cutting machine is constructed so that it may be used to cut dough into strips for twist bread, or into pieces of any other shape desired. In the preparation of dough by this process, it is utterly unnecessary for the hands to come into contact with it, except to guide it as it passes through the rollers. The mixer, the preparer, and the cutter form a connected line of machinery, capable of preparing a barrel of flour for the oven in six minutes, converting it into one- or two-pound loaves. Immediately after being taken from the oven the bread is placed in boxes, each containing a hundred pounds, ready for delivery.
>
> It is baked in pans, some containing twelve two-pound and others eighteen one-pound loaves, all the loaves being joined together, so that, when separated from each other, they have, with the exception of the outside ones, very little crust. The shape of this bread renders it very convenient to handle and put up for exportation.
>
> Only four hours are required to convert flour into bread by our process, while at least ten to thirteen hours are consumed by any other; less change, therefore, takes place in the saccharine principle of the flour. This fact enables us, with little care and watchfulness, always to have sweet bread, even in the warmest weather.[1]

In Europe politicians and policy makers had long debated the "bread question," the challenge of providing ample quantities of the staple foodstuff at a price even the poorest could afford. Beginning in the late eighteenth century, they decided that one answer to this problem was the mechanization of the baking process. In the United States leaders eager to spur the nation's industrial development felt a similar need to increase production of bread. Inventors on both sides of the Atlantic began to tinker with mechanical devices that could replace human hands, arms, and backs at every stage of the baking process. This included kneaders to perform the first mix of wet and dry ingredients, molders (Hecker's "preparers") to roll out and degas the risen dough, and cutters that divided the dough into pieces.

Traditional wood-fired ovens, which workers started by lighting a fire inside them, were also inadequate because they were relatively small and couldn't provide uniform heat over long periods of time. During the nineteenth century the old "direct" oven design was gradually replaced by devices using indirect sources of heat, usually below or behind the baking chamber. One great advantage of the new ovens was that bakers could fire them with coal or coke, which burned hotter and cleaner and were significantly cheaper than wood. Some manufacturers introduced ovens heated by coils of pipes running with pressurized steam, but these could reach only about 300 degrees Fahrenheit, not enough for all baking uses. Further innovations took place inside the baking chamber. The drawback of traditional ovens was that bakers had to frequently shift the loaves around the interior, leading to loss of heat through the open door. Oven makers introduced draw plate ovens, in which the loaves were placed on a steel sheet that could move in and out on rollers, and rotary ovens in which bread was baked on a rotating metal carousel. For the largest bakeries, however, the dream was the "traveling" or "continuous flow" oven (now commonly called a "tunnel" oven). Unlike other ovens this device was operated at two ends. At the front end bakers would open the door and place pans of risen dough on a conveyor belt inside the capacious baking chamber. The belt would slowly clank around its track, and eventually bakers at the back end would open the door and pull out row after row of perfectly browned loaves.

John Hecker's Lower East Side factory was not the only automated bakery in operation at the time. An inventor named Hiram Berdan patented a massive two-story oven that allowed bakers to roll pans of bread on little carts into the chamber. Inside, the carts would be carried through the oven on a vertical carousel (something like a Ferris wheel) and then would roll out another door holding the finished loaves. Berdan sold the concept of a "Mechanical Bakery," complete with kneading, molding, and dividing devices, to investors in Brooklyn, Boston, Philadelphia, and other cities and—for a while—showed that he could produce vast numbers of loaves at a lower price. The only problem was the hazard caused by the employment of all this new technology. In 1862 the weight of Hecker's machinery caused a side of his bakery to collapse, killing a neighbor's child and injuring several more. Berdan's Brooklyn bakery was destroyed by fire, and a few years later another conflagration, triggered by a spark that ignited flour dust, razed his Boston factory. Unable to find new investors, Berdan turned his inventing talents to gun manufacture (the Civil War had just started).

Developing the proper machinery was just one part of building a viable, high-volume bakery. Other crucial components included the availability of compressed yeast, introduced by Fleischmann in 1868, and the arrival of consistent, white, roller-milled flour in the 1880s. However, what happened outside the bakery was just as important as the process inside the walls. If you were turning out thousands of loaves a day, you needed to be able to reach large numbers of consumers willing to buy your product. In 1890, 80 percent of all bread was made at home, and in rural areas it was closer to 95 percent. The big bakeries all rose in the largest cities, where women were increasingly finding jobs outside the home and didn't have time to bake. These firms were able to produce so much bread that it was no longer enough to just sell loaves from the counter at the factory store. They delivered their wares to grocery stores in horse-drawn wagons colorfully painted with the bakery name. Some, such as Freihofer's in Philadelphia, also developed a profitable line delivering loaves directly to homes. To distinguish themselves from the competition, they gave their product catchy brand names—"Holsum," "Tip Top," "Butter-Nut"—and wrapped them in wax paper printed with the company logo. Two or three big bakeries competing in a market led to price wars, billboards advertising their wares on every available city wall, and gimmicks to draw consumers such as free gifts (bread boxes, collectible postcards, etc.) and contests. These usually ended when the company with the deepest pockets bought out the competition and took control of the entire market.

One businessman who thrived in this new world was Robert B. Ward, who was born into a bread-making family of humble roots. In 1850 his father, Hugh Ward, arrived in New York amid the thousands of immigrants fleeing the Irish Potato Famine. He started a small bakery on Broome Street but after only a few years moved to the burgeoning industrial town of Pittsburgh to find his fortune. His sons Robert B. (aka "R. B.") and George grew up in the family business, making and delivering bread before and after school. As soon as he was of age, R. B. opened his own bread business, and by the 1890s his company's wagons were seen all over Pittsburgh delivering his "pure, light and nutritious" loaves. Joined by his brother George, R. B. was noticed as a local go-getter by a Pittsburgh banker named Andrew Mellon (later US secretary of the treasury), who financed his acquisition of the city's big Mackey biscuit and cracker bakery. In 1903, Ward-Mackey opened a massive new bread-making factory, incorporating all the latest "ideas, devices and improvements" and capable of producing as many as one hundred thousand loaves a day. The company's leading product was "Mother's Bread," a loaf "more moist, more wholesome, more nourishing" and less expensive than its competitors. Having conquered

Pittsburgh and the surrounding region, the Ward brothers looked for new fields of battle.

The era between 1890 and 1910 was the heyday of "consolidation in industry"—an anodyne term for building monopolies. When John D. Rockefeller Sr. started out in oil refining, he described his tactics as "rationalizing" the production and distribution of his product. The industry was then divided between dozens of small and medium-sized refineries. Rockefeller would make a rock-bottom offer to buy out a competitor; if they refused, he would undercut their prices, ruin their business, and take over their market. As his business grew, he took advantage of economies of scale to negotiate highly advantageous deals with the suppliers and railways that shipped his oil, increasing his bottom line and further squeezing competitors. By 1892, Rockefeller's Standard Oil not only controlled the American oil market but had grown into the largest corporation in the country. Leaders in other industries took note of Rockefeller's tactics and built similar monopolies in steel, copper, railways, tobacco, sugar, ice, lumber, and so on. The Mellon National Bank, flush with profits from metal refining and railroads, was happy to fund the ambitious Ward brothers as they sought to consolidate the nation's baking industry.

Under either the Ward-Mackey or Ward-Corby corporate umbrella, the Wards began their campaign to "roll-up" major bakeries in Washington, DC, and then moved on to Cleveland, Chicago, Saint Paul, Providence, and Boston. In each place they installed their own managers and machinery and began to make breads using their proprietary recipes. Introduced in 1905, the flagship loaf was now "Ward's Tip Top Bread" costing merely five cents. What would the consumer get for their nickel? R. B. Ward was a pioneer in using all the methods of advertising to promote his products. Cities were plastered with colorful billboards showing enormous Ward loaves wrapped in wax paper. He took out newspaper advertisements proclaiming that his bread contained more gluten than the competition, good for building "more nourishment, more brain, more brawn." However, the real lure to housewives was the fact that a few of the loaves sold each week contained either silver or gold thimbles that you could redeem for five or ten dollars at a local bank. A Mrs. Pratt of Cleveland usually made her own bread but one day decided to buy a loaf of Tip Top at the local grocery. She was just about to give up hope of finding the prize, when "the very next stroke of the knife revealed the missing Gold Thimble and Mrs. Pratt was the most delighted woman in Cleveland."[2]

In 1909 the Ward brothers announced their biggest move yet: they would build two factories, one in Brooklyn and the other in the Bronx, to bring Tip Top loaves to the biggest market in the Western Hemisphere. The bakeries didn't begin production until 1911, but in the meantime R. B. made a study of what would sell in New York City. Just at that time, a thick government report was issued about the horrors of the city's cellar bakeries—the coal dust and vermin, consumptive workers coughing over the loaves, and sewage water dripping into the baking rooms. Ward called the report a "happy accident" that gave a huge boost to his efforts (though he denied any participation in the investigations): "When we were ready to advertise we simply came forward with the facts about our own products, and told the truth in paid space. The response was instantaneous."[3]

According to advertisements running in every major city newspaper, Ward's bread-making plants were the antithesis of the old, immigrant-owned Lower East Side cellar bakeries (including probably the one opened by Hugh Ward). One ad reprinted a newspaper article titled "Cellar Bakeries in Shocking State" and showed next to it a picture of the stern-faced physician who examined all Ward job applicants for contagious diseases before allowing them to work. What's more, customers were guaranteed that "the human hand never touches dough or bread at Ward bakeries." Tip Top was made in the "brightest, whitest, cleanest places in all New York," which they called not factories but "Snow-White Temples of Industrial Cleanliness."[4] Rather than being hidden in dingy cellars, the factories were ringed with large windows that allowed sunlight to shine on every step of the process. In fact, the public was invited to tour the factories and view with their own eyes what Ward meant by "Purity Absolute." This focus on cleanliness and whiteness also extended outside the factory walls. In another ad a housewife declared that she refused to eat a bakery-made loaf. Why? "Because yesterday I observed a bread wagon driver feeding his horse—handling the harness, adjusting the feed bag, etc., and then and there I resolved to eat no more baker's bread."[5] That is, until Ward began delivering Tip Top in electric vans driven by men "dressed and gloved in white," with "no horses, no stables, no odors—save the appetizing one of crisp, fresh bread."[6]

Outside New York City, Tip Top was sold by Ward-owned factories across the Midwest and Northeast but also by dozens of independent bakeries in other markets to whom Ward had licensed use of the recipe and logo. The deal also included prepackaged advertising copy and artwork, almost all aimed at the primary bread-buyer in the family: the housewife. Some ads took advantage of women's anxieties over their children's health: "TIP-TOP BREAD is pure, wholesome and delicious and rich in body-building nourishment. If you would have sturdy boys and girls, teach them the TIP-TOP habit." Other ads aimed at the many housewives who still baked their family's bread. In one ad a chic woman tells a friend: "Between you and me, TIP-TOP BREAD is better than my own baking. The whole family like it—the children will have nothing less, and I confess, too, have a preference for TIP-TOP. Glad? Well, I should say! For buying TIP-TOP BREAD has made my baking day a day of rest." Another ad depicted three housewives on a front porch enjoying their leisure reading and playing with children above the tagline: "Yes, TIP-TOP BREAD saves hours in the kitchen."

This effort to convince women to stop baking at home and buy bakery loaves was not limited to the Ward companies. Around 1911 the National Association of Master Bakers, of which the Wards were

Figure 17. Mrs. Ethel Hassler bakes bread at home, ca. 1915.
Source: Museum of the City of New York.

members, began a nationwide campaign to "educate" women about the superiority of the factory-baked loaf. Part of this was a reaction to the cellar bakery scandal. Some of the era's food influencers, including the *Chicago Tribune*'s Marion Harland, were advising women to shun bakeries, all of them. She recalled a visit to one shop, where she saw flies crawling all over the loaves. The baker told her: "We can't be bothered keeping the things covered all the time. Most people don't mind a few little flies having touched the things." Instead, Harland told women that baking homemade bread was worth the trouble: "Emancipate your family from the baker and see if change doesn't pay in every way."[7]

To counter that argument, Paul Schulze, president of the National Association of Master Bakers (and owner of Chicago's big Schulze bakery), gave the keynote speech at the association's 1911 annual convention. The center of that speech was an anecdote about a woman who came to his office one day with a loaf of her homemade "health bread" hoping to sell her recipe. She claimed that all her neighbors were "crazy" about it:

> I told her I'd be very glad indeed to look at her bread, so she unwrapped it. Before she got the paper off I had lifted the package and made up my mind if it was bread at all it was half baked, for it was as heavy as a brick. I found it a very nice looking loaf on the outside, the crust was a little hard, but it looked good and appetizing. I then asked her if I might cut the loaf. Certainly, she said, that was her idea in bringing it; she wanted me to examine it and see for myself how good it was. I got a knife and cut the loaf, and found as I had expected, that while it was nice part way in, the center wasn't baked at all—it was just so much dough. I called her attention to this, and she was highly indignant that I should question its wholesomeness. "Perhaps you get most of your loaves more thoroughly baked than this, madam?" I suggested. "Why no!" she said. "They're all just liked that—the loaf is perfectly baked!" And I think she really thought it was.
>
> Now that woman is unquestionably committing murder. I refrained from asking how many of her neighbors had died of indigestion since they commenced to eat her Health Bread.[8]

To Schulze, the average American housewife was "an earnest and sensible individual, but set in her ways.'" As a result, "the long-suffering stomachs of their family continue to pay the penalty for their mistaken sense of duty." The cure, Schulze said, was to convince women to break with custom: "One thing we bakers in the larger cities see most plainly today is the absolute necessity of the need of educating the housewife to quit baking at home. . . . To stimulate this change and guide it along the proper channels, we must use that greatest of modern persuasive forces—educative advertising."[9]

Figure 18. Workers shaping dough for pan loaves, Dugan Brothers Bakery, 1938. *Source*: DeGolyer Library, Southern Methodist University.

Newspapers reports about Schulze's speech brought an immediate angry reaction from housewives. Mrs. A. W. Hester of Chicago told a reporter: "Of course, there is poor home made bread, just as there is poor baker's bread. But the question of the merits of the two kinds is not worthy of discussion, because the home made bread is so much better than bakery bread."[10] Schulze, however, put his money where his mouth was, paying for large newspaper advertisements enumerating all the ways that the American housewife didn't measure up to professional bakers: she wasn't trained; her equipment was inadequate; her kitchen stove didn't possess "the *germ-killing power* of the modern baker's great ovens"; and, perhaps worst of all, she didn't understand what made modern bakery bread superior. The National Association of Master Bakers followed up with a slick, color pamphlet titled "The Story of the Staff of Life," which explained the methods of professional bakers:

They used the latest scientific techniques to ensure the best ingredients and processes; their facilities were equipped with the latest machinery and noted for "absolute cleanliness"; and their loaves were scarcely touched until they reached the housewives' hands. The moral of the story? "The best bread is baker's bread."[11]

R. B. Ward died in 1915, but his family continued to expand the Ward baking empire. His son William B. trained in the family business but then moved up to Buffalo to start his own factory bakery. His business acumen apparently impressed backers, because in 1922 he began a buying spree that eventually reached across the continent. Under the umbrella of the United Bakeries Corporation, by 1924 he had gained control of forty bakeries in thirty different cities. He then formed the Ward Baking Corporation to buy out his father's old Ward Baking Company in New York, forcing the resignation of his uncle George S. Ward. William did not end there, however, creating further heavily capitalized holding companies (often with his involvement hidden), which within two years swallowed one hundred factories in the United States and Canada. (One of these was as Indianapolis firm called Taggart Baking, which had just introduced a loaf called Wonder Bread.) By early 1926 a super-holding-company called Ward Food Products controlled about 20 percent of the nation's bread production. A bakery map of the country shows hundreds of Ward bakeries scattered from East to West in every state except for North Dakota. In each of those plants bakers were instructed in the Ward way: economy, efficiency, the latest machinery, better packaging design, better organized delivery routes, and professional advertising. These methods worked, because sales rose, and investors ate up the stock, giving Ward more money for expansion.

The Ward empire's leading product was its pan-baked, white flour loaf. Depending on the location, they also sold wheat and rye, but white bread was always the biggest seller. William Ward apparently decided that the Tip Top brand had become stale, because he sidelined it in favor of a new loaf, Ward's Fine Bread, sold by Ward Baking Company's plants from Maine to Missouri. In other regions he retained brand names such as Taystee, Holsum, and Bond already known to customers. All of these loaves displayed the same characteristics: The loaf was golden brown, its top either smooth or split, and its crust crisp yet tender. It had good volume, which meant that it was neither flat and bricklike nor puffed up like a balloon but somewhere in between. If you squeezed it, it would bounce back when released. Inside, the silky crumb was white or creamy white, with a sweet, nutty aroma redolent of wheat. No large holes marred the crumb; small cells evenly distributed gave it a firm, close-knit texture—what one baking expert called "dense sponginess."

During the 1920s the big factory bakeries produced their loaves using various recipes and processes. As the decade progressed, however, these methods began to converge toward one simplified baking routine. The old-school way was called "sponge and dough": Workers mixed together a sponge of flour, water, and yeast; let it rise for roughly five hours; then added more flour, water, and yeast as well as sugar, shortening, milk, salt, and perhaps malt. The main reason for using sponges was that they ensured a good rise to the dough in a time when that yeast leavening agents were not always reliable. For a speedier bake, bakers eliminated the sponge, using the "straight dough" process that mixed together all the same ingredients at once, cutting hours off the schedule. Some still preferred using the sponge method, however, because the loaves kept longer. In 1922 the Fleischmann Company introduced its "No-Time Dough Method," which of course employed its brand-name compressed yeast. The key to this process was keeping the dough warmer than the customary routines. No-time doughs were mixed, folded twice rather than kneaded, divided, placed in pans, and allowed to rise for 45 minutes. From there they went straight to the oven. Total time from start to golden brown loaves: 160 minutes, half the time of the straight-dough method. Not only did this save money, but baking experts reported that no-time loaves tasted better and remained fresh longer.

Despite the differences in methods, the ingredients of these white pan breads remained similar across all the large bakeries: flour, water, milk, sugar, shortening, salt, and yeast. The New York Public Library holds the archives of Albert E. Tolley, who began his career as an apprentice at Ward Baking Company and eventually rose to executive vice president. As head of bread production, it was Tolley's job to oversee the recipes for dozens of plants across the nation. The archive contains the leather notebooks in which he kept the formulas for white, wheat, and rye loaves expressed in baker's shorthand. Here's his 1924 recipe for one batch of Ward's Fine Bread:

WARD'S FINE BREAD

Dough	80°	4 hrs
784	lbs	Spring pat.
18	"	Sugar
15 1/2	"	Lard
48	"	Milk
16	"	Salt
9	"	Yeast
490	"	Water[12]

The first ingredient is the flour, equivalent to today's all-purpose. The sugar is to sweeten the bread and boost the rising power of the yeast. Bakers added the lard, made from hog fat, to produce a springy loaf and soften the crust and crumb. They mixed in the milk (probably condensed) for added dough softness and silkiness and to enhance the bread's nutrition, making up for whatever had been taken out of the flour by the steel roller milling process. The 80° refers to the temperature the dough is kept during its four-hour rise. Tolley's recipe for Tip Top Bread differs mostly in the production method:

TIP TOP BREAD

Sponge	76°	5 hrs
500	lbs	Spring pat.
300	”	Water
7	”	Yeast
4 lbs 9oz.		Arkady
Dough	81°	1/2 hr
300	lbs	Spring pat.
22	”	Sugar
16	”	Lard
28	”	Milk
13 1/2	”	Salt
2	”	Yeast
145	”	Water[13]

This is sponge dough, so the baker would mix the flour, water, yeast, and Arkady (more on that in a moment) and let it ferment for five hours. This would be added to the other ingredients and the whole would be kneaded and given a half-hour rise before being divided and heading toward the oven. What we don't know, however, is whether American homemakers could taste a real difference between a loaf of Ward's Fine, Tip Top, or any of the other top-selling brands produced in 1920s America.

According to Ward advertisements, one of the skills their employees possessed—and housewives lacked—was the ability to use the latest scientific techniques to produce the best loaf. Thanks to advances in fields like microbiology, chemistry, and botany, bakers had a much greater understanding of ingredients like flour, water, salt, and yeast and how they interacted during the baking process. They were eager to employ that knowledge to enhance the quality of their breads, and increase their bottom line. Their first focus was boosting the rising power of yeast. In 1909, George S. Ward asked Pittsburgh's Mellon Industrial Research Institute (funded by Andrew Mellon) to come up with a method to help standardize loaves made in plants in different parts of the country that had water supplies with very different mineral content. The result was Arkady, a "yeast food" made of mineral salts, mainly calcium sulphate, ammonium chloride, and potassium bromate. Arkady heightened the leavening so well that bakers only had to use half the amount of yeast, a significant cost saving, and the bread tasted better as well.

Ward Baking introduced Arkady with its customary big advertising campaign but quickly encountered pushback: Mayor Curley of Boston accused Ward of putting plaster of paris (i.e., calcium sulphate) into its bread to make the loaves heavier. Distinguished scientists testified that the chemical was actually a good source of calcium and the bread was safe to eat, but it was years before the cloud over Arkady finally lifted. (It's still used as a baking ingredient today.) Other "bread improvers" used by bakers included malt flours and malt extracts, which helped the yeast convert starch to sugar and encouraged rising. The author of a popular professional baker's manual told his reader: "There are many varieties of yeast foods, so-called, on the market today. All of them have some good qualities. . . . I advise their use whenever possible."[14]

While Ward and the other big baking conglomerates were racing ahead with their plans to expand and industrialize the production of white loaves, scientists were gaining a clearer idea of the nutritional benefits of foodstuffs, including the various varieties of bread. Scientists such as Elmer V. McCollum had discovered that the human body didn't just use food as fuel but needed specific combinations of proteins, carbohydrates, and minerals to thrive. Among these compounds were newly discovered "vitalizing elements" that came from what came to be called vitamins A, B, C, D, and so on. Researchers began analyzing American foods for these ingredients, including white and whole wheat flour. They discovered that the steel roller–milling process stripped the wheat kernel of those darker parts that contained most of its nutrients, particularly vitamin B. When they fed rats in two separate cages on wheat or white flour, the results were clear: "The 'wholemealers' are sleek and healthy in appearance, while animals fed on white bread show obvious signs of debility, are listless in movement, are losing their hair, and show every sign of dying."[15] The Ward Baking Company responded the best way it knew, with a splashy newspaper ad campaign. In Chicago it featured the city's health commissioner explaining to readers the nutritional benefits of bread and particularly why white bread *made with milk*, like Ward's, was full of vitamins and perfect for the growing child (and, presumably, lab rats).

How could the American housewife sort out all these conflicting claims? Eat white bread or whole wheat? Buy baker's bread or make it at home? Mrs. Ida Bailey Allen, one of the country's most widely read food columnists and host of a popular cooking radio show, provided some guidance. In the mid-1920s she embarked on a ten-state lecture tour during which she naturally noticed what she ate: "I found it almost impossible to secure anything but white bread at the bakers. In each case I asked why entire-wheat bread was not on sale. In every instance the answer was the same: 'There is no demand!'" For her, whole wheat loaves were clearly the best: "When a whole-grain bread is served . . . vitally needed minerals are introduced, make it unnecessary to use so many other mineral foods."[16] If you fed the family white bread, however, you had to give the menu more variety: "White bread must be used in proper combination with other foods which supply the lacking elements else the body is liable to suffer." Beyond the nutritional issue, Allen offered lukewarm praise for factory-made bread: "Baker's bread, generally speaking, is good, wholesome, of fine grain and texture, and well flavoured, and where the family is small and not much bread is eaten, it is oftentimes more profitable to buy than to make, but we do grow tired of baker's bread."[17] Homemade bread, however, she praised as a "delicious treat." Her basic recipe for homemade white bread produces four loaves:

WHITE BREAD

1 compressed yeast cake

2 teaspoonfuls sugar

1 quart lukewarm liquid (Milk or water or a mixture of the two)

2 tablespoonfuls shortening

3 quarts bread flour

3 teaspoonfuls salt

Put the yeast and sugar together in a cup and work them with the back of a spoon until the yeast liquifies. Add two-thirds cupful of lukewarm liquid and one tablespoonful of flour, beating the flour into the liquid, and set aside to rise while preparing the other ingredients. Sift the flour and salt together into a large mixing bowl, make a hollow in the centre, and into this pour the remainder of the liquid in which the shortening has been dissolved; add also the prepared yeast. Gradually work in part of the flour, beating smoothly with a large spoon. As soon as the mixture is thick, work in the remainder of the flour with the hands and knead until smooth and elastic—this will take about ten minutes. Turn smooth side uppermost into an oiled bowl, brush over with a little vegetable oil or melted shortening to prevent the formation of a crust, cover and set aside in the proof box or in some moderately warm place—75 to 80 degrees F.—free from draughts until the dough has doubled in bulk—from three to four hours. Now turn the dough out on to a floured board, divide into loaves, knead slightly, place in oiled bread pans, cover, and again let rise until it has doubled its bulk—about one hour. Bake as directed from forty to sixty minutes according to the size of loaves.[18]

The sugar was added to give a touch of sweetness and to activate the yeast (not yet as reliable as today's instant yeast). The shortening, which helped soften the crumb, was usually lard, as in baker's bread of the era. Given the use of these ingredients, this homemade loaf wouldn't have been that different from Ward's Fine Bread, except for the fact that factory bread was probably springier, spongier, and more uniform in quality.

In 1926, William B. Ward's dream of dominating the North American bread industry came to a sudden end. Following complaints from labor and consumer groups and progressive politicians, the US Department of Justice charged Ward Food Products, and its subsidiaries (the Ward, Continental, and General baking companies) with violations of the Sherman and Clayton antitrust acts. William Ward denied controlling these companies, but his claim ran hollow in face of the reality that he was their largest stockholder, their corporate offices occupied the same building, they shared the same attorney, and they had interlocking directorships. After two months of negotiations, a judge approved a consent decree dissolving Ward Food Products and separating the three baking companies from each other. William Ward retained control of Ward Baking but had to sell his stock (which had plummeted in value) in the other two bakeries. Three years later, at the age of forty-four, he died of a heart attack while working at his desk in the Ward offices atop its Bronx bakery. The end of the Ward conglomerate gave some respite to smaller regional bakeries. This, however, did not slow the move toward the greater industrialization of the nation's bread production.

For the American homemaker the great advantage of baker's bread was convenience—no more drudgery, mess, or failed loaves. In 1928 a Chillicothe, Missouri, bakery added the ultimate innovation by using a new machine, invented by an Iowan named Otto Rohwedder, to slice their Kleen-Maid loaves before sale. The bakery's announcement claimed: "Every slice perfect and CORRECT, far better than you could cut it yourself. But MORE, each slice is fresh and good—the same wholesome, tasty Kleen Maid Bread that has won so many friends. By a patented process the loaf is held firmly together and WILL REMAIN FRESH AS LONG AS ANY UNCUT LOAF. Remove as many slices as you desire and still the loaf is held firmly together."[19] Somewhat to the bakery's surprise, housewives pounced on the loaves. No longer did they have to cut their own bread, with the risk of squashing the spongy loaf and causing crumbs to spread over the kitchen counter. They simply opened the wrapping of the Kleen-Maid Pre-Sliced Bread, removed however many slices they needed, then closed the wax paper again to keep it fresh. Other bakeries quickly bought the machines and found that their sales jumped by as much as a third after they introduced sliced bread. The reason, one marketing expert said, was that "the modern housewife . . . wants to do less and less work all the time."[20] The only problem was that the loaves tended to fall apart when they were unwrapped, so bakers started placing them in cardboard trays before wrapping. All of these machines and added steps in the production process cost money, so they had to raise the price of their loaves by one cent. That didn't mean much to consumers in 1929, but their calculus would soon change.

Between 1930 and 1939, the Great Depression, and its accompanying unemployment, misery, and hunger, infected every aspect of the American economy, including bread baking. After years of consistent gains, commercial bread production dropped as families no longer had money to spend on store-bought loaves. Many smaller mom-and-pop bakeries were forced to close, while big factory bakers held on, although with fewer workers and less to spend on improvements. Women, who were often first to be laid off from jobs, returned to baking homemade bread, both for the nutrition and as a cheap way of keeping their family's stomachs full. For the neediest, another source of bread was handouts of loaves, or the flour to make them, via various local and national relief programs, school lunch plans, and at the end of the decade food stamps. Nevertheless, years of chronic malnutrition suffered by millions of Americans took their toll. In 1940, with the war in Europe looming, the Roosevelt administration restarted the draft of young men into the military. More than 40 percent failed their physical due to poor diet and inadequate medical and dental care. The main reason, nutritionists said, was the lack of vitamins and minerals in their food. A major cause was that bread, the staple, had been stripped of most of its nutritional content, particularly the B vitamins present in wheat grain, by the steel roller–milling process.

In May 1941, President Roosevelt convened the National Nutrition Conference for Defense in Washington, DC. A key question for the meeting, which gathered leading nutritionists, home economists, food industry leaders, Secretary of Labor Frances Perkins, and Eleanor Roosevelt, was what to do about white bread. Some nutritionists suggested that bakeries scrap white flour altogether and only sell Grahamite whole wheat loaves, but bakery executives protested that consumers were too much in love with their factory bread to give it up. Others proposed that white flour be merely restored to its original nutritional content by adding B vitamins. Eventually, however, the meeting arrived at the consensus that flour mills must not just restore some components to white flour but fortify it—that is, give it a nutritional boost by adding thiamine (vitamin B1), niacin (vitamin B3), iron, and perhaps also riboflavin (vitamin B2) and calcium—making it *almost* as nutritious as whole wheat flour. At the same time, the USDA and its Department of Home Economics enlisted newspapers and radio shows nationwide to educate Americans about the importance of vitamins and eating the so-called protective foods, including milk, vegetables, fruit, and eggs, that would keep them healthy and build healthy children.

Consuming enriched flour and bread now became a patriotic duty, and the flour and baking industries wasted no time in turning it into a selling opportunity. Gold Medal Flour advertised: "Take a tip from Uncle Sam! For a stronger, more healthy nation, the United States Government urges everyone to eat more foods baked from Vitamin-and-Mineral Enriched Flour. It's part of our defense program to make *stronger Americans* by serving *more nutritious* foods."[21] A Ward Baking Company ad showed a fighter pilot smiling down toward two youngsters above the lines: "You, too, have a WAR JOB . . . Give your family vitamins and minerals in this delicious bread. Amazing new WHITE

Figure 19. In this ca. 1951 advertisement the nurse approves of buying Wonder Bread for your children's health. *Source*: National Library of Medicine.

bread—enriched to give you better health—better morale in these trying times."[22] These campaigns worked. By 1945 more than 80 percent of all bread consumed in the United States was purchased from a commercial baker. This was partly due to the fact that many women had gone to work while their husbands were off fighting and didn't have time to bake. However, it was also generated by housewives' fear that their homemade loaves were somehow inadequate. In another Wonder Bread ad a doctor asked mothers: "What kind of bread are you feeding your child? Is it chalky-white in color? *Is it made from refined flour that's been robbed of its precious natural minerals and vitamins?* And your children? Are they thin? Nervous? Underweight? Lacking in strength, energy?"[23] Wonder Bread was the "RIGHT FOOD" to build strong bodies—and so convenient!

The big wholesale bread bakeries flourished during World War II. However, they were constrained by government restrictions from raising prices. As soon as controls were lifted, the price for a loaf of white jumped from nine to twelve cents. Americans apparently did not mind,

Figure 20. Wonder Bread is sliced and wrapped, Continental Bakery building, Century of Progress Exposition, Chicago, 1934. *Source*: Industrial Life Photograph Collection, Baker Library, Harvard Business School.

because by 1950 almost 90 percent of the bread they consumed came from a bakery, as fewer and fewer housewives baked at home. Most of their loaves were produced by big wholesale bakeries such as Continental Baking (Wonder Bread), American Baking (Taystee Bread), and General Baking (Bond Bread). Depending on the region, their bakeries also made wheat and rye breads as well as rolls, but by far their biggest seller was the white pan loaf. Thanks to better roads, larger trucks, and more preservatives in their products, bread factories could now distribute their products across a wider region to grocery stores, restaurants, and the new supermarkets beginning to appear. In fact, their biggest competition came not from mom-and-pop bakeries but from grocery chains such as A & P, which had opened bakeries and sold their own branded loaves. The new battle was over shelf space, over how many feet were given to each brand to display its loaves, and it was the grocer who became the ultimate arbiter.

The rise in prices gave the big bread wholesalers the ability to invest in larger plants and machinery that could produce loaves faster, more efficiently, and with fewer workers. For millennia bread had been mixed batch by batch: bakers would mix one batch of dough, put it into a tub for fermentation, and start with another batch. In 1953 an equipment company introduced the first continuous mixer into which pneumatic tubes pumped a constant stream of vitamin-enriched flour, water, salt, yeast, and other ingredients (including yeast foods and mold inhibitors). Out the other end came a continuous flow of dough that was sent for quick fermentation sped up by the addition of a dough conditioner such as potassium bromate. Continuous mixing allowed bakeries to reduce their production line, traditionally divided into a twelve-step process, to as little as six steps, with a corresponding decrease in workers needed. They could make a finished, wrapped loaf of bread in three to four hours instead of six to eight. Those bakeries that installed these systems could greatly increase production and lower expenses, giving them the ability to undercut the prices of smaller regional firms. The disadvantage was that they lost the ability to produce variety breads such as rolls and Italian and French hearth breads. Investing in the new technology locked them into making a very limited range of pan-baked product—some wheat and rye but most of all squishy, golden-crusted, white flour loaves.

To ensure of the fealty of their customer base (i.e., housewives), wholesale bakeries relied on massive and relentless advertising campaigns. Some of these highlighted the loaves' positive attributes, such as "soft as a cloud," "extra tasty," "oven-rich flavor," and "silky smooth texture." But by far the most common focus was on how eating these breads would improve your family's and particularly your children's health. The most aggressive campaign was promoted by Continental Baking to drive sales of Wonder Bread, the country's best-selling loaf between the 1930s and the 1970s. In 1941, Continental hired the newly formed Ted Bates Agency to craft their message. The campaign was led by the agency's legendary Rosser Reeves, whose approach was the "unique selling proposition" (USP). Translated from adspeak, USP campaigns were based on hammering home one concrete promise until it was burned into consumers' brains. In the case of Wonder Bread, the pledge was first that it "HELPS BUILD STRONG BODIES 8 WAYS" and, from the mid-1950s on, "HELPS BUILD STRONG BODIES 12 WAYS." Wonder loaves included, supposedly, as much protein as a steak, as much calcium as a serving of cottage cheese, as much phosphorus as an egg, and so on—provoking mothers' anxiety that the other foods that they were feeding their families were somehow not enough. They also made the pitch directly to kids themselves by sponsoring their favorite shows on the new medium of television. One Boston homemaker told a reporter: "My choice of bread has been dictated by a puppet who came into our home via TV some four years ago. Howdy Doody had a bread to praise and he convinced my children that it was the best. I like it as well as any other so go along with the children's choice. Maybe it convinces them to eat more which I feel is good for them. Evidently the puppet has sold me on the food value of bread, too."[24]

Despite the relentless hard sell, from time to time bakery executives became aware of rumbles of discontent about their loaves. In 1953 the *Wall Street Journal* ran an article on the country's largest flour mills closing plants due to the fact that wheat consumption had plummeted to 130 pounds per person—compared to 225 pounds in 1900. The causes discussed were dieting, competition from other foods, and the disappearance of home baking. Americans had forgotten what fresh-baked bread smelled like, so their appetites for the product were dulled. This article didn't ruffle too many feathers, because bakers had been aware of these problems for years. A week or two later, however, the *Journal* published five letters from readers across the country in response to the article. Each lashed out at what Big Baking called "bread." A Texan declared that bakers' loaves were "absolutely tasteless and can be rolled up into a solid ball just like a handful of putty." One Illinois man griped: "People eat less and less bread because it is getting lousier and lousier. It is a wonder they sell any at all, tasteless and half cotton." A Californian asked: "Can fine display, pretty packaging, and misleading, flamboyant, comic-strip advertising serve to cover up slipshod workmanship, synthetic substitutes, and lack of quality?" What this country needs, he said, "is a GOOD loaf of bread."[25]

Bakery executives were incensed, first at the *Journal* for publishing these letters and second at the public for daring to question their product. (Said the maker of Holsum bread: "These people must be stopped in their tracks regarding their vilification of the baking industry.") The leading trade journal ran a multipage feature with rebuttals from top executives. While a few allowed that perhaps their loaves could be improved (and maybe made less squishy), most bakery executives were unwavering in their belief in their product: "No bread is lousy or cotton tasting. It can't be. If everybody thought like this chap, that baker wouldn't last 24 hours. The baking industry, which includes all bakers, like any other industry has progressed tremendously in the last quarter century. We found better ingredients, better equipment, with better shops and better men to make the best loaf of bread our country has ever seen. The baking industry can only survive if it makes what the people want." As in 1911, the answer was to hammer home the "real facts" about "the vital role played by bread in the nation's nutrition" through a national "educational advertising campaign."[26]

In the case of the *Journal* article, bakery leaders could find comfort in telling themselves that the letter-writers were cranks with a grudge against their industry. However, they nevertheless knew that the "average" consumer had issues with white bread. In 1961 the Institute for Motivational Research, founded by the psychologist and marketing expert Ernest Dichter, convened a group of sixteen housewives to explore their feelings about the products of Continental Baking, including Wonder Bread. After "projective tests, intensive group discussions and a taste test," researchers reported the following results: "Wonder Bread is rather definitely an inferior product in the eyes of these women respondents, who describe it as spongy, pasty, doughy, bland, tasteless and indigestible."[27] Another of the institute's studies, for Tip Top Bread, revealed the reasons women continued to buy what they called "mainline bread" (i.e., factory-made, sliced pan loaves): it was usually fresh (i.e., squeezably soft), it was cheap, and their children demanded it for their school sandwiches. But if parents were allowed to choose their own loaves, the bread on the table would be different: "French, Italian or bakery white bread, rolls or variety types" valued for their flavor rather than as toast or a carrier of other ingredients.[28]

12

HIPPIE BREAD

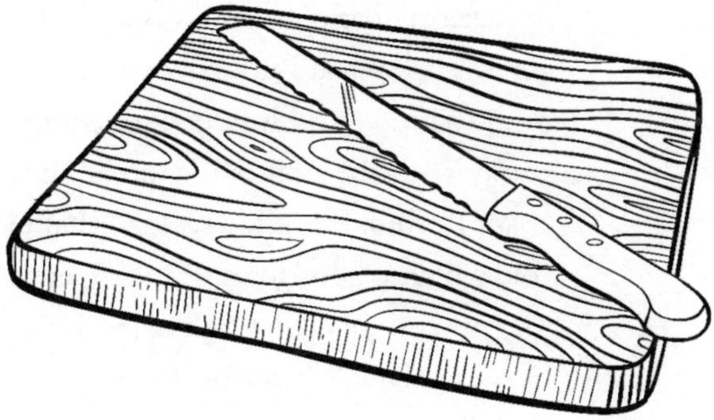

IN 1944 THE AUTHOR HENRY MILLER sat down in front of his typewriter in a cabin overlooking the Pacific Ocean south of Big Sur and began to write:

> Bread: prime symbol. Try and find a good loaf. You can travel fifty thousand miles in America without once tasting a piece of good bread. Americans don't care about good bread. They are dying of inanition but they go on eating bread without substance, bread without flavor, bread without vitamins, bread without life. Why? Because the very core of life is contaminated. If they knew what good bread was they would not have such wonderful machines on which they lavish all their time, energy and affection. A plate of false teeth mean much more to an American than good bread. Here is the sequence: poor bread, bad teeth, indigestion, constipation, halitosis, sexual starvation, disease and accidents, the operating table, artificial limbs, spectacles, baldness, kidney and bladder trouble, neurosis, psychosis, schizophrenia, war and famine. Start with the

> American loaf of bread so beautifully wrapped in cellophane and you end on the scrap heap at forty-five. . . .
>
> What do I find wrong with America? Everything. I begin at the beginning, with the staff of life: bread. If the bread is bad the whole life is bad. Bad? Rotten, I should say. Like that piece of bread only twenty-four hours old which is good for nothing except perhaps to fill up a hole. Good for target practice maybe. Or shuttlecock and duffle board. Even soaked in urine it is unpalatable, even perverts shun it. Yet millions are wasted advertising it. Who are the men engaged in this wasteful pursuit? Drunkards and failures for the most part. Men who have prostituted their talents in order to help further the decay and dissolution of our once glorious Republic.[1]

Then fifty-three, Henry Miller had settled in Big Sur after living for more than a decade in France and Greece. After the outbreak of war forced his return to the United States, he embarked on a yearlong journey across the country, an expedition he documented in his travelogue *The Air-Conditioned Nightmare*. Used to the products of his local Paris boulangerie, he was forced to swallow whatever bread was available on his American travels. When he sat down in a restaurant, he would ask the waitress:

> "Do you have anything but white bread?" If the answer is not a flat No, it is: "We have whole wheat," or "We have graham bread." Whereupon I usually mumble under my breath, "You can stick that up your ass!" When she says, "What did you say?" I reply, "Do you have any rye bread by any chance?" Then, before she can say no, I launch into an elaborate explanation of the fact that I don't mean by rye bread the ordinary rye bread, which is no better than white, graham, or whole wheat, but a succulent, tasty, dark sour rye such as the Russians and the Jews serve. At the mention of these two suspect nationalities a scowl spreads over her face.[2]

Miller's essay on bread, called "The Staff of Life," was first published in a small West Coast art journal and then in *Remember to Remember*, a collection of essays he intended as volume two of *The Air-Conditioned*

Nightmare. Hitting bookstores just after the war, when patriotic enthusiasm still ran high, neither of the books, with their caustic exploration of American culture, found many enthusiastic readers. The *New York Times* called *Nightmare* "self-conscious, overwritten, without organization or sequence, occasionally cheaply vulgar and crashingly boring."[3] The *Daily Worker* accused him of being passé and decried his "outhouse vocabulary." Out of step with American tastes, the books didn't sell, and Miller was forced to beg money from patrons and former lovers to keep his family afloat. Two decades later, the larger culture caught up with Henry Miller.

In 1966 hundreds of young men and women who had dropped out of high schools, colleges, and the American rat race began to drift into the Haight-Ashbury District of San Francisco. They were drawn by rumors of psychoactive drugs, psychedelic music, alternative religions, sex without hang-ups, and the possibility of building a community without the need of money, cops, or government. (Henry Miller had no use for drugs or rock and roll but was all in on sex, Eastern gurus, and giving the middle finger to the Establishment.) Many of these young people quickly ran out of money and, half-starved, were forced to start panhandling on street corners. At the same time, some members of the radical San Francisco Mime Troupe broke off to form an anarchist group named the Diggers—the name taken from a seventeenth-century British agrarian movement espousing shared property and the abolition of money. The San Francisco Diggers envisioned a "Free City" where cash was useless and inhabitants could build a communal existence apart from the laws and morals of the larger society. They printed manifestos, staged street performances (including a mock "Death of Hippie" funeral), and began to ladle out free turkey stew from stolen milk cans in the Panhandle, a park just north of Haight-Ashbury.

Seeing the need to feed more people, the Diggers opened a Free Store in an old garage where they prepared soup, stew, and other dishes using whatever they could cadge (or steal) from the city's wholesale food market. After police harassment scared their landlord, the operation moved to the nearby All Saints Episcopal Church, where the pastor offered them use of the church kitchen to help feed the neighborhood's growing hungry population. In the spring of 1967 a bearded, suit-and-tie-wearing engineer from Palo Alto named Walter Reynolds and his wife, Ruth, drove up one day with a batch of loaves to drop off at the church. He only baked with whole wheat flour, he told the *Berkeley Barb*: "It has all the life in it. I don't like the de-vitalized white stuff. You could live on whole wheat alone."[4] He figured that healthy bread was just what the young people needed. The couple delivered their loaves every Saturday for a month until the Diggers finally asked them, how do we bake that bread ourselves? The following weekend, Walt and Ruth packed their car with dozens of empty coffee cans and four hundred pounds of whole wheat flour and headed to Haight-Ashbury for the first "Bake-In."

Walt Reynolds's recipe was of his own devising, engineered to be as simple as possible, using only coffee cans, a large bowl, flour, water, yeast, honey or sugar, powdered milk, salt, and an oven. The Diggers published the recipe in leaflet form and handed it out to anyone who wanted to replicate their bakery on their own:

FREE BREAD RECIPE

We bake in 2-lb cans and sometimes 1-lb cans. This recipe makes one loaf in the 2-lb can and two in the 1-lb cans.

Wet mixture:

2–1/2 cups warm water (not over 85 degrees—if it's too hot it will kill the yeast, which can survive at freezing but not at high temperatures)

1 cake or package of yeast (this is still enough if the recipe is doubled, tripled)

1 tablespoon flour

1 tablespoon sugar, honey, molasses (more may be added, or some of each—we like to use molasses because it's so rich in minerals and vitamins)

This can be mixed in your 1-lb coffee can—2 cups water fills it to the middle line.

Let the wet mixture stand while preparing the dry ingredients.

Dry mixture:

1 level 1-lb coffee can whole-wheat flour, or 4 cups

2 teaspoons salt, or to taste

1/4 to 1/2 cup dry milk

MIXING THE TWO: In a large bowl mix the wet mixture into the dry mixture. Let the dough stand in the bowl until it rises by half, about two hours. The bowl should be put in a warm place, such as over the pilot light on top of your stove, and it should be covered. Again, too much heat will kill the yeast, but at about 80 degrees it is at peak activity.

THEN KNEAD . . . drop into a greased coffee can—the 2-lb can takes 2–1/2 lbs dough, the 1-lb can about 1–1/4 lbs—after shaping the dough into a ball making sure no flour is on the surface. Let rise again until it's just getting to the top of the can, about 45 minutes.

BAKE at 390 degrees for the 1-lb can, 55 minutes; or 400 degrees for the 2-lb can for 60 minutes. Oven should be preheated.

The Diggers played with this recipe by adding rye or soy flour, wheat germ, raisins and other dried fruit, and extra honey. There was, however, one taboo ingredient: "White flour, or bleached whole-wheat, is not allowed for Free Bread." At the end of the recipe they gave one additional instruction: "Please take this recipe home and start making bread. The only stipulation is that you always give it away."[5]

The Diggers baked twice weekly, handing out a couple of hundred loaves on Tuesdays and Saturdays to hungry street kids and anyone else who showed up at the church. In 1968 they moved the bread operation up to a commune at Rancho Olompali in Marin County. There, the bakers' practice was to do their work topless, or completely in the nude, both men and women, which the *Berkeley Barb* publicized with a large and uncensored photo. (*The Hippie Cookbook*, published in 1970,

Figure 21. Enjoying the sun at Rancho Olampali in Marin County, north of San Francisco, members of the Diggers knead bread, 1968. *Source*: *Berkeley Barb*, courtesy of Raquel Scher. All rights reserved.

stated: "Contrary to public opinion, nude cooking is good for your head, your body and your food. While your pores are flashing on the air, the rest of you will get behind turning on the food, and it'll taste like it."[6]) (Sylvester Graham must have turned in his grave.) The following year, the commune closed and the Diggers began to disperse, but the free bakery tradition continued. The Diggers' oven was inherited by the Grove Street Free Bakery in Oakland, which after a few years passed on its baking equipment to the Kaliflower commune in San Francisco. These bakeries traded the Diggers' coffee cans for standard baking pans, but they still followed the somewhat slapdash outline of the Diggers' recipe and always used whole wheat flour.

By the time of the Summer of Love, Sylvester Graham, the high priest of whole grain, 100 percent whole wheat bread, had largely been forgotten. However, his spiritual descendants—often derided in the mainstream press as "health faddists"—still touted the benefits of whole grain flour. Graham had promoted the flour to combat dyspepsia and constipation. For twentieth-century nutrition experts, who ranged from Columbia University chemists to the eccentric "father of physical culture" Bernarr MacFadden, the principal reason to consume whole wheat bread is that it contains the vitamins and minerals that had been stripped out of white bread by the milling process. In 1954, Adelle Davis, the most widely read nutritionist of the midcentury (who later gave financial support to the Grove Street Free Bakery), wrote:

> I have had no white flour in the house for perhaps 20 years. All my flour is stone-ground whole wheat; usually it is "organically grown," that is, grown on soil rich in humus, without commercial fertilizers. Such flour has a flavor infinitely more delicious than that of ordinary varieties. The machinery which grinds ordinary flour creates such heat of friction that the flour is precooked; it's comparable to last night's chops reheated. So-called "enriched" flour is my idea of outright dishonesty; at least 25 nutrients are largely removed during refining, and one-third the original amount of iron, vitamin B1, and niacin. Such flour is "enriched" just as you would be enriching someone stealing 25 dollars from you and returning 99 cents.[7]

Nutrition scientists, however, realized that whole wheat flour was not really a complete food. Although it contained more vitamins and minerals than white flour, the difference wasn't all that significant—and not all of its nutrition was assimilated due to the bran that caused it to be passed more rapidly through the body. During the 1920s and 1930s scientists experimented on rats to see if they could produce the most nutritionally complete bread. They started by feeding laboratory rats white bread and whole wheat bread and discovered that whole wheat was definitely better—the white bread rats sickened and died. Rats fed solely on whole wheat bread didn't die, but they did lose weight and didn't have the sleek and glossy look of healthy, well-fed animals. Next researchers mixed various additives into the dough and found that small amounts of powdered milk, wheat germ, or soy flour gave the bread a nutritional boost by adding calcium, protein, and B vitamins. The rats remained happy and healthy.

One scientist who ran these experiments was Cornell's Clive M. McCay, who in 1948 was asked by the commissioner of New York State mental hospitals to formulate a recipe for a high-protein loaf to feed his patients. The result was Cornell Bread, made from unbleached flour, water, salt, yeast, sugar or honey, and oil—and significant amounts of powdered milk, soy flour, and wheat germ. *Harper's Magazine* reported: "Laboratory rats fed on this bread as their sole diet thrive and grow. When they are restricted to run-of-the-market white bread, they pine and die."[8] By 1950 health-conscious housewives could either buy Cornell Bread at the store—the university had licensed the "Cornell Triple Rich" formula to dozens of bakeries nationwide—or, after *Ladies Home Journal* published the recipe in 1953, bake it at home. In 1951 the new edition of the best-selling *Joy of Cooking* got on the bandwagon—with the help of Adelle Davis—adding detailed information on why whole grains were better than white flour and how to enhance bread's nutrient value by adding wheat germ, soy flour, and so on. These efforts spurred a small craze in the early 1950s for making healthy bread at home. It soon petered out, however, as big bakeries' relentless advertising campaigns and the convenience of supermarket shopping continued to pull housewives into the store to buy white bread.

What was different about the radical youth of the 1960s and 1970s is that they turned bread making into part of a counterculture, antiestablishment world view. Mick Wellwood and Lini Lieberman, who wrote a food column syndicated in a number of alternative newspapers, began their 1970 article on "The Art of Making Bread" with the start of Henry Miller's "The Staff of Life": "Bread: prime symbol. Try and find a good loaf. You can travel fifty thousand miles in America without once tasting a piece of good bread. Americans don't care about good bread. They are dying of inanition but they go on eating bread without

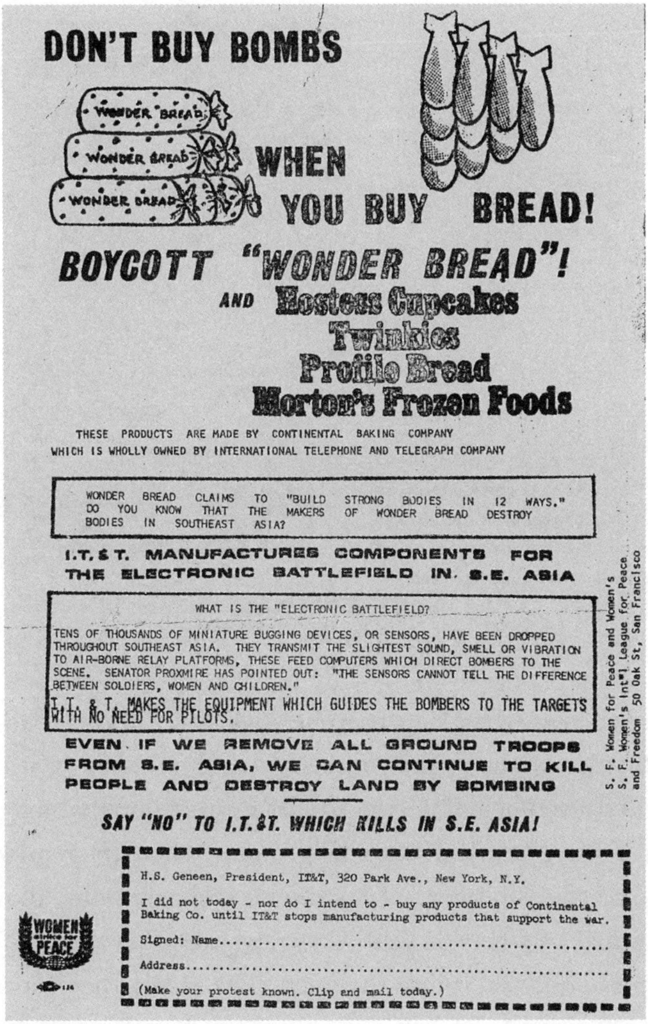

Figure 22. During the Vietnam War protesters boycotted Wonder Bread because it was owned by IT&T, which also made devices used to bomb the Vietnamese. *Source*: Andrew Coe Collection.

substance, bread without flavor, bread without vitamins, bread without life." Wellwood and Liberman believed that not only was the American store-bought white loaf bad but that most of its main ingredients, including white flour, yeast, and sugar, were harmful to our health. The answer was to return to the wheat kernel itself, which was

Figure 23. Edward Espe Brown's *Tassajara Bread Book* (Shambhala Publications, 1970) taught a generation how to bake healthy, whole wheat bread. *Source*: Andrew Coe Collection.

"specifically designed by Nature to be a *whole* nutritional package."[9] If you couldn't grow the grain yourself, you should buy it at a feed or health food store. They preferred freshly ground flour, which they processed in a hand-cranked Corona grinder. Then they mixed flour, water, and a little salt, kneaded it and let it rise overnight, allowing the "natural yeasts" to help it rise. The next day they gave the dough another knead and slid it into the oven. The result, they claimed, was the "chewiest, most flavorful, most nutritious bread you've ever eaten. This bread will *not* dissolve instantly in your mouth like store-bought yeasted bread. In fact, *it must be chewed to bring out its finest flavor.*"[10] Like the Grahamites of the previous century, Wellwood and Liberman intended this recipe to return bread to its most primal form, free from the poisons of industrial society and closer to Nature.

Around the time that the Diggers were first coalescing, Edward Espe Brown, a student of Zen Buddhism, was performing his daily meditations in what would become a Zen monastery at the Tassajara Hot

Springs in the rugged mountains about fifteen miles east of Big Sur. When he wasn't meditating, his job was to wash the dishes, sharing the kitchen with a gay couple who cooked the community's meals and baked the bread. Their previous job had been at Alan Hooker's quasi-vegetarian Ranch House restaurant down in Ojai, California, where they had learned how to bake Hooker's famous Ranch House Stone Ground Whole Wheat Bread. Brown loved the loaf, with its sweet whole wheat flavor and faint redolence of honey, and asked them to teach him: "There was no recipe. You start with some water and add about this much yeast and flour and this much sweetening and powdered milk. We let it rise as a sponge. Then we added oil, salt, and the rest of the flour. Pretty soon I was washing the dishes and baking the bread."[11]

The next year, Brown was named the Tassajara Zen Mountain Center's head cook, preparing all the meals for residents and summer guests. They all loved the bread, and he began thinking about assembling the notes for a cookbook. Brown sent his manuscript to Shambhala Publications, specializing in Buddhism and Eastern religion, which in 1970 published the first edition of *The Tassajara Bread Book*. The book begins with a promise:

> Bread makes itself, by your kindness, with your help, with imagination running through you, with dough under your hand, you are breadmaking itself, which is why breadmaking is so fulfilling and rewarding.
>
> A recipe doesn't belong to anyone. Given to me, I give it to you. Only a guide, only a skeletal framework. You must fill in the flesh according to your nature and desire. Your life, your love will bring these words into full creation. This cannot be taught. You already know. So please cook, love, feel, create.[12]

And if the recipe didn't come quite like you had envisioned, no matter, because there are no mistakes: "You might do it differently next time, but that's because you did it this way this time. Perfect, even if you say too much this too little that."[13]

For his ingredients Brown chose those that embodied "wholeness" and particularly those that were the "most life-containing, life-giving," such as whole wheat flour. He begins with Tassajara Basic Yeasted Bread, which is his adaptation of the Ranch House recipe. It may be the longest bread recipe published up to that time, seventeen pages of detailed instructions accompanied by line drawings illustrating every step of the process, perfect for those who had never made bread at home before. For those who didn't need all that guidance, he also gives an abbreviated version producing four loaves:

I. 6 c lukewarm water (85–105°)

2 T yeast (2 packages)

1/2–3/4 c sweetening (honey, molasses, brown sugar)

2 c dry milk (optional)

7–9 c whole wheat flour (substitute 2 or more cups unbleached white flour if desired)

II. 2 1/2 T salt

1/2–1 c oil (or butter, margarine, etc.)

6–8 c additional whole wheat flour

2–3 c whole wheat flour (for kneading)

Dissolve yeast in water.

Stir in sweetening and dry milk.

Stir in whole wheat flour until thick batter is formed.

Beat well with spoon (100 strokes).

Let rise 60 minutes.

Fold in salt and oil.

Fold in additional flour until dough comes away from sides of bowl.

Knead on floured board, using more flour as needed to keep dough from sticking to board, about 10–15 minutes until dough is smooth.

Let rise 50 minutes.

Punch down.

Let rise 40 minutes.
Shape into loaves.
Let rise 20 minutes.
Bake in 350° oven for one hour.
Remove from pan and let cool, or eat right away.[14]

The Tassajara loaf is soft, slightly sweet, and fragrant with wheat—not that different from Cornell Bread or the whole grain loaf in *The Joy of Cooking*. What sets Brown's book apart is that he transforms the baking process into a spiritual task. The more love and attention you put into the process, he tells you, the better your bread will turn out. When dealing with the occasionally erratic performance of yeast, he advises: "Waiting-on-yeast is to feed, keep house, clean its air, empty its garbage, and cater to its whims. Getting angry at its failings does not help. To provide patient loving care and food for growth does."[15] Once you've mastered the basic Tassajara bread, you can also experiment with his recipes for more than a dozen variations using rye flour, millet, oats, bananas, dried fruit, and so on. For those who shunned yeast, like those following the macrobiotic diet, he includes a whole section of unyeasted breads, which he praises as "basic whole, natural food."

Wrapped in a rough, earth-brown jacket and printed on off-white paper, *The Tassajara Bread Book* was issued in a first run of five thousand copies. A few months later, Alicia Bay Laurel, a winsome twenty-two-year-old resident of a California commune, published her hand-drawn book *Living on the Earth*, a countercultural guide to back-to-nature living, which included the recipe for Diggers' bread. *Living on the Earth* was the first paperback to make the *New York Times*'s bestseller list, selling more than 350,000 copies, while over the decades the public has bought more than 800,000 copies of *The Tassajara Bread Book*. The books helped inspire a generation to start making their own breads.

One was Crescent Dragonwagon, a seventeen-year-old member of a Brooklyn commune: "Nobody taught me how to do it, I just learned from a book. And kneading is just like you imagine, just like they show you in cartoons, very natural."[16] In 1972 she published her own contribution to the genre, *The Commune Cookbook*, featuring her take on whole wheat bread using nutritional yeast instead of powdered milk. A visitor liked the loaf so much that he asked the commune to make sixteen loaves a week for him. They tried it for a couple of weeks but realized that they were only making two dollars a day after costs (not counting the gas bill). They cut back on the quality of ingredients and convinced the buyer to add on two dollars an hour for labor costs. That meant that one of their loaves cost two dollars, as opposed to thirty-five cents for a loaf of Wonder at the supermarket. Finally the commune gave up: "There you have another step in the radicalizing of one more person—burnt irrevocably and emotionally . . . into her brain is the legend: *Capitalism can't work*."[17] Others of Dragonwagon's generation had better luck making the system work, up to a point. After the Digger-inspired free bakeries petered out, young bakers began to open independent baking collectives in which workers shared in the profits and decision making. Their loaves were mostly whole grain, whole wheat, and often were enriched with soy flour, herbs, kelp, brown rice, millet, vegetables, cheese, and so on. More than a dozen of the collectives banded together into the Cooperative Whole Grain Educational Association, which lasted almost two decades before disbanding due to the financial pressures that had caused its bakeries one after another to shut down.

In the early 1970s the fad for making homemade whole wheat bread also seeped from the counterculture into the larger society. According to a writer from the *Washington Post*: "Bread-making is no longer limited to bakeries and the health food cult. It got much impetus from young people going off to live on farms and communes. But today, bread is made by suburban housewives over 30, consumer advisers, government workers, musicians, teachers, secretaries. It's part to the back-to-living-off-the-earth lifestyle. It's part of the ecology kick that rejects preservatives and opts for natural ingredients; part of the new consciousness that values human endeavor and personal freedom over mechanized perfection and bureaucratic rules."[18] Some of this was due to *The Tassajara Bread Book*, *Living on the Earth*, and the *Whole Earth Catalog*, which printed Edward Brown's recipe for unyeasted whole wheat bread. However, home cooks also picked up volumes such as James Beard's *Beard on Bread* and Bernard Clayton Jr.'s *The Complete Book of Breads*, both published in 1973. They contain recipes for loaves with the "whole-wheat-and-honey" profile for the health conscious but also feature recipes for Southern corn bread, Russian black rye, French rolls, and sourdoughs. Beyond whole wheat bread, they opened home bakers' senses to a whole world of bread-making traditions that our immigrant ancestors knew but had been forgotten in the rush to industrialize.

13

ARTISAN BREAD

ONE SUMMER AT THE END OF THE 1970S, Steven Sullivan, a busboy at Chez Panisse, spent his vacation bicycling around France, traveling light, and sleeping in ditches. He had begun his journey in London, where Alice Waters suggested he meet up with Chez Panisse chef Jeremiah Tower, who was helping Richard Olney compile his *The Good Cook* series of Time-Life cookbooks. On the shelf at Olney's office, Sullivan saw a title that intrigued him: *English Bread and Yeast Cookery* by Elizabeth David. He bought his own copy and carried it with him to France, reading it in cafés and in the odd ditch until daylight failed. The more he delved into it, the more he became intrigued and enthused about the idea of baking bread. Not necessarily English bread but more like what he ate in Paris every morning—a fresh, crisp-crusted baguette with a soft but flavorful crumb spread with apricot jam.

Sullivan was one of the small group of bakers who came of age during the heyday of counterculture, whole grain breads yet who aspired to produce something different. Daniel Leader baked his first loaf, from the *Tassajara Bread Book*, as a student at the University of Wisconsin, and then decided to attend the Culinary Institute of America. His first chef jobs were at classic New York French restaurants like Le Veau D'Or and La Grenouille. During the August break Leader traveled to France with a list from his fellow chefs of restaurants and bakeries to try. One day he stopped off for a late lunch at an empty small-town restaurant:

> Feeling a little uncomfortable, I seated myself at a small table at the edge of the room. Then a woman came from the kitchen carrying a harvest basket full of fresh loaves of all kinds of breads. There was seeded rye, *levain*, wheat loaves studded with hazelnuts, golden loaves of raisins and sesame seed, black breads, herbed rolls, and *baguettes*. She offered me my choice of breads for the meal, and from that moment on all my discomfort melted. I was home.[1]

Leader was growing disenchanted with the relentless pressures of working in high-end New York restaurants, yet he still wanted to stay in the food world. Maybe the answer was to open a bakery?

Another young baker, Michael London, had dropped out of academia after deciding, perhaps under the influence of psychedelics, that he wanted to work with his hands. London began baking bread in his tiny New York apartment and bicycling the loaves around the city looking for customers. He finally found a job running the ovens at Ananda East, a Greenwich Village organic bakery, making hippie whole wheat, Jewish rye, and other yeast loaves for the health food crowd and fell in love with Wendy, the pastry cook. They married between batches of cheesecake and decided to open a bakery in Saratoga Springs. Mrs. London's bakery opened in 1977, selling loaves a lot like London had produced at Ananda East. During the post-Christmas slack season they traveled Paris to do a little bread tourism, attending the big Europain exposition and visiting well-known bakeries, including a boulangerie named Poilâne at 8 rue du Cherche-Midi.

Poilâne occupied a unique position in the bread world of late twentieth-century Paris. In the difficult years after the end of World War II, many boulangeries had succumbed to pressure to increase production, turning their shops into little factories for mass-producing breads, particularly baguettes. Pierre Poilâne, who opened his bakery back in 1932, refused. His flagship loaf was the rustic, two-kilo Poilâne sourdough, an urban version of the country loaves turned out by prewar village bakeries. Parisians appreciated the quality of his loaves—as did tourists thanks to its location in the heart of the Left Bank—and lines grew outside the door. Whenever young American bakers knocked on his door, Pierre's son Lionel was happy give them a tour of the *fournil*, or production floor. They walked through the traditional first floor shop, passing through the office whose walls were covered with paintings of breads, and then down to the cellar with its arched brick walls dating back to the seventeenth century. Here one or two workmen, shirtless and dressed in the traditional white shorts and shoes, presided over the baking process. They mixed stone-ground wheat flour, water, Guérande salt, and a piece of *mère*, or "mother" dough left over from the last batch. The dough was proofed (with one piece reserved as the *mère* for the next bake), then cut, shaped, and placed in wicker baskets for the final rise before sliding into the century-old wood-fired stone oven. The Americans were entranced by the timelessness and integrity of the process—and by the quality of the loaves. London remembers: "The first time I visited Poilâne, I took a piece of leavening and put it in my pocket. I didn't know what to do with it, I just knew it was something important."[2]

Back in the United States the young bakers faced a steep learning curve as they tried to replicate crusty, European-style loaves. The only cookbooks that could give them an idea of French bakers' methods were Bernard Clayton's *The Complete Book of Breads* (1973) and *The Breads of France* (1978). Most of Clayton's doughs, however, are either straight yeast or overnight preferments. The closest he comes to a sourdough is his take on re-creating the Poilâne loaf over a three-day period. ("Poilâne approved it," Clayton claims.) On the East Coast Michael London and Daniel Leader sought guidance at the handful of bakeries that had already uncovered the secrets of making Old World breads. They got advice from Chuck Conway and Carla Kevorkian of O-Bread Bakery in Shelburne, Vermont, and Baldwin Hill Bakery in Massachusetts, where Herman "Hy" Lerner was making sourdoughs using the Belgian *desem* method. Their biggest influence, however, was Jules Rabin, an ex-anthropology professor who had fallen in love with French bread while visiting a commune in southern France. Back home in Vermont, Rabin and his wife, Helen, built a fieldstone and brick wood-fired oven modeled on French village communal ovens and started to teach themselves how to make sourdough breads using just flour, water, and salt. To support themselves, they began baking—without hired help—two hundred loaves four times a week using flour they ground themselves, a pace they kept up for thirty-six years before retiring. What Leader and London admired was their knowledge and devotion to their craft (though their work/life balance may have been a bit too ascetic for their own lives).

For Steven Sullivan a pivotal experience was a visit he made (on Richard Olney's recommendation) to the Domaine Tempier vineyard in southern France. As he and Lucien Peyraud, the vineyard owner, enjoyed some bread and wine, they discussed how fermentation was crucial to the production of both. Peyraud revealed that many bakers used grape skins, which are covered with yeasts and lactic acid bacteria, as the seed for their sourdough starters. Back home in California, Sullivan collected some grapes from his father's backyard, crushed them in cheesecloth, and mixed the juice with flour and water. His previous attempts at sourdough starters had turned into rank messes, but after a few days his grape starter smelled fresh and lovely, with a fruity, almost apple-y aroma. This became the nucleus of the starter he has used ever since. Now he could make sourdough bread. The only problem was that Chez Panisse, where he had taken on the job of making

Figure 24. Steven Sullivan in the early years of the Acme Bread Company. *Source*: Susan Sullivan Collection.

yeast-raised baguettes, *pain d'épi*, and boules, didn't have room for his starters or a full-scale bread operation.

Sullivan and Leader opened their own bakeries within weeks of each other in 1983. Sullivan's Acme Bread Company was located in Berkeley, right next to Chez Panisse's Cafe Fanny, while Leader's Bread Alone opened in Boiceville, a hamlet up in New York State's Catskill Mountains. Acme sold its bread to retail customers at the bakery shop, but from the beginning, it was also producing baguettes, both yeast-leavened and sourdough, as well as pain au levain and multigrain boules for Chez Panisse and other restaurants. Leader received a precious ball of sourdough from his friend Basil Kamir of Paris's Le Moulin de la Vierge bakery and brought it back to Boiceville as the seed of his first sourdough, a pain au levain. Kamir introduced Leader to the mason André Lefort, who came to Boiceville to build its two wood-fired ovens (still in operation). In addition to the pain au levain, Leader formulated recipes for peasant, Jewish rye, pumpernickel, and walnut

Figure 25. Michael London scoring loaves in his bakery, 1987. *Source: Albany Times Union*/ Hearst Newspapers.

breads that remain Bread Alone staples today. He sold locally at first but soon acquired a couple of trucks to ship his loaves to New York City's restaurants, gourmet stores, and greenmarkets.

Michael London obtained his sourdough after his parents told him that a bakery near their home in Monterey, California, was making a better sourdough loaf than anything in San Francisco. Until then, London's sourdough experiments had been unsuccessful; he needed expert advice. On a 1981 trip to Monterey, he asked the baker for some tips, but the man refused until London offered to swap it for his knowledge of making Danishes and brioches. One of the employees had spent years on the floor at Boudin Bakery and revealed the secrets of the San Francisco treat, sending him home with a twelve-pound bucket of prime "mother." Soon, Mrs. London's was selling "absolutely authentic San Francisco sourdough bread" (leading to a cease-and-desist letter from Boudin Bakery). However, Michael and Wendy didn't expand their line of naturally leavened loaves until they left Mrs. London's in 1985. The duo spent a year developing their sourdough breads and then opened Rock Hill Bakehouse out of their 1805 farmhouse. With the help of three young partners, they began sending van loads of bread down to New York City.

By the mid-1980s customers and the press began to notice this crop of new bakeries. As one tongue-in-cheek article noted, bread lines began to form in front of certain Bay Area store:

> It is 9:30am on a foggy Tuesday morning in Berkeley. A line of shivering, half-starved men and women stretches from the front door of Acme Bread Company across a parking lot jammed with blue Volvos.
>
> Skinny as Italian breadsticks, the pale, bearded men stare vacantly as the line inches forward. The women, too, are skin-and-bones, their frail running shorts and flimsy tank tops offer no protection from the cruel wind, the piercing cold, the vacant stares of the pale, bearded men.
>
> Bread, they are waiting for bread. They are lined up, hollow cheek to absent jowl, waiting for designer bread—sourdough rye, crusty Levain, spicy Fougasse, and Rye Raisin Rabbits.[3]

In 1987 the *San Francisco Examiner* ran a tasting of city sourdoughs from more than a dozen bakeries, including a few of the famous sourdough producers. The expert panel, which included Alice Waters, gave the award to the newcomer: "When the ballots were tallied, the baguette and *pain au levain* from Acme Bread Company were the clear winners, at the top of almost everyone's list. As one judge noted, 'They have a good hearty flavor that combines with other foods without competing.'"[4]

On the East Coast, Craig Claiborne of the *New York Times* rated the best whole wheat breads in the city and surrounding area. At the top of the list, which was otherwise populated by products from Italian and Eastern European bakeries, stood Bread Alone's walnut loaf, which he called "appealingly chewy" and "dense but lightly moist, tastes lightly of smoked ham."[5] This led an Associated Press reporter to travel up to Boiceville, where Daniel Leader revealed that in three years Bread

Alone had gone from a small country bakery to a company that expected to earn $300,000 in revenue that year and was selling its loaves all over New York State and the surrounding region. Many of those ended up sliced for restaurant bread baskets, which had become an integral part of the meal. One food writer said: "Call me a breadaholic, but I often judge a meal's worth by the bread I'm served. . . . Opening the napkin on a bread basket at a dinner table is not unlike watching the curtain go up on a play. That first glance is everything, setting the tone for all the rest to follow."[6]

As these bakeries ramped up operations, their owners realized that there was one aspect of their process that they could no longer take for granted: the flour. Then, as now, the American milling industry was dominated by behemoths such as General Mills, Conagra, and Archer Daniels Midland whose main business was turning out millions of tons of bleached white flour for use in industrial bakeries. However, there still existed regional mills that had the ability to produce stone-ground flours for the health food market. When bakeries such as Acme and Bread Alone opened, they were happy to simply buy the ingredient from the nearest mill. The only requirement was that it be stone-ground, and preferably organic. After a year or two, however, Leader and Sullivan began to notice that the flour, even if of the same variety and from the same mill, could vary greatly from batch to batch. As their needs grew, they found that local mills couldn't supply sufficient and consistent product.

At one point Sullivan discovered that he was using more organic wheat than was grown in all of California. He discussed the issue with Leader, and they decided that they needed to learn more about the grain they were using. The best way to do this was follow the flow of wheat all the way back to the farm. Leader found himself in North Dakota walking through the wheat fields at harvest time and discussing the crop with farmers. They tested various varieties and discovered which strains would work the best in their loaves. Not coincidentally, these produced flours that highly resembled Old World flours, particularly those used in France, such as French Types 65, 80, and 110. These numbers refer to the ash (or mineral) content of the flour. Compared with American flours, which were graded by protein content, this system gave bakers of Old World breads a more accurate way to determine which flour worked best for each recipe. This knowledge—and the power they gained as fast-growing customers—allowed Leader and Sullivan to take control of their grain supply chains.

In the West a crucial figure in the movement to produce European-style flour was Keith Giusto. His grandparents founded San Francisco's Golden Crescent health food emporium, selling, among other things, whole wheat bread and flour ground in a fifteen-inch mill in the back of the store. Giusto's first jobs were in the bakery, running the grain mill and making deliveries to local health food stores. In the early 1950s his father Al Giusto started Giusto's Specialty Foods, a South San Francisco wholesaler of organic grains, beans, seeds, and flour. Giusto went to work for the company and built contacts with a number of Bay Area bakeries, including Acme, whose bread he loved. To meet their requirements, Giusto began to travel all over the West to find farmers who could grow the correct organic grains. In 1996 he and some partners bought a mill in Logan, Utah, and founded Central Milling to provide high-grade flours to the new crop of European-style bakers. To help Acme, Giusto and Rick Kirkby, the bakery's production manager, would work through a variety of flour varieties, selecting those with the optimum color and flavor for baguettes and more rustic breads. In turn, this input would inform Central Milling's decisions on formulating the flours it sold to other bakeries. Seeing the growing market, even the largest mills developed products for the new wave of bakers, such as General Mills's Harvest King, "designed primarily for making European-style handmade breads."

When their bakeries opened in the early 1980s, Sullivan and Leader felt like lonely voices in the wilderness, with only a few other like-minded bread businesses scattered on the East and West Coasts. A decade later the country was home to dozens of bakeries making traditional Old World breads. The roster included Gayle's Bakery, La Brea Bakery, Wild Flour Bread, Artisan Bakery, and Grace Baking Co. in California; New York City's Eli's Bread, Tom Cat Bakery, Amy's Bread, Sullivan Street Bakery, and Ecce Panis; Clear Flour Bread, Hi Rise Bakery, and Berkshire Mountain Bakery in Massachusetts; Central Baking in Seattle; Neighborhood Baking Co. in Portland, Oregon; Bread Furst in Washington, DC; and Standard Baking in Portland, Maine. Michael and Wendy London helped seed some of these bakeries by selling licenses to their recipes and training staff on how to handle sourdoughs and other parts of the process. Among them were a Texas-based health food market called Whole Foods and Zingerman's Bakehouse, which continues to sell tens of thousands of handmade sourdough loaves a year through the Ann Arbor Zingerman's store and its vast mail-order operation.

While the bakeries proliferated, home bakers lagged behind on producing their own baguettes and crusty country loaves. Cookbooks such as *The Laurel's Kitchen Bread Book* gave detailed instruction on the care of sourdough starters, but their recipes were limited to San Francisco sourdoughs, whole wheat loaves, and Jewish ryes. The difficulty of the learning curve was illustrated by Jeffrey Steingarten's 1990 article on how to make a simple *pain au levain naturel* just like Monsieur Poilâne's famous loaf. He discovers that it takes at least six days, beginning with making the starter. He follows Steven Sullivan's recipe using mashed farmer's market grapes mixed with flour and is taken aback when it bubbles and seethes all over his kitchen counter. Undeterred, Steingarten orders some Giusto's flour and attempts his first loaves. They come out purple, and too sour. He acquires a copy of Lionel Poilâne's cookbook, *Faire son pain*, and follows the recipe through the six-day process. The final loaf is bread, but not à la Poilâne: "The crust is crisp and tender, the aroma and crust are complex and nutty if a little bland. But it is overly sour and its crumb is dense and gray." Steingarten bakes again and again, but his loaves remain too dense. Disappointment sets in, and he decides he needs professional guidance. He travels up to Saratoga Springs with a loaf of his homemade bread and four ounces of his starter to consult with Michael London. After spending a couple of days watching London turn that starter into Michael London–quality bread, Steingarten realizes: "The secrets, it seems, lie in the baker's art and intuition, not just in the bacterial composition of the air, the flour, or the grapes." Apparently, enough of London's art rubs off on him, because after returning home he makes bread "more than good enough to eat, and some days it is so good we eat nothing else."[7] The entire process takes only eleven months.

In 1993 the first two American cookbooks appeared with instructions on how to make European-style hearth breads: Daniel Leader's *Bread Alone* and *The Village Baker* by Joe Ortiz of Gayle's Bakery in Capitola, California. Both were ostensibly aimed at the home baker but at the same time discuss techniques and formulas more of interest to professionals. Both identify the traditional sourdough *pain au levain* as one of their iconic loaves. Of the two recipes, *The Village Baker*'s version is slightly less complicated:

PAIN BLANC AU LEVAIN

The Refreshment

1 1/4 cups organic, unbleached white (or all-purpose) flour

1/2 cup warm water

3/4 cup sourdough starter or an 8- to 10-hour piece from yesterday's loaf

The Dough

1 package (2 1/2 teaspoons, 1/4 ounce) active dry yeast

2 cups warm water

4 1/2 cups organic, unbleached white (or all-purpose) flour

All of the refreshed *levain* from the previous step (about 2 1/2 cups)

1 tablespoon salt (1 scant teaspoon if the original starter comes from a salted bread dough)

Glaze: 1 egg white whisked into 1/2 cup cold water

To refresh the starter, make a fountain with the flour and in the middle put the starter or old dough that has been broken up into little pieces. Pour in the warm water and dissolve the old dough completely by mixing it with the water and slowly pulling in the flour, little by little, from the rim of the fountain until you have a paste that can be stretched and pulled with 2 or 3 fingers of your mixing hand. Make sure that the old dough is well broken up in the early stages and evenly distributed through the new dough. Add the rest of the flour, a little at a time, and clean off the mixing fingers with a plastic dough scraper and then with some of the remaining flour. As the dough begins to come together, knead it on the table for 5 or 6 minutes until it becomes firm but elastic. Let the dough rise, covered, in a warm place for between 4 and 5 hours.

To make the dough, first proof the yeast in 1/2 cup of the warm water and set it aside until it is creamy. Make a fountain with the flour. Break up the refreshed *levain* and dissolve it in the rest of the warm water in the center of the flour, making sure that the *levain* is well diluted. Gradually pull in the flour from the edges. As the mixture become pasty and elastic, develop the gluten by whipping the wet dough with wide sweeping motions of one hand. Add the yeast mixture and then pull in most of the rest of the flour. When only about 1 cup of the flour is left, sprinkle the salt over the dough. Gradually add the last of the flour and knead for 3 or 4 minutes. You will have a soft, very wet dough. You do not have to knead it much at this stage because the gluten was well developed in the paste stage.

Let the dough rise, covered, for 1 hour. Punch it back and allow it to rise for another 30 minutes.

Shape the dough into 1 round loaf and 2 *baguettes*. The doughs may be set to rise in *couches* or *bannetons* for the baking stone method or directly on baking trays.

Let the loaves rise, covered with a damp cloth, for between 1½ and 2 hours in a cool place. Slash each *baguette* diagonally with a razor 3 or 4 times on top and the large loaf in a criss-cross pattern. Glaze all the loaves.

Bake the bread in a preheated 450° oven. The *baguettes* will take between 15 and 20 minutes and the round loaf will take 40 minutes. The loaves will be golden brown when done and sound hollow when thumped on the bottom.

Cool on a wire rack.[8]

The *Chicago Tribune* called *The Village Baker* "an exhaustive theory-and-practice treatise" on the baker's art and advised: "This is not necessarily a book for beginning bakers, although novices will do just fine if they plow through the recipes step by step."[9]

In the early 1990s America was in the midst of a bread revolution, with great baguettes, sourdough *levains*, and other loaves available not just on the coasts but in the heartland. However, one bakery owner, Tom McMahon of Pittsburgh's The Breadworks, decided that this new class of bakeries needed a little nudge to achieve even greater success. He initially envisioned starting a newsletter in which bakers could meet other like-minded peers and trade information. This soon morphed into an organization, founded in 1992 with McMahon as executive director, called the Bread Bakers Guild of America. The first question the Guild had to answer was: Who was it for? It was meant as a gathering place for bakers—decidedly not producers of industrial, pan-baked loaves—who made breads they called "country," "rustic," "farm," "handmade," "traditional European," and so on. Eventually, McMahon and the other Guild founders decided that these bakers should be called "artisans," so the loaves they produced were "artisan bread." However, this term had different meanings to different people. Maggie Glezer, author of *Artisan Baking Across America*, tried to pin it down:

> So I decided to conduct a poll among some well-respected bakers to see what their definitions might offer. While I got a variety of answers, they all agreed on one thing: For bread to be considered "artisan," at least one part of its production must be performed by hand. Beyond that, artisan

bread is *most likely* to be crusty, European-style bread, sometimes sourdough, sometimes not; hopefully weighed, rounded, and slashed by hand; and baked directly on a hearth in a "deck oven."[10]

Along with forming a community of like-minded bakers, another of the Guild's missions was education, both to hone the skills of established bakers and to help young people learn the techniques needed to make this kind of bread. At the time, baking training in America was solely aimed toward jobs in industrial bakeries. What was needed, McMahon saw, was a wholesale transfer of knowledge of European, and particularly French, artisan techniques to the United States. Guild members Michel Suas and Olivier Frot, who had come to the States as representatives of a French oven company, passed on information about European equipment designed specifically for artisan bakeries and arranged seminars for American bakers at some of the best boulangeries in France. McMahon brought over Didier Rosada, who had trained at France's rigorous top baking school and then baked professionally for a decade, to oversee instruction in classic bread-making practices. Rosada helped open the National Baking Center in Minneapolis, specifically geared toward artisan bakers, and found the Americans to be eager students: "Despite not having formal baking education, they were super motivated to take the extra step to making great bread, with a purist attention to quality. And unlike the French, who are very attached to tradition, they weren't afraid to try anything."[11] This led to the daring step of forming a team to vie for the Coupe du Monde de la Boulangerie, the competition for the best bakers in the world. In 1996, the second year they competed, Baking Team USA won first place in the bread category, marking the arrival of American artisan bakers on the world stage.

The spread across the United States of bakeries selling crusty *pains au levain* and other European-style loaves stimulated a wave of interest in making artisan breads at home. At the time, bread machines were the latest fad, allowing consumers to make pan loaves with a minimum of work and mess. For the new crop of artisan home bakers, however, shortcuts were anathema. They were purists, willing to do whatever it takes to achieve the best crust and optimal crumb structure and draw out the most flavor from the dough. Publishers launched cookbooks such as *Amy's Bread* (1996) by Amy Scherber and Toy Dupree, *Nancy Silverton's Breads from La Brea Bakery* (1996), *Crust & Crumb* (1998) and *The Bread Baker's Apprentice* (2001) by Peter Reinhart, and Jeffrey Hamelman's *Bread* (2004). The Reinhart and Hamelman books in particular straddled the line between professional and amateur markets, offering recipes with advanced techniques and formulas that could easily be adapted for commercial uses.

The apotheosis of this style of cookbook arrived with the 2010 publication of Chad Robertson's *Tartine Bread*. Like Daniel Leader, Robertson was one of the rare Culinary Institute of America graduates who decided to make bread baking his life. He apprenticed with Richard Bourdon of Berkshire Mountain Bakery, who taught him the value of naturally leavened, long-fermented, high-hydration doughs. After working for a couple of years in France, Robertson and his wife opened their first bakery, with a wood-fired oven built by the famous oven guru Alan Scott, in Point Reyes, California. Their goal was making loaves like they had eaten in France:

> I had fallen in love with the sweet, creamy flavor of bread fermented with wild yeast leavens that contradicts the widespread perception of "sourdough." I wanted a deep auburn crust to shatter between the teeth, giving way to tender, pearlescent crumb. I wanted my baker's signature, the score made with a blade on top, to rise and fissure, and the crust to set with dangerous edges. Rustic forms from the forge of the oven would be the final expression of the process.[12]

In 2002 they moved down to San Francisco and opened their famous Tartine bakery at Eighteenth and Guerrero Street, where lines quickly formed for the only 240 loaves its oven produced every day.

In *Tartine Bread*, Robertson revealed—to the relief of those who couldn't obtain one— the secrets of his "basic country bread," essentially a *pain au levain*. Its ingredients were simple: flour, water, and Guérande sea salt—the same as the Poilâne *pain de campagne*. The instructions, however, ran to thirty-eight pages, with Robertson meticulously describing every step, each illustrated with numerous photos. The recipe ends after the loaves are pulled from the oven: "As each baked loaf cools, the crust contracts slightly. Listen for a faint crackling sound—the song of the bread."[13] One reviewer noted: "Baking bread of this caliber is challenging and, even with the advice from Robertson, folks need to realize that it is a lifestyle."[14] Luckily the book found its audience of compulsive amateur bakers, many of whom it seems were men in the tech industry who loved Robertson's analytical approach. Soon websites such as The Fresh Loaf were filled with photos of readers' own versions of long-fermented, high-hydration, naturally leavened loaves with thin, dark crusts and glossy crumb opening into tunnels and pockets. Boasted one baker: "Listening to them sing right now!"

For many home bakers, however, making a traditional sourdough loaf at home, whether from *Tartine Bread* or another of the artisan cookbooks, remained aspirational. The multiple steps and the time involved were too daunting. It seemed much easier to turn to a method that had burst onto the scene in 2006. A food columnist recounted: "My bread epiphany came in a phone call from my daughter Linda, who never bakes bread. 'Mom,' she said, 'you've got to try this recipe. It will change your life.'"[15] Its name was "No-Knead Bread," as formulated by Jim Lahey, owner of New York's Sullivan Street Bakery. Lahey had started out as an art student but found that making bread was a more fruitful direction for his restless and obsessive personality. Unlike most other artisan bakers, he found his muse in the Italian bread tradition, first via Carol Field's *The Italian Baker* and then on numerous trips to Italy.

On a baking gig in Miami for his mentor, the restaurateur Joe Allen, Lahey noticed that the only way to make his bread in that city was not to knead it, surmising that the minerals in the local water were causing the dough to break down. He worked out a no-knead technique and a couple of years later decided to teach a class in it, sending a teaser to the *New York Times* food writer Mark Bittman: "I'll be teaching a truly minimalist breadmaking technique that allows people to make excellent bread at home with very little effort. The result is surprisingly simple—I think a four-year-old could master it—and the results are fantastic."[16] Bittman took the bait and, enthused by the result, in 2006 wrote an article calling the process one of the greatest innovations in bread's six-thousand-year history. That, it turned out, was not true: The technique was probably millennia old (as Lahey himself has said) and had already been described in books like Suzanne Dunaway's 1999 *No Need to Knead: Handmade Italian Bread in 90 Minutes* and Pillsbury Flour's 1946 *Bake the No-Knead Way*. However, it was Lahey's recipe, Bittman's promotion, and the platform of the *New York Times* that launched the craze for no-knead bread. Essentially, it is another *pain au levain*, using a tiny bit of yeast and a very long preferment rather than a sourdough. Lahey mixes flour, salt, yeast, and water into a very wet dough, lets it sit for twelve to eighteen hours and then moves the loose ball to a board for a quick shape. He lets this rise for an hour or two, plops it into a preheated lidded pot or Dutch oven, and slides it into the oven. Less than an hour or so later, out comes a beautiful, dark, and crusty boule.

Those who tried Lahey's no-knead recipe became instant fans, posting their results on food blogs and social media. Even Jeffrey Steingarten was won over by this "wonderful" loaf:

> Since late November, I have baked nearly 100 loaves of nearly perfect bread. Ok, possibly only 90 of them were nearly perfect. We baked them faster than we could eat them—even though they were fantastically good to eat and even though bread is the best of all possible foods. . . . They

> were all made according to a dazzling new method of producing irresistible bread at home with hardly any work at all—less than 15 minutes spread over 20 hours or so. And the ingredients cost next to nothing—30 cents' worth of flour, water, yeast and salt.[17]

Another food columnist, whose husband liked to make Dan Leader's "time-consuming and messy" but still "wonderful" recipes, had a more critical take on Lahey's bread: "The result is a round, rustic loaf with a chewy crust and an interior with irregularly shaped holes. This is not a fine-textured bread, like my husband's, but is similar in appearance to an Italian ciabatta. It's not full of flavor nuance, but it's good and makes great crostini."[18] Although many food writers, including Bittman himself and chef and food writer Kenji Lopez-Alt, have tweaked Lahey's recipe, almost two decades later the fervor for his loaves remains undimmed.

In early 2020 the number of Americans who baked at home surged for an unanticipated and unwelcome reason. In response to the rapid spread of the deadly COVID-19 virus, in mid-March the United States began to close down. Federal, state, and local governments banned large gatherings and closed schools, restaurants, theaters, gyms, and other nonessential businesses. Americans stocked up on toilet paper and food and hunkered down at home for weeks or perhaps months. Isolated from their normal routines, they streamed online entertainment, took up hobbies, and cooked, both for pleasure and for necessity. Just two days after the state of Maine closed down, a local newspaper suggested: "If you are stuck inside for days, why not try making sourdough bread from scratch? The secret ingredient is sourdough starter, which takes several days to develop, but all you need to get started is flour, water and a little patience."[19]

Thousands of Americans had the same idea. However, the act of baking quickly became more than a fun activity. People now made bread as a form of meditation, using their hands to create something and distract from the grim news outside their doors, posting their results under Instagram hashtags like #coronavirusbaking and #stress-bread. Some home bakers even opened pop-up bakeries, selling loaves at their kitchen door or lowered down from their apartment window in a basket. In fact, so many Americans started making bread that they stripped supermarket aisles bare of flour and yeast. Nevertheless, they managed to fill online communities with photos of their sourdough starters (often named like children) and loaves coming out of the oven. The main show-off bread was the traditional *pain au levain*, with its golden-burnished and scored crust. Beginners used Lahey's no-knead recipe, while the most ambitious attempted the Tartine country bread. They posted videos of slicing the loaf down the middle and then opening the boule to reveal its perfect crumb structure.

The following year, Bittman wrote: "American is no longer a Wonder Bread nation. Gone are the days when bleached, sliced and plastic-wrapped bread from the supermarket was the default. Increasingly, Americans feast on ciabatta, tortillas and pita breads and Instagram their home baked loaves."[20] That view was somewhat overoptimistic. Based on consumption statistics, Americans still eat more industrial white pan bread than any other variety. Thanks to our experience during the pandemic, however, we also know that we have the possibility of making flavorsome loaves in our own kitchens: all it takes is flour, water, salt, and leavening.

Acknowledgments

I wrote this book in the haven that is the Wertheim Study of the New York Public Library's Vartan Gregorian Center for Research in the Humanities. I am beholden to all the NYPL librarians who helped me in my research and also to that institution for its vast resources of materials and databases. I relied on the collections of New York University's Bobst Library's Special Collection Center for books and archival materials relating to bread and labor unions. Both for this book and in my past writing, I have reached out to numerous bakers who have helped me understand the bread world, both its history and the current practice. In no particular order, I am deeply grateful to William Rubel, Michel Suas, Eli Zabar, Apollonia Poilâne, Michael London, Julia O'Malley, Jim Lahey, Allan Zuchowski, Amy Scherber, Melissa Weller, Kamel Saci, Steven Sullivan, Daniel Leader, Zachary Golper, Matthew Tilden, Didier Rosada, Keith Giusto, Tom MacMahon, Karen Bornarth, Abe Faber and Christy Timon, Louis Volle, Esther Kramer, Peter Endriss, Keith Cohen, Anton Duke, Nathan Berg, Amy Halloran, Genevieve Bardwell, and Roger Gural for their time and insights. Darra

Goldstein helped bring this project into existence, and both she and Paul Freedman came to its aid at a crucial time. I would like to thank my editor, Kate Marshall, for her determination in bringing this book into the world. Finally, thank you to Jane, Buster, and Edward for putting up with all the baking, bags filled with flour, visits to bakeries, and my obsession with all things bread.

American Bread Timeline

1000 CE: Maize, or corn, enters eastern North America as a food crop. Over the next five hundred years, Indigenous peoples as far north as New England adopt maize as their dietary staple.

1607: Jamestown is established by employees of the Virginia Company of London on the banks of the James River.

1619: A group of about twenty abducted Africans are sold at auction in Virginia, becoming the first enslaved men and women in Britain's North American colonies.

1620: The Pilgrims, a group of Protestant separatists, found the Plymouth Colony on the coast of Massachusetts.

1624: The Dutch West India Company sets up a trading post on the southern tip of Manhattan Island, which is given the name New Amsterdam. Within a year, both a horse-powered grist mill and a windmill are built to grind grain.

1632: The first windmill is erected in Boston.

1651: In response to complaints from citizens, the government of New Amsterdam established the first assize of bread to regulate the size, price, and quality of loaves.

1680: The government of New York forbids the bolting of flour anywhere except New York City, ensuring the city's dominance of the colony's booming flour trade.

1776: Citizens of North America's Thirteen Colonies declare their independence of Britain and royal rule.

1780s: The Delaware engineer Oliver Evans designs the first fully automatic, water-powered flour mill, revolutionizing the flour industry.

1796: Amelia Simmons publishes *American Cookery*, the first cookbook written by an American author and containing native dishes.

1804–1806: The Lewis & Clark Expedition opens the land route from the Mississippi River to the Pacific. The settlers that follow learn how to make bread on the move, using chemical, salt-rising, and sourdough leavens.

1820s: Saleratus, which could either be sodium bicarbonate (baking soda) or potassium carbonate, becomes popular as a bread leaven, taking the place of yeast.

1824: *The Virginia House-Wife* is published by Mary Randolph. This is the first cookbook containing recognizably Southern dishes, including breads.

1832: The first cholera epidemic hits the United States. Reverend Sylvester Graham, a temperance orator, begins his crusade for whole wheat bread as a cure for all ills.

1843: The first single-acting baking powder, a chemical leavening agent, goes on sale in England.

1848: Gold is discovered at Sutter's Mill in California. Thousands of adventurers rush to the Pacific Coast to earn their fortunes, including French bakers.

1850: A Vienna brewer named Adolf Ignaz Mautner wins the prize for developing a method to produce compressed yeast, which gives bakers their first reliable source of yeast leavening.

1850s: German immigrants arrive in the United States after the 1848 Revolution. They find jobs in the baking industry and begin to make their favored rye loaves.

1858: John Hecker opens the first mechanized bread-making factory in New York City.

1860s: Chemist Eben Norton Horsford and partner develop the first double-acting baking powder, which goes on sale under the Rumford brand name.

1861: Outbreak of the American Civil War.

1863: The Emancipation Proclamation, signed by President Abraham Lincoln, orders that the legal status of enslaved African Americans be changed to free men and women.

1868: Émigrés Charles and Max Fleischmann begin producing their Fleischmann's Yeast in Cincinnati.

1871: The crushing of the Paris Commune leads to an exodus of French men and women to New York City. They bring French food and baking techniques to Manhattan.

1873: At the Vienna International Exposition, Americans learn about European advances in flour milling and baking. They taste Vienna bread, then considered the best in the world.

1876: At the Philadelphia Centennial Exposition the Fleischmann brothers open the Vienna Model Bakery, introducing Americans to Viennese-quality baking.

1878: The Washburn Crosby Company of Minneapolis begins installing a Hungarian-style roller mill, allowing them to produce the finest and whitest flour Americans had ever seen.

1880–1914: Thousands of Eastern European Jews and Italians from southern Italy arrive from Southern Italy. Many of them settle in New York and other big cities and find work in the baking industry.

1889: *Aunt Babette's Cookbook*, the first German cookbook written in America, is published. It includes recipes for rye breads.

1890: By now, 80 percent of American bread is made at home, while 20 percent is store-bought. In rural areas housewives make nearly all the loaves that their family consumes.

1904: James N. Alsop patents a mechanism for bleaching flour to make it whiter.

1911: The National Association of Master Bakers begins a campaign to convince women to stop making bread at home and buy store loaves.

1913: The governor of New York signs bills attempting to ban cellar bakeries and give workers better conditions.

1914–1918: World War I, and the United States enters the war in 1917.

1925: The Beigel Bakers Union is founded to help bagel men earn better pay and working conditions. For the next forty years the union dominates the city's bagel industry.

1926: The Ward baking interests control 20 percent of the national bread trade. The federal government charges them with violating the Sherman Anti-Trust

Act and sues to break up their monopoly. The Ward family is forced to sell most of their bakeries to other companies.

1941: With another world war looming, the National Nutrition Conference for Defense in Washington, DC, advocates adding vitamins to white bread, which had been criticized as unhealthy. Vitamin-enriched flour becomes the norm for supermarket bread.

1941: Wonder Bread begins an ad campaign proclaiming that its loaf "Builds Strong Bodies 8 Ways," later changed to "Builds Strong Bodies 12 Ways."

1941–1945: World War II. War has been raging in Europe since 1938, but the United States enters the war following Japan's December 7, 1941, attack on Pearl Harbor.

1950: By now, 80 percent of the loaves consumed by Americans are store-bought. Home baking falls out of favor as housewives choose the convenience of feeding their family cellophane-wrapped, presliced white bread.

1962: Daniel Thompson patents the automatic bagel-rolling machine.

1965: The Lender family opens the first fully automated bakery using bagel-rolling machines, altering the face of bagels across the United States.

1966: The radical street theater group called the Diggers is formed in San Francisco. The next year they begin distribution of free bread in the city.

1970: *The Tassajara Bread Book*, written by Edward Espe Brown, is published, becoming a surprise bestseller for its recipes for healthy loaves.

1973: The United States withdraws its troops from Vietnam, ending the Vietnam War.

1973: A team of USDA scientists isolates *Lactobacillus sanfranciscenis*, the lactic acid bacteria that gives San Francisco sourdough its particular tang.

1977: Michael and Wendy London open Mrs. London's Bakery in Saratoga Springs, New York, which becomes one of the country's first artisan bakeries.

1983: Two pioneering artisan bakeries open: Daniel Leader's Bread Alone in Boiceville, New York, and Steven Sullivan's Acme Bread in Berkeley, California. Selling both retail and to restaurants, these bakeries pave the way for dozens of other young bakers.

1985: Carol Field publishes *The Italian Baker*, the first cookbook to give detailed instructions on how to make the great breads of Italy.

1992: The Bread Bakers Guild of America is founded to promote the needs of artisan bakers through outreach, meetings, and education.

1993: The first two artisan bread cookbooks are published: *The Village Baker* by Joe Ortiz and *Bread Alone* by Daniel Leader and Judith Blahnik.

1996: Keith Giusto and partners open Central Milling, the first flour mill devoted to the needs of artisan bakeries. Many of their products are modeled after European-style, and particularly French, flours.

2006: The *New York Times* publishes article on Jim Lahey's method for making no-knead bread, sparking a baking trend that continues today.

2010: Chad Robertson publishes *Tartine Bread*, one of the most detailed and obsessive artisan baking cookbooks.

2018: The Washington State University Bread Lab introduces the Approachable Loaf, a 100 percent whole wheat loaf meant to compete with supermarket white bread.

2020: Millions of Americans enter lockdown due to the COVID-19 pandemic crisis. With lots of free time on their hands, they begin baking bread and posting photos of their loaves on social media.

Glossary

BAKING POWDER First developed in the mid-nineteenth century, baking powder is a chemical leavening agent made from an alkali salt like sodium bicarbonate and one or two acids, most commonly monocalcium phosphate and sodium aluminum sulfate. These are usually mixed with cornstarch to keep them from reacting until water is added. When mixed into a dough, baking powder releases carbon dioxide over an extended period, including in the oven, to ensure a good rise. Despite the hopes of manufacturers, baking powder has never gained wide acceptance as a bread leaven, except for quick breads. However, it is widely used for cakes, cookies, and biscuits.

BAKING SODA Sodium bicarbonate, or baking soda, is an alkali salt used mostly as a leavening agent for quick breads. It is usually mixed into a dough containing an acidic liquid, such as buttermilk or yogurt, and the ensuing chemical reaction causes the production of carbon dioxide gas. This raises and lightens the loaf. Baking soda is also sometimes added to sourdoughs to reduce their sour flavor. In the nineteenth century, baking soda was also called "saleratus" and, due to the crude processing methods of the day, often created a harsh, bitter flavor in breads.

BOLTING After the grain passes through the mill, it is sent to a succession of sifters that separate out the various components of flour. Until the twentieth century this step was known as bolting. Early sifters were made of bolting cloths (usually horsehair, linen, or silk) of various degrees of fineness that sorted the coarse bran from the finer flour. This was first done by hand using circular sieves shaken by the mill worker, but by about 1800 various types of bolting machines were used in newer mills. Today mills use oscillating machines called plansifters that automatically sift and grade their product.

CORN Also known as maize (*Zea mays*), corn is a Native American crop first domesticated in Central Mexico about nine thousand years ago. (In England "corn" also refers to cereal crops in general, leading to occasional confusion in the literature.) In precontact North America maize was the primary staple for most Native American groups and at the center of their religious culture. They consumed it in various forms of corn cakes and mushes. When the first European settlers arrived, they relied on corn to keep themselves alive and gradually learned to incorporate it into their own cuisine. Corn does not contain gluten, however, so a dough made of 100 percent cornmeal does not rise. New England settlers learned how to mix it into rye loaves, while Southerners used corn to make pone, hoe cakes, and the like. In the early nineteenth century, Southerners began to use saleratus and other chemical leavenings to produce cornbread, a staple of Southern cuisine today. Beyond these regional specialties, corn rarely appears in American loaves.

FERMENTATION After a loaf's ingredients are thoroughly mixed, the dough is left to rest so that it can ferment. During this process natural or chemical leavens produce carbon dioxide bubbles that become trapped in the dough's matrix of gluten molecules. They also generate flavor elements that add to the taste of the finished bread. Fermentation occurs at a number of stages in the baking process, including in the preferment (if used), after the first mix, during the various stages of rising and proofing, and even while baking. If the fermentation is allowed to go on too long, the leavens consume all available sugars and the dough collapses.

LEAVENING Without leavening, bread made from flour and water would become a dense gummy mass, consumable only by gnawing. Leavening agents such as yeasts, sourdoughs, and various chemicals react with the other ingredients to produce carbon dioxide gas. These bubbles become trapped within the dough structure, causing it to rise and develop holes both large and small. This increases the volume of the bread and gives the crumb better mouthfeel and texture. Depending on the leavening agent, it can also affect the loaf's flavor in both positive and negative ways.

MALT This is made from barley that has been germinated (i.e., malted) and then dried and ground. It usually comes in dried or syrup form. Malt in a dough increases yeast activity, improves a bread's flavor, and gives it a browner crust. It also adds a slight sweetness but much less than sucrose. Malt is an essential ingredient in classic New York bagels.

MILLING Milling is the process in which grain is ground into small pieces, ranging from coarse meal to fine white flour. Native Americans and the first European settlers prepared their corn by pounding it in versions of a mortar and pestle. Soon settlers imported circular stone grindstones to turn grain into flour. The smaller ones, called querns, could be turned by human strength, while heavier grindstones needed animals or wind or water power to be set in motion. Toward the end of nineteenth century, big American millers began to install new steel rollers that could grind wheat into the finest white flour. The downside was that the rollers stripped grain of many of its most important nutrients. Mills in cities like Buffalo, New York, and Minneapolis, Minnesota, were so sophisticated that they could divide a kernel of wheat or rye into streams of its constituent parts, some only fit for cattle feed, others perfect for making the lightest breads and biscuits. Periodic protests over the lack of nutrition in factory bread have led to millers trying to replace many of the elements they removed during production. This includes vitamins, replaced during World War II, and more recently wheat germ, bran, and fiber.

MIXING This is the initial combination of the main ingredients: flour, water, salt, leavening, and so on. This can take from five minutes (in high-speed mixers used by factory bakers) to twenty minutes with artisan bakers. During mixing, water combines with flour causing its proteins to form into long strands of gluten that give dough its structure. The flour hydration exposes the sugars that the yeasts and bacteria will feed upon, beginning the fermentation process. The churning of the mixing arms also causes air bubbles to be trapped in the dough, encouraging the rise.

PREFERMENT This is a mixture of flour, water, and leavening that is allowed to ferment and is then added to the final dough ingredients in the mixing process. Sourdough is a preferment. Other varieties include old dough (dough from the previous bake is added to the next batch), poolish, biga, and sponge. The advantage of a preferment is that it can boost the yeast, improve a loaf's texture, and add flavor elements.

PROOFING After a dough undergoes its first rise (after mixing), it is generally kneaded to degas it and then shaped. Then the loaf is allowed to proof, often in a warm environment, so that fermentation resumes, allowing it to rise a second time. Proofing is the last stage before breads are put into the oven.

RYE *Secale cereale*, or rye, is a grass originating in Neolithic-era western Asia. Due to its tolerance of poor soil and cold weather, rye became the most common grain planted in eastern and northern Europe. In countries like France and England rye breads—darker and coarser than fine white loaves—were considered lower status and more likely to be consumed by poorer and more rural classes. Rye is rich in proteins, minerals, and fiber but contains less gluten than wheat, so rye breads are generally denser than wheat loaves. In the United States most rye breads contain mostly wheat flour and a smaller amount of rye for flavor and texture. In immigrant communities many rye breads contain much higher amounts of rye and are often made with sourdough starters due to tradition and flavor preferences.

SALT Sodium chloride is added to bread as a taste enhancer. It also strengthens the gluten structure so that it holds more gas bubbles and slows the fermentation process. Without salt, fermentation proceeds too quickly, giving less time for flavors to develop. The Tuscany region of Italy is one of the few parts of the world where saltless bread is an important part of the culinary tradition.

SALT-RISING Women living on the American frontier developed the leavening technique known as salt-rising. After mixing a slurry of flour, cornmeal, water, and baking soda, they would put it in front of a fire to keep it warm overnight. The next morning, if the starter took, the mixture would have a head of foam and smell something like rotten eggs. The aroma was caused by the bacteria *Clostridium perfringens* (a common cause of food poisoning). When mixed with flour, the starter would generate hydrogen gas, causing the bread to rise. Baking the bread killed the bacteria (no illnesses have ever been reported from eating a salt-rising loaf), which nevertheless gave the bread a distinct but not unpleasant cheesy flavor.

SHORTENING Also known as fats, shortenings used in bread making include butter, lard, oils, and margarine. They can soften a loaf's texture, improve mouthfeel, increase shelf life, and boost richness and flavor. Breads in which shortening and also sugar and eggs are added are called enriched breads, including brioche and challah.

SOURDOUGH The first leavened breads were probably sourdoughs. These are made from a starter culture of wheat or rye mixed with water, which after a few days begins to bubble and develop a fresh, sour aroma. This reaction is caused by lactic acid bacteria and wild yeasts from the surrounding environment. When the starter is mixed into the dough, the bacteria and yeasts ingest the sugars in the wheat or rye and give off ethanol and CO_2 gas. This causes the loaf to rise, but it also gives a more complex (often slightly sour) flavor profile to the bread and extends keeping time. While the knowledge of how to make sourdough breads has been shared widely across regions, its popularity is highly culturally specific. Only recently has sourdough gained widespread acceptance in the United States.

SUGAR Bakers add sugar to bread to promote yeast activity during fermentation, to improve a loaf's texture, flavor, and shelf time, and as a sweetener. Sugar also helps the crust to brown due to the Maillard reaction. Aside from plain sugar (i.e., sucrose), other sweeteners include honey, molasses, brown rice syrup, and high fructose corn syrup.

WATER This is a fundamental ingredient in all breads. Water dissolves salt, sugar, baking powder, baking soda, and other components. It activates the yeast, starting the fermentation process. It releases the starches and sugars from the flour and hydrates the gluten so it forms into strands. The amount of water added affects the moisture content of the finished bread. Bakers also use the water added to a recipe to regulate the temperature of the dough. Water quality can vary greatly from region to region, so bakers in a city where the water has a high mineral content may have to treat their doughs very differently than those in areas with fewer minerals.

WHEAT *Triticum aestivum*, or common wheat, is by far the most common grain used in American bread production. Other varieties of wheat include einkorn, spelt, emmer, and durum. Wheat is a grass, first domesticated in West Asia, that produces seeds, or kernels, that may be milled into flour. It spread to Europe, where it was grown everywhere from Sicily to southern England. From at least Roman times on, fine white wheat loaves became a preferred food of the upper classes. Wheats used for baking are divided into hard and soft varieties. Hard, with higher protein content (leading to stronger gluten formation), is the primary bread wheat, while soft wheats with less protein are preferred for biscuits, cakes, and pastries. Each wheat kernel is enclosed in a husk that is removed to expose the edible wheat berry, made of the bran, germ, and endosperm. Each of these elements contains various amounts of vitamins, protein, fiber, and pigmentation. To make the white flour used in supermarket white bread, millers only use the endosperm containing minimal pigmentation that is then bleached out. The many different types of whole wheat flour—from coarse, dark "Irish-style" to white whole wheat—contain larger amounts of bran and wheat germ. American flours are graded primarily by their protein content but also by the amount of ash (i.e., minerals from bran and germ) they contain. European countries use different numbering systems but all refer to the ash content of their flours.

YEAST The single-celled microorganism *Saccharomyces cerevisiae*, also known as baker's yeast, has been helping humans turn flour and water into risen bread for thousands of years. When mixed into a dough, this fungus begins to consume the sugars in the flour and produces ethanol and carbon dioxide. The latter causes the dough to rise, while the former contributes to bread's flavor and aroma. In western Europe for many centuries an important form of yeast was liquid brewer's yeast, a by-product of the beer production process. Housewives also used fermented fruit and hops to produce a similar liquid leavening agent. In the second half of the nineteenth century, baker's yeast, first compressed and later dried and powdered, hit the market and is now by far the dominant form of yeast in the world baking market.

Notes

1. RYE AND INDIAN

1. William Bradford, *Bradford's History of the Plymouth Settlement, 1608–1650* (E. P. Dutton & Company, 1920), 65.

2. These early details as recounted in *Mourt's Relation, or Journal of the Plantation at Plymouth* (John Kimball Wiggin, 1865), 21.

3. Bradford, *Bradford's History*, 69.

4. Rembert Dodoens, *A New Herbal, or Historie of Plants* (By Edward Griffin, 1619), 333.

5. Eliza Acton, *The English Bread Book* (Longman, Brown, Green, Longmans & Roberts, 1857), v.

6. *Mourt's Relation*, 97.

7. Edward Johnson, *Wonder-Working Providence of Sions Saviour in New England* (Warren F. Draper, 1867), xvii.

8. Johnson, *Wonder-Working Providence*, 84.

9. John Gerard, *The Herball, or Generall Historie of Plants* (John Norton, 1597), 77.

10. Fulmer Mood, "John Winthrop, Jr., on Indian Corn," *New England Quarterly* (March 1937), 130

11. Mood, "John Winthrop, Jr.," 130.

12. Domestic Matters," *New England Farmer*, August 15, 1832, 5 (the article originally appeared in the *Northampton Courier*).

13. "Messrs. Dunlap and Claypoole," *Dunlap's Pennsylvania Packet*, October 10, 1788, 3.

14. "Rye and Indian Bread," *Poughkeepsie Journal*, May 8, 1847, 1 (the article originally appeared in the *Massachusetts Ploughman*).

15. "Beer & Bread," *The American Farmer*, November 16, 1821, 271; emphasis in the original.

16. [no article title], *Public Ledger*, June 23, 1840, 2.

17. "Steam Cooker Free," *Boston Globe*, November 7, 1888, 4.

2. CORN BREAD

1. Edward D. Neill, *The History of the Virginia Company of London* (Joel Munsell, 1869), 11.

2. Captain John Smith, *A True Relation of Virginia* (Wiggin and Lunt, 1866), 13.

3. William A. Kelso, *Jamestown: The Truth Revealed* (University of Virginia Press, 2017), 185–203.

4. Robert Beverley, *The History and Present State of Virginia* (Richard Parker, 1705), 55–56.

5. "Household Affairs," *Prairie Farmer*, May 1847, 156.

6. Mrs. Mary Randolph, *The Virginia House-Wife* (Davis and Force, 1824), 172.

7. Col. George Bailey, "The Crime of Cornbread," *Clinch Valley News*, May 27, 1921, 2 (the article was reprinted from the *Houston Post*).

8. "Longing for Dixie," *Atlanta Constitution*, July 29, 1907, 4.

9. The Bentztown Bard, "Maryland Musings," *Baltimore Sun*, January 16, 1915, 6.

10. Frederick Law Olmsted, *A Journey in the Seaboard Slave States* (G.P. Putnam's, 1904), 102–103.

11. Theodore Weld, *American Slavery As It Is: Testimony of a Thousand Witnesses* (American Anti-Slavery Society, 1839), 31.

12. Olmsted, *Journey*, 109.

13. Anne L. Bower, ed., *African American Foodways* (University of Illinois Press, 2007), 103.

14. Quoted in Herbert C. Covey and Dwight Eisnach, *What the Slaves Ate* (Greenwood Press, 2009), 56.

15. Wilbur O. Atwater and Charles D. Woods, *Dietary Studies with Reference to the Food of the Negro in Alabama* (Government Printing Office, 1897), 21.

16. Michael Twitty, *The Cooking Gene: A Journey Through African American Culinary History in the Old South* (Harper Collins, 2017), 348.

3. WHEAT BREAD

1. Quoted in J. Franklin James, *Narratives of New Netherland, 1609–1664* (Charles Scribner's Sons, 1909), 48.

2. James, *Narratives of New Netherland*, 76.

3. Michaelius as quoted in James, *Narratives of New Netherland*, 130.

4. Charles T. Gehring, ed., *Laws & Writs of Appeal, 1647–1663* (Syracuse University Press, 1991), 22–23.

5. Gehring, *Laws & Writs of Appeal*, 25–26.

6. A.J.F. Van Laer, ed., *Minutes of the Court of Albany, Rensselaerwyck and Schenectady* (University of the State of New York, 1928), vol. 2, 480–81.

7. A.J.F. Van Laer, ed., *Correspondence of Maria van Rensselaer* (University of the State of New York, 1935), 39.

8. I.N. Phelps Stokes, *The Iconography of Manhattan Island* (Robert H. Dodd, 1922), vol. 4, 384.

9. Quoted in Albert Cook Myers, ed., *Narratives of Early Pennsylvania, West New Jersey, and Delaware* (Barnes & Noble, Inc., 1953), 327, 331.

10. Quoted in J.P. Brissot de Warville, *New Travels in the United States of America* (J.S. Jordan, 1792), 187–88.

11. Quoted in Greville Bathe and Dorothy Bathe, *Oliver Evans: A Chronicle of Early Engineering* (Historical Society of Pennsylvania, 1935), 12.

12. Quoted in Bathe and Bathe, *Oliver Evans*, xiv.

13. Stokes, *Iconography of Manhattan Island*, vol. 5, 1142.

14. [no title] *Vermont Intelligencer*, November 23, 1818, 1.

15. Maria Rundell, *A New System of Domestic Cookery* (R. M'Dermut & D.D. Arden, 1814), 238.

16. Sarah Josepha Hale, *The Good Housekeeper* (Weeks, Jordan and Company, 1839), 22.

17. Hale, *Good Housekeeper*, 21–22.

18. "Bread," *Moore's Rural New Yorker*, February 7, 1850, 43.

19. Eliza Leslie, *Directions for Cookery in Its Various Branches* (Carey & Hart, 1844), 376.

20. Arriet Van Rensselaer, *Receipt Book from 1816–1835*, New York Heritage Digital Collections, https://cdm16694.contentdm.oclc.org/digital/collection/CherryHill/id/1351/rec/10, p. 27.

21. Leslie, *Directions for Cookery*, 376.

4. GRAHAM BREAD

1. "Dyspepsia: Extracts from a Diary," *Boston Daily Advertiser*, April 28, 1820, 2; emphasis in the original.

2. "Bread," *New England Farmer*, August 31, 1827, 3 (reprinted article from the *New York Mirror*).

3. Edward Hitchcock, *Dyspepsy Forestalled* (J. S. & C. Adams, 1831), 2

4. "Dyspepsia Bread," *New England Farmer*, August 13, 1830, 27.

5. "Bread," *New England Farmer*, August 31, 1827, 3.

6. "Bread. Wheat. Bran Bread," *Agricultural Almanack*, 1823, 9; emphasis in the original.

7. "Temperance Cause in Pennsylvania," *Philadelphia Recorder*, December 11, 1830, 37.

8. Sylvester Graham, *Lectures to Young Men on Chastity* (Light & Stearns, 1837), 137.

9. "Flour—again," *New York Evangelist*, July 15, 1837, 8.

10. "Adulteration of Food," *Boston Cultivator*, September 9, 1848, 290.

11. Sylvester Graham, *A Treatise on Bread, and Bread-Making* (Light & Stearns, 1837), 47–48.

12. Graham, *Treatise on Bread*, 105–106.

13. "A Temperance Lecture and a Critic," *Workingman's Advocate*, July 2, 1831, 2.

14. Graham, *Treatise on Bread*, 93.

15. Graham, *Treatise on Bread*, 34.

16. Graham, *Treatise on Bread*, 26–27.

17. Graham, *Treatise on Bread*, 29.

18. Graham, *Treatise on Bread*, 100.

19. Sylvester Graham, *Lectures of the Science of Human Life* (Fowler & Wells, 1858), 43.

20. Caleb Ticknor, *The Philosophy of Living* (Harper & Bros., 1836), 81–82.

21. "Large Bread," *Evening Post*, New York, May 1, 1833, 3.

22. As reported in Joel R. Peabody, *A World of Wonders* (Robert S. Davis, 1838), 151.

23. "Thanksgiving Sermon," *Free Enquirer*, October 26, 1834, 1.

24. "The Graham Boarding House," *Liberator*, June 16, 1837, 7; emphasis in the original.

25. "Sylvester Graham," *Home Journal*, October 11, 1851, 41.

26. D. Fraser, "Fermented and Unfermented Bread," *Herald of Health*, December 1864, 4.

27. W. A. Alcott, "Healthy Bread," *New England Farmer*, February 1857, 9.

28. William Alcott, *Vegetable Diet* (Fowler and Wells, 1859), 293.

29. Alcott, *Vegetable Diet*, 293.

30. Russell Trall, *The Hygeian Home Cook-Book* (S. R. Wells, Publisher, 1874), 10.

31. Ronald L. Numbers, *Prophetess of Health: Ellen G. White and the Origins of Seventh-Day Adventist Health Reform* (University of Tennessee Press, 1992), 81

32. John Harvey Kellogg, *A Household Manual of Hygiene, Food and Diet* (Office of the Health Reformer, 1878), 51.

33. "What the National Biscuit Company Has Done and Is Doing," *Kansas City Star*, March 11, 1904, 9.

34. "Necessity of a Varied Diet," *Muscatine News-Tribune*, October 18, 1907, 3.

35. "Unsifted: Recipes and Words," November 2021, https://s3.wp.wsu.edu/uploads/sites/2616/2021/11/Unsifted-Pamphlet-PDF_112221.pdf.

5. SOURDOUGH BREAD

1. Diary entry of May 26, 1804, *Journals of the Lewis & Clark Expedition*, edited by Gary Moulton, Center for Great Plains Studies, University of Nebraska–Lincoln, https://lewisandclarkjournals.unl.edu/item/lc.jrn.1804-05-26, published by Bison Books, 2002.

2. Diary entry of November 30, 1805, *Journals of the Lewis & Clark Expedition*, https://lewisandclarkjournals.unl.edu/item/lc.jrn.1805–11-30#lc.jrn.1805-11-30.03.

3. Quoted in Glenda Riley, ed., *Prairie Voices* (Iowa State University Press, 1996), 6.

4. "To make excellent bread without yeast," *American Magazine*, October 1789, 292.

5. "Bread and Bread Making," *Indiana Farmer*, March 1859, 421.

6. "A Bread Riot," *Indiana State Sentinel*, September 19, 1889, 1.

7. Randolph B. Marcy, *The Prairie Traveler* (Harper & Brothers, 1861), 35–36.

8. T. H. Jefferson, *Map of the Emigrant Road from Independence, Mo., to St. Francisco, California* (California Historical Society, 1945), 9.

9. In Clifford Merrill Drury, ed., *The Mountains We Have Crossed: Diaries and Letters of the Oregon Mission, 1838* (University of Nebraska Press, 1999), 99.

10. Mrs. Cornelius, *The Young Housekeeper's Friend* (Charles Tappan, 1846), 25.

11. Edward Hazen, *The Panorama of Professions and Trades* (Uriah Hunt, 1836), 28.

12. Maria Rundell, *American Domestic Cookery* (E. Duyckinck, 1823), 259.

13. William Henry Brewer, *Fermentation in Its Household Relations* (Case, Lockwood & Brainard, 1880), 232–33.

14. "Aged Dough," *Rochester Democrat and Chronicle*, December 21, 1896, 2.

15. Ralph Raven, *Golden Dreams and Leaden Realities* (G. P. Putnam & Co., 1853), 174.

16. Oliver Nelson, *The Cowman's Southwest* (Arthur H. Clark Company, 1953), 56.

17. Ramon F. Adams, *Come an' Get It* (University of Oklahoma Press, 1952), 78.

18. Adams, *Come an' Get It*, 79.

19. Jack London, "Housekeeping in the Klondike," *Harper's Bazaar*, September 15, 1900, 1227.

20. "Out of Alaska's Kitchens," *Ketchikan: The Ketchikan Alaska Chronicle*, 1947, 79–80.

21. Quoted in "'Mush!,'" *Nebraska Farmer*, October 13, 1934, 10.

22. "1,000,000 Flapjacks," *New York Times*, May 10, 1953, SM71.

6. VIENNA BREAD

1. "Thurlow Weed on Vienna Bread," *Buffalo Morning Express*, June 22, 1852, 2.

2. Eben Norton Horsford, *The Theory and Art of Bread-Making* (Welch, Bigelow and Company, 1861), 8.

3. E.N. Horsford, *Report on Vienna Bread* (Government Printing Office, 1875), 1.

4. Lily Haxworth Wallace, *The Rumford Complete Cookbook* (Rumford Chemical Works, 1908, 1918), 121.

5. Quoted in Horsford, *Report on Vienna Bread*, 1.

6. Horsford, *Report on Vienna Bread*, 99.

7. Horsford, *Report on Vienna Bread*, 103.

8. "Compressed Yeast," *Cincinnati Enquirer*, September 13, 1873, 5.

9. Bayard Taylor, "World's Exposition," *New York Tribune*, August 22, 1876, 1.

10. Estelle W. Wilcox, *The New Practical Housekeeping* (Home Publishing Company, 1890), 30.

11. Maria Parloa, *Miss Parloa's New Cook Book* (Estes and Lauriat, 1881), 382.

12. Quoted in John Storck and Walter Teague, *Flour for Man's Bread* (University of Minnesota Press, 1952), 222–23.

7. FRENCH BREAD

1. Quoted in Malcom J. Rohrbough, *Rush to Gold: The French and the California Gold Rush* (Yale University Press, 2013), 27.

2. J.D. Borthwick, *Three Years in California* (William Blackwood and Sons, 1857), 365.

3. Borthwick, *Three Years in California*, 73–74.

4. Steven L. Kaplan, *The Bakers of Paris and the Bread Question* (Duke University Press, 1996), 51.

5. T.A. Barry and B.A. Patten, *Men and Memories of San Francisco* (A.L. Bancroft & Company, 1873), 160.

6. "City Bakeries," *San Francisco Chronicle*, September 27, 1883, 3.

7. "San Francisco Uses More Kinds of Bread Than Any Other City in the Country," *San Francisco Chronicle*, March 6, 1904, 7.

8. "Do You Like Genuine Sour French Bread?," *Woodland Daily Democrat*, January 24, 1922, 4. "Better Bread," *Tracy Press*, August 3, 1928, 2.

9. "For That Real, Sour Dough French Bread," *The Southwest Wave*, December 19, 1930, 9.

10. "Food: Newest Products Include French Bread," *New York Times*, July 29, 1960, 28.

11. USDA, "Sour Dough French Bread," US Patent 3,734,743, May 22, 1973, 1.

12. Mark Stein, "Bakers Waging the Battle of the Baguette," *Los Angeles Times*, November 19, 1983, 37.

13. "The French Quarter of New York," *Scribner's Monthly*, November 1879, 1.

14. Rodolphe E. Garcynski, "Bread," *Appleton's Journal*, March 29, 1873, 434.

15. Paul Richards, *Paul Richards' Book of Breads, Cakes, Pastries, Ices and Sweetmeats* (The Hotel Monthly, 1907), 103.

16. Marion Harland, *Common Sense in the Household* (Charles Scribner's Sons, 1882), 272.

17. Richards, *Paul Richards' Book*, 103.

18. "Freihofer's Famous French Bread," *Atlantic City Daily Press*, November 9, 1920, 7.

19. Quoted in "It's French Bread—but It Proudly Carries a Made-in-New York Label," *New York Times*, October 23, 1971, 38.

20. Mimi Sheraton, "A Toast to Ethnic Bakeries, and Noble Loaves of Splendor," *New York Times*, April 20, 1977, 57.

8. RYE BREAD

1. F. W. Bogen, *The German in America* (B. H. Greene, 1851), 7.

2. Bogen, *German in America*, 33.

3. "Germans in America," *New York Daily Times*, June 27, 1855, 1.

4. "The Staff of Life," *Scientific American*, September 23, 1871, 200.

5. "The Madison Bakery," *Wisconsin State Journal*, December 18, 1863, 1.

6. Henriette Davidis, *Pickled Herring and Pumpkin Pike: A Nineteenth-Century Cookbook for German Immigrants to America* (Max Cade Institute for German-American Studies, 2002), 415.

7. Aunt Babette (Bertha Kramer), *Aunt Babette's Cookbook* (Bloch Publishing, 1889), 160–61.

8. Jane Eddington, "Rye Breads," *Chicago Tribune*, September 27, 1925, C2.

9. "Our New York Letter," *Burlington Free Press*, November 15, 1888, 6.

10. "Sunbeams," *The Sun*, August 21, 1894, 6.

11. Quoted in "Bakery Inspection Law," *New York Times*, May 16, 1896, 9.

12. Emil Braun, *The Baker's Book* (Emil Braun, 1901), vol. 1, 284.

13. Julius Wihlfahrt, *A Treatise on Baking* (Fleischmann Division, 1935), 373.

14. Clementine Paddleford, "Makers of Rye Bread Since 1885 Now Hearth-Baking White Loaf," *New York Times*, September13, 1949, 26.

15. Robert Glatzer, *The New Advertising* (Citadel Press, 1970), 53.

16. Advertisement "All Right, All Right," *New York Times*, October 28, 1954, 24.

17. Libby Rosof quoted in "Rye Bread: Like a Lot of Us, It Has Gone Soft, *Philadelphia Inquirer*, May 15, 1977, 1-H.

9. ITALIAN BREAD

1. "First Steps in America," *New York Times*, April 25, 1887, 8.

2. "Over Four Thousand Immigrants," *New York Tribune*, April 10, 1887, 9.

3. "Bread of All Nations in New York City," *Baker's Helper*, January 1904, 78.

4. "The Italians of New York," *The Cosmopolitan*, January 1888, 398.

5. Clarence Pullen, *In Fair Aroostook* (Bangor & Aroostook Railway Co., 1902), 16.

6. US Senate, Reports of the Immigration Commission, *Immigrants in Industries, Part 24: Recent Immigrants in Agriculture* (Government Printing Office, 1911), 324.

7. US Senate, *Immigrants in Industries*, 125.

8. Jerre Mangione, *Mount Allegro* (Columbia University Press, 1981), 132–33.

9. Braun, *Baker's Book*, vol. 2, 526.

10. "They Like Italian Bread," *Los Gatos Mail*, January 4, 1912, 6.

11. Edgar Lee Masters, *Songs and Satires* (Macmillan Company, 1916), 29.

12. Michael Parenti, "The Blessings of Private Enterprise," in *Studies in Italian American Social History: Essays in Honor of Leonard Covello*, ed. Francesco Cordasco (Rowman and Littlefield, 1975), 81.

13. Parenti, "Blessings of Private Enterprise," 83.

14. Paul Richards, "Jewish and Italian Breads," *Bakers' Helper*, July 15, 1927, 179.

15. Samuel A. Matz, *Formulas and Processes for Bakers* (Pan-Tech International, Inc., 1997), 169–70.

16. Jane Nickerson, "News of Food," *New York Times*, October 1, 1952, 36.

17. Carol Field, *The Italian Baker* (Harper & Row, 1985), 99.

18. Field, *Italian Baker*, 122–24.

19. Quoted in Vincent M. Mallozzi, "In East Harlem, Another Vestige of the Old Days Bids Farewell," *New York Times*, September 18, 2007, B3.

10. BAGELS

1. Der Tunkeler [Josef Tunkl], "Wilno, A Chapter in My Life," translated by Gloria Berkenstat Freund, 1951, https://www.jewishgen.org/yizkor/lita/Lit1279.html.

2. Arje Rolnicki, "Small Businesses in Our Town," translated by Zeva Shapiro, 1973, https://www.jewishgen.org/yizkor/dzialoszyce/dzi090.html#Page101.

3. Abraham Cahan, *Grandma Never Lived in America: The Journalism of Abraham Cahan*, ed. Moses Rischin (Indiana University Press, 1985), 386.

4. "Bagles [*sic*] Are Higher," *Hartford Courant*, April 3, 1899, 12.

5. Quoted in David Wise, "Luchese Lists Mayor, Judge As Men He Knows," *New York Herald Tribune*, November 15, 1952, 3.

6. Elizabeth May, "Through Bakeshop Windows," *New York Herald Tribune*, February 19, 1933, SM 18.

7. Clementine Paddleford, "Bagels and Lox Delivered for Breakfast in Bed," *New York Herald Tribune*, December 5, 1947, 32.

8. "Bread and Filth Cooked Together," *The Bakers' Journal*, October 6, 1894, 1.

9. Quoted in "Bread and Filth Cooked Together," 1.

10. "Kosher Bakers' Joyous Parade," *New York Tribune*, July 3, 1909, 14.

11. Mike McGrady, "Confessions of a Bagelphile," *Newsday*, September 26, 1964, 118.

12. "Bagel Baking," *The Bakers' and Confectioners' Journal*, March 1950, 7.

13. "Excerpts from the Thirty-Third Annual Session of the General Executive Board of the Bakery & Confectionery Workers International Union of America," 1937, 6.

14. "Strike Ends, Bakers Begin the Bagel," *Newsday*, January 2, 1954, 5.

15. Irving Pfefferbilt, "The Bagel," *Commentary*, January 1, 1951, 478–79.

16. Daniel T. Thompson, Apparatus for Making a Toroid, US Patent 2,584,414, filed February 10, 1966, and issued March 6, 1968, https://patents.google.com/patent/US3371624A.

17. "BONANZA in BAGELS," *Newsday*, October 13, 1969, 68.

18. Mimi Sheraton, "The Bagel Finagle," *New York Magazine*, August 6, 1973, 60.

19. Bromated flour is made with potassium bromate, a chemical that makes dough stronger and helps it rise. The ingredient has been found to be carcinogenic in rats. While it's banned in western Europe and other parts of the world,

the USDA allows its use in small amounts. Many bagel bakeries today use high-gluten, bleached, enriched, and bromated flour manufactured by companies such as General Mills.

20. Sheraton, "Bagel Finagle," 61.

21. Quoted in Robert Metz, "Bagel Maker Crosses Ethnic Lines," *New York Times*, August 20, 1973, 41.

22. Leah Leonard, *Jewish Cookery* (Crown Publishers, 1949), 104.

23. Stanley Ginsberg and Norman Berg, *Inside the Jewish Bakery: Recipes and Memories from the Golden Age of Jewish Bakeries* (Camino Books, 2011), 99–100.

24. Samuel A. Matz, *Formulas and Processes for Bakers* (Pan-Tech International Inc., 1997), 255.

25. "Newest Bagel," *Peninsula Time Tribune*, November 19, 1974, 9.

26. Arthur Schwartz, "Food Guide to Woodbury/Syosset," *Newsday*, January 19, 1977, 102.

11. WHITE BREAD

1. Quoted in "The Staff of Life," *American Phrenological Journal* (October 1863), 107.

2. "Thimbles Found," *The [Cleveland] Plain Dealer*, May 29, 1905, 12.

3. Quoted in Paul T. Cherington, *Advertising as a Business Force* (Doubleday, Page & Co., 1913), 23.

4. Quoted in "The Story of an American Business Success," *New York Times*, November 8, 1911, 5.

5. "I Will Not Eat Baker's Bread," *The National Bakery*, October 1912, 43.

6. "Delivering Ward's Tip Top Bread," *Brooklyn Eagle*, November 22, 1911, 6.

7. Marion Harlan, "Concerning Home Made Bread," *Chicago Tribune*, January 5, 1913, F3.

8. Schulze's keynote in "Report of Fourteenth Convention National Association of Master Bakers," National Association of Master Bakers, 1911, 11–13.

9. Schulze, "Report of Fourteenth Convention National Association of Master Bakers," 11–13.

10. Quoted in "Critic of Loaves Stirs City Women," *Chicago Tribune*, August 24, 1911, 9.

11. *The Story of the Staff of Life* (National Association of Master Bakers, 1911), 22.

12. "Ward's Fine Bread," in *Recipe Notebook, Tolley Baking Records, 1887–1979,* New York Public Library, Box 2, Folder 2.

13. "Tip Top," in *Recipe Notebook, Tolley Baking Records, 1887–1979,* New York Public Library, Box 2, Folder 2.

14. F. L. Gienandt, *The Twentieth Century Book for the Progressive Baker* (Fritz L. Gienandt, 1927), 176.

15. "British Press Discusses Bread," *The Crawford Tribune*, November 11, 1927, 6.

16. Ida Bailey Allen, *Mrs. Allen on Cooking, Menus, Service* (Doubleday, Doran & Company, 1929), 189.

17. Allen, *Mrs. Allen on Cooking*, 188.

18. Allen, *Mrs. Allen on Cooking*, 199–200.

19. "Announcing," *Constitution-Tribune*, July 6, 1928, 8.

20. Walter Warrick, "Sliced Bread," *Baker's Helper*, August 31, 1929, 516.

21. "Take a tip from Uncle Sam!," *Montgomery Advertiser*, May 2, 1941, 20; emphasis in the original.

22. "You, too, have a WAR JOB," *Daily News*, February 10, 1942, 28.

23. "Now! The First White Bread of Its Kind in Human History!," *Sioux City Journal*, April 22, 1942, 7; emphasis in the original.

24. Quoted in "Why—Did You Buy That Particular Kind of Bread?," *Baking Industry*, January 16, 1954, 40.

25. Letters to the Editor, *Wall Street Journal*, July 15, 1953, 10.

26. Quoted in "Bakers and Millers Reply to Critics," *Baking Industry*, September 12, 1953, 56–61.

27. "The *New York Times* Grocery Research Workshop Report, Continental Baking," Institute for Motivational Research, November 14, 1961, Ernest Dichter Papers, Hagley Museum, Delaware, 2.

28. "A Motivational Research Study on the Sales and Merchandising of Tip-Top Bread," Institute for Motivational Research, January 1962, Ernest Dichter Papers, Hagley Museum, i.

12. HIPPIE BREAD

1. Henry Miller, *The Intimate Henry Miller* (Signet/New American Library, 1959), 71–72.

2. Miller, *Intimate Henry Miller*, 79.

3. Orville Prescott, "Books of the Times," *New York Times*, December 19, 1945, 23.

4. "Bake-In Spreads Joy in Haight," *Berkeley Barb*, June 30, 1967, 11.

5. "Digger Bread & the Free Baker(ies)," Digger Archive, https://www.diggers.org/diggers/digbread.html.

6. Gordon and Phyllis Grabe, *The Hippie Cookbook* (Paisley Shawl Publishing Co., 1970), 24.

7. Adelle Davis, *Let's Eat Right To Keep Fit* (Harcourt, Brace & World, Inc., 1954), 107.

8. James Rorty, "Bread, and the Stuff We Eat," *Harper's*, March 1, 1950, 45.

9. Mick Wellwood and Lini Lieberman, "The Art of Making Bread," *Los Angeles Free Press*, January 23, 1970, 40.

10. Wellwood and Lieberman, "Art of Making Bread," 43; emphasis in the original.

11. Brown as quoted in Jonathan Kauffman, *Hippie Food* (William Morrow, 2018), 123.

12. Edward Espe Brown, *The Tassajara Cookbook* (Shambhala Publications, 1970), front matter.

13. Brown, *Tassajara Cookbook*, 3.

14. Brown, *Tassajara Cookbook*, 44–45.

15. Brown, *Tassajara Cookbook*, unpaginated page vii.

16. Crescent Dragonwagon, *The Commune Cookbook* (Simon & Schuster, 1972), 126.

17. Dragonwagon, *Commune Cookbook*, 128.

18. Heidi Sinick, "Bread Makes Itself by Your Kindness," *Washington Post*, July 15, 1971, D1.

13. ARTISAN BREAD

1. Leader, in Daniel Leader and Judith Blahnik, *Bread Alone* (William Morrow and Company, Inc., 1993), 15.

2. Michael London, interview by the author, April 2025.

3. Oscar London, "The Bread Lines of Berkeley," *San Francisco Chronicle*, August 24, 1986, Sunday Punch section, 2.

4. Doris Muscatine, "The Proof Is in the Tasting," *San Francisco Examiner*, January 18, 1987, 294.

5. Craig Claiborne, "The Whole Wheat Story," *New York Times*, July 9, 1986, C1.

6. Dena Kleiman, "Judging a Meal by Its Bread," *New York Times*, August 2, 1989, C2.

7. Jeffrey Steingarten, "Food: Primal Bread," *Vogue*, November 1990, 310.

8. Joe Ortiz, *The Village Baker* (Ten Speed Press, 1993), 95–96.

9. Pat Daily, "Cook's Books," *Chicago Tribune*, December 2, 1993, Section 7, 8.

10. Maggie Glezer, *Artisan Baking Across America* (Artisan, 2000), x.

11. Didier Rosada, interview by the author, April 2025.

12. Chad Robertson, *Tartine Bread* (Chronicle Books, 2010), 28.

13. Robertson, *Tartine Bread*, 68.

14. Blair Anthony Robertson, "Serious About Sourdough," *Sacramento Bee*, January 26, 2011, D2.

15. Carole Kotkin, "Homemade Bread—Without the Need to Knead," *Grand Forks Herald*, March 12, 2008, C2.

16. Mark Bittman, "The Secret of Great Bread: Let Time Do the Work," *New York Times*, November 8, 2006, F1.

17. Jeffrey Steingarten, "Easy Riser," *Vogue*, May 2007, 275.

18. Debbie Moose, "No-knead Bread Meets a Need," *News & Observer*, January 28, 2007, 8D.

19. Sam Schipani, "Self-quarantined and Stuck Inside? Here Are Five Things You Can Try," *Bangor Daily News*, March 15, 2020, https://www.bangordailynews.com/2020/03/15/homestead/self-quarantined-and-stuck-inside-here-are-5-things-you-can-try/.

20. Mark Bittman, "Your Sourdough Starter Can Be a Time Machine," *New York Times*, November 27, 2021, A21.

Bibliographic Essay

There are no other histories of American bread. In my research I relied on the perspective given in a number of world histories of bread, particularly William Rubel's *Bread: A Global History*, H. E. Jacob's *Six Thousand Years of Bread: Its Holy and Unholy History*, and Bernard Dupaigne's *The History of Bread*. Although it focuses mostly on bread's history in Britain, *Breads White and Brown* by R. A. McCance and E. M. Widdowson also provides an excellent introduction to bread in Europe from Greek and Roman times through the Middle Ages. Stanley L. Kaplan's *The Bakers of Paris and the Bread Question* only focuses on the history of bread in France from 1700 on. However, his work is a model of culinary history and provides a fascinating window into the French bread traditions that landed on American shores in the nineteenth and twentieth centuries. I wrote this book because I love bread but also due to my admiration of Elizabeth David's *English Bread and Yeast Cookery*. My first idea was to write the American version of her book, but then I realized that it couldn't be copied. Still, in its own way this book is an homage.

CHAPTER 1

My narrative of New England's rye and Indian bread begins with the arrival of European settlers to the Massachusetts coast. My primary sources for this story were first-person accounts written by the Plymouth Pilgrims and early Puritans. I used William Bradford's *Of Plymouth Plantation* (in the Modern English rendition by Harold Paget for clarity) and *Mourt's Relation*, with text written primarily by Edward Winslow and William Bradford. For the culture and history of corn-growing and processing in precontact eastern New England, my primary source was Andrew Lipman's excellent *The Saltwater Frontier*. I also consulted numerous books on the history of corn among Native Americans, among them *Indian Agriculture in America* by R. Douglas Hurt and the essay collection *Corn and Culture in the Prehistoric New World*, edited by Sissel Johannessen and Christine A. Hastorf.

European scholars were able to cultivate and study corn decades before the Pilgrims arrived in the New World and formed definite opinions as to its utility. The most prominent early botanical tracts were Rembert Dodoens's *A New Herbal, or Historie of Plants* and John Gerard's *The Herball or Generall Historie of Plants*. For sixteenth- and seventeenth-century English bread my main informants were Elizabeth David's *English Bread and Yeast Cookery* and Peter Brears's *Cooking and Dining in Tudor and Early Stuart England*. For the story after the American Revolution, I had to dig deep into online newspaper archives to find rye and Indian recipes and accounts of people eating the loaf. I used Arthur W. Brayley's *Bakers and Baking in Massachusetts* for information on milling and the baking trade in that state from the colonial era through the early twentieth century. *America's Founding Food: The Story of New England Cooking* by Keith Stavely and Kathleen Fitzgerald was a helpful guide through nearly every part of this history.

CHAPTER 2

The story of the English colonists who landed on the Virginia coast in 1607 is dramatically told by its leader, Captain John Smith, in his *The Generall History of Virginia, New England & the Summer Isles*. The best source on the Indigenous groups on whom the colonists depended for their survival is Helen C. Rountree's *The Powhatan Indians of Virginia: Their Traditional Culture*. William M. Kelso's *Jamestown: The Truth Revealed* uncovers the archaeological evidence about life in the early settlement, including remains of bread ovens and signs of cannibalism during the "Starving Time." For bread baking during the colonial era, I consulted numerous travelers' accounts and diaries and, most important, Robert Beverley's *The History and Present State of Virginia.* Mary Randolph's groundbreaking *The Virginia House-Wife* was a crucial source for cornbread recipes, and I also found many in period newspapers.

I am indebted to William Rubel's online seminar on American bread culture for illuminating the link between cornbread and white Southern (racist) identity. There exists a large amount of excellent work about African American culinary traditions, both under enslavement and afterward. Among the books I used were a number of early nineteenth-century antislavery tracts as well as *African American Foodways*, edited by Anne L. Bower, and *What the Slaves Ate*, by Herbert C. Covey and Dwight Eisnach. As my guide through the many African American cookbooks, I followed Toni Tipton-Martin's *The Jemima Code: Two Centuries of African-American Cookbooks.* Finally, this chapter could not have been written without the help of Jessica Harris's books, particularly *High on the Hog*, and Michael Twitty's *The Cooking Gene: A Journey Through African American Culinary History in the Old South.*

CHAPTER 3

For information on bread in New York City during the Dutch and English colonial eras, my most important source was I. N. Phelps Stokes's six-volume *The Iconography of Manhattan Island*, containing reports on everything from windmills to bread laws. I consulted J. Franklin Jameson's *Narratives of New Netherland* for accounts by early Dutch explorers and landowners. An invaluable resource of writings on Dutch New York is the New Netherlands Institute website, containing links to hundreds of original documents and scholarly books and articles. I mined it while researching grain growing and trading on Upstate New York plantations. For a more general picture of the history and culture of New Amsterdam, I relied most on Edwin G. Burrows and Mike Wallace's *Gotham: A History of New York to 1898* and *The Island at the Center of the World* by Russell Shorto.

Peter G. Rose is the foremost expert on Dutch cooking in the New World, particularly her *History on Our Plate: Recipes from America's Dutch Past for Today's*

Cook and *The Sensible Cook: Dutch Foodways in the Old and the New World*. For information on the inventor Oliver Evans, I used his own *The Young Mill-Wright's and Miller's Guide* and *Oliver Evans: A Chronicle of Early Engineering* by Greville Bathe and Dorothy Bathe. The essential book on the history of American flour mills is Herman Steen's *Flour Milling in America*. While investigating wheat bread recipes, I turned to the cookbooks of Maria Rundell, particularly her *A New System of Domestic Cookery*, Sarah Josepha Hale's *The Good Housekeeper*, and many others. The *Manuscript Cookbooks Survey* (online at https://www.manuscriptcookbookssurvey.org/) is by far the best resource for anyone wanting to consult handwritten recipe books from the eighteenth through the twentieth centuries.

CHAPTER 4

Sylvester Graham was a prolific writer. His *A Treatise on Bread and Bread-Making*, *Lecture to Young Men on Chastity*, and *Lectures on the Science of Human Life* are essential reading for scholars interested in his life and work. For a doctor's eyewitness report on New York's 1832 cholera epidemic, the most important text is *Reports of Hospital Physicians, and Other Documents in Relation to the Epidemic Cholera of 1832*, edited by Dudley Atkins. (Anyone interested in how we respond to pandemics today should read this book.) Published by some of his acolytes, *The Graham Journal of Health and Longevity* fills out the picture of Grahamism during the era of his greatest fame. The primary scholarly texts on Graham are Stephen Nissenbaum's *Sex, Diet, and Debility in Jacksonian America: Sylvester Graham and Health Reform* and *Eros and Modernization: Sylvester Graham, Health Reform, and the Origins of Victorian Sexuality in America* by Jayme Sokolow. For a broader perspective on health reform, I consulted *Crusaders for Fitness: The History of American Health Reformers* by James C. Whorton, while Kyla Wazana Tompkins's *Racial Indigestion: Eating Bodies in the Nineteenth Century* has an excellent chapter on the links between Graham's notions about sex, bread, and the idea of the American home.

CHAPTER 5

The principal source for information about Lewis and Clark's journey to the Pacific is the account by the explorers themselves, published in the multivolume *Journals of the Lewis and Clark Expedition*, edited by Gary E. Moulton. It is also available online at https://lewisandclarkjournals.unl.edu. For information on the breads consumed by the settlers, I consulted numerous journals, collections of letters, and guidebooks for travelers heading to the West. The best (and only) book on the history and culture of salt-rising bread is Genevieve Bardwell and Susan Ray Brown's *Salt Rising Bread: Recipes and Heartfelt Stories of a Nearly Lost Appalachian Tradition*. This chapter and the next delve into the early history of chemical leavens, which we use today as baking soda and baking powder. The essential text on this subject is Linda Civitello's *Baking Powder Wars: The Cutthroat Food Fight That Revolutionized Cooking*. The California Gold Rush unleashed not only a race to the gold fields but dozens of travelers' accounts of life in the Far West that I scoured for bread information. My information on later Western sourdough cookery comes from books on cowboy culture and life on the Alaska frontier. The Anchorage food writer Julia O'Malley helped me understand Alaska sourdough culture today.

CHAPTER 6

The scientist Eben Norton Horsford was a pivotal figure in the bread world of the late nineteenth century. His *Report on Vienna Bread* helped bring the latest advances in European bread-making techniques to America, and he was also a pioneer in the chemical leavening industry. Given the Fleischmann family's importance to bread making and many other aspects of national culture, it is surprising that there isn't a family archive or much published material about them. I was able to glean my information from newspaper accounts and Christian P. Klieger's photo-history *The Fleischmann Yeast Family*. Much of my information on the nineteenth-century flour industry, including about the start of bleaching, comes from *Wheat Flour and Diet* by C. O. Swanson and John Storck as well as Walter D. Teague's *Flour for Man's Bread*.

CHAPTER 7

The best book on the exodus of French adventurers to California gold country is Malcolm J. Rohrbaugh's *Rush to Gold: The French and the California Gold Rush*. My information on the bread culture of France in the early nineteenth century comes from the masterful *The Bakers of Paris and the Bread Question* by Stanley

L. Kaplan. As in the sourdough chapter, I used Gold Rush travelers' accounts for information on French bread in early San Francisco. We are still waiting for an in-depth history of French settlement and culture in New York City. I relied on period magazine accounts and newspaper articles on the city's French community as well as on directories of French businesses on both the West and East Coasts. By the late nineteenth century the baking and milling industries were becoming professionalized and the first trade journals began to appear. Among those that I used are *Baker's Helper, Bakers Weekly, The Baker's Digest, The American Baker, Bakers Review, Baking Industry, The Retail Bakery*, and *American Miller.* Bread experts on the staffs of some of those journals also produced professional baking manuals that provide a window into the methods of big bread manufacturers (and how they co-opted immigrant bread). These books include Paul Richards's *Book of Breads, Cakes, Pastries, Ices and Sweetmeats*, Emil Braun's *The Baker's Book*, Samuel Maltz's *Bakery Technology and Engineering, Equipment for Bakers*, and *Formulas and Processes for Bakers*, and Julius Wihlfahrt's *A Treatise on Baking.*

CHAPTER 8

Almost as soon as the first large wave of German immigrants began to arrive in New York City around 1850, journalists and other writers began to record their culture, including their bread habits. Aside from period newspapers and magazines, the best source on their community is Stanley Nadel's *Little Germany: Ethnicity, Religion, and Class in New York City, 1845–80*. For a more general picture on immigrants in the city, I used *Immigrant Life in New York City, 1825–1863* by Robert Ernst. German cookbooks both recorded and helped shape immigrant cooking. The most important are *Aunt Babette's Cook Book* by Bertha Kramer and Henriette Davidis's *Practical Cookbook*, both of which were published in numerous editions in Germany and the United States. In 1901 the immigrant baker Emil Braun published *The Baker's Book*, a two-volume world encyclopedia of baking that I mined for insights into the German-dominated bread industry in this country. The vile sanitary condition of "cellar bakeries" was a major scandal during that era. The best place to start on this topic is the comprehensive *Report on Bakeries and Bakers in New York City, 1912*, compiled by

J. B. Lyon for the New York Factory Investigating Commission. For the more recent history of rye bread, the authority is Stanley Ginsberg, author of *Inside the Jewish Bakery: Recipes and Memories of Jewish Baking* (with Norman Berg) and *The Rye Baker*, which contains my favorite recipe for corn rye.

CHAPTER 9

For a detailed picture of life and bread-baking traditions in a poor southern Italian village, Charlotte Gower Chapman's *Milocca: A Sicilian Village* is a key resource. Much of my information on Italian immigrant bread culture in the United States comes from *South Italian Folkways in Europe and America* by Phyllis H. Williams and memoirs such as Jerre Mangione's *Mount Allegro* and Michael Parenti's essay in *Studies in Italian American Social History: Essays in Honor of Leonard Covello*. In 1911 the US Senate's Immigration Commission published a massive report on immigrant workers. Part 24, covering "Recent Immigrants in Agriculture," is a trove of information on Italian and other immigrant workers across the United States. As I noted in this chapter, for many years Italian bread was considered primitive compared to the French baking tradition. This attitude finally began to change with the publication of Carol Field's *The Italian Baker*, one of the twentieth century's most important bread cookbooks.

CHAPTER 10

The one and only book on the history of the bagel is Maria Balinska's essential *The Bagel: A Surprising History of a Modest Bread*. I also consulted the bagel entry in *The Encyclopedia of Jewish Food* by Gil Marks. The memories of bagels in Eastern Europe come from the Bobruisk and Dzialoshitz *yizkor* ("memory") books. Produced by survivors of the Holocaust to memorialize their lost European communities, *yizkor* books are an incredible source of information on Jewish Old World culinary culture. Hundreds of them have been translated and may be accessed via the JewishGen *yizkor* book collection at www.jewishgen.org/yizkor. Ginsberg and Berg's *Inside the Jewish Bakery* is filled with information on bagel bakeries as they transitioned from the union era to the current free-for-all.

CHAPTER 11

An introduction to how technology began to replace human labor in bakeries is found in *Mechanization Takes Command* by Sigfried Giedion. For insights into the industrial bread business, I used the New York Public Library's *Tolley Baking Records, 1887–1997.* Albert Tolley was a longtime bread expert at the Ward Baking Company, the largest bread baker in the United States, and then went on to formulate loaves for many competitors. His archives contain dozens of recipes for the biggest selling brands as well as a trove of baking ephemera and business records. Carl Alsberg's *Combination in the American Bread-Baking Industry* and the Federal Trade Commission's report to the US Senate, *Bakery Combines and Profits*, provide a detailed record of how the Ward company attempted to build a national bread monopoly. I found the bread marketing reports by the Institute for Motivational Research in the online archive of Delaware's Hagley Museum and Library, which is an indispensable resource for anyone interested in the history of American industry.

CHAPTER 12

Jonathan Kauffman's *Hippie Food* was my guide to the growth and spread of counterculture cuisine from the 1960s through the 1980s. I supplemented it with insights from *Food for Dissent: Natural Foods and the Consumer Counterculture Since the 1960s* by Maria McGrath. San Francisco's radical Diggers remain active and have collected their archives, containing documents on their free bakeries and bread recipes, at diggers.org. The era's alternative newspapers reflect the counterculture's interest in breaking free from the industrial food system, including by baking your own bread. The best way to access these newspapers is through JSTOR's Independent Voices digital collection.

CHAPTER 13

I based much of my information in this chapter on personal interviews with some of the pioneer artisan bakers, including Steven Sullivan, Michael London, Daniel Leader, Apollonia Poilâne, Amy Scherber, Keith Giusto, Abe Ferber, Christy Timon, Tom MacMahon, Michel Suas, Didier Rosada, Jim Lahey, and Karen Bornath, director of the Bread Bakers Guild of America. The past issues of *Bread Lines*, the BBGA's magazine, provide insights into the organization and trajectory of the artisan bread movement. Maggie Glezer's cookbook, *Artisan Baking Across America*, includes not only recipes but profiles of some of the most important bakers circa 2000.

Bibliography

Acton, Eliza. *The English Bread Book*. Longman, Brown, Green, Longmans & Roberts, 1857.

Adams, Ramon F. *Come an' Get It*. University of Oklahoma Press, 1952.

Alcott, William. *Vegetable Diet*. Fowler and Wells, 1859.

Allen, Ida Bailey. *Mrs. Allen on Cooking, Menus, Service*. Doubleday, Doran & Company, 1929.

Alsberg, Carl. *Combination in the American Bread-Baking Industry*. Stanford University Press, 1926.

Atkins, Dudley, ed. *Reports of Hospital Physicians, and Other Documents in Relation to the Epidemic Cholera of 1832*. G. & C. & H. Carvill, 1832.

Atwater, Wilbur O., and Charles D. Woods. *Dietary Studies with Reference to the Food of the Negro in Alabama*. Government Printing Office, 1897.

Aunt Babette (Bertha Kramer). *Aunt Babette's Cookbook*. Bloch Publishing, 1889.

Balinska, Maria. *The Bagel: A Surprising History of a Modest Bread*. Yale University Press, 2008.

Bardwell, Genevieve, and Susan Ray Brown. *Salt Rising Bread: Recipes and Heartfelt Stories of a Nearly Lost Appalachian Tradition*. St. Lynn's Press, 2016.

Bathe, Greville, and Dorothy Bathe. *Oliver Evans: A Chronicle of Early Engineering*. Historical Society of Pennsylvania, 1935.

Bay Laurel, Alicia. *Living on the Earth*. Vintage Books, 1970.

Beard, James. *Beard on Bread*. Knopf, 1973.

Bennett, M. K. "The Food Economy of the New England Indians," *Journal of Political Economy* (October 1955): 369–396.

Beverley, Robert. *The History and Present State of Virginia*. Richard Parker, 1705.

Bobrow-Strain, Aaron. *White Bread: A Social History of the Store-Bought Loaf.* Beacon Press, 2012.

Bogen, F. W. *The German in America*. B. H. Greene, 1851.

Borthwick, J. D. *Three Years in California*. William Blackwood and Sons, 1857.

Bower, Anne L., ed. *African American Foodways*. University of Illinois Press, 2007.

Bradford, William. *Bradford's History of the Plymouth Settlement, 1608–1650*. E.P. Dutton & Company, 1920, 65.

Braun, Emil. *The Baker's Book*. Vols. 1 and 2. Emil Braun, 1901.

Brayley, Arthur W. *Bakers and Baking in Massachusetts*. Master Bakers' Association of Massachusetts, 1909.

Brears, Peter. *Cooking and Dining in Tudor and Early Stuart England*. Prospect Books, 2015.

Brears, Peter. *A Taste of History: 10,000 Years of Food in Britain*. English Heritage, 1993.

Briggs, Rachel V. "The Hominy Foodway of the Historic Native Eastern Woodlands." *Native South* 8 (2015): 112–148.

Brissot de Warville, J. P. *New Travels in the United States of America*. J. S. Jordan, 1791.

Brown, Edward Espe. *The Tassajara Bread Book*. Shambhala Publications, 1970.

Burrows, Edwin G., and Mike Wallace. *Gotham: A History of New York City to 1898*. Oxford University Press, 1999.

Cabell, N. F. *Early History of Agriculture in Virginia*. Printed by L. Towers, 1899?.

Cauvain, Stanley. *Technology of Breadmaking*. Springer, 2015.

Chapman, Charlotte Gower. *Milocca: A Sicilian Village*. Schenkman Publishing Co., 1971.

Cheney, Brock. *Plain but Wholesome, Foodways of the Mormon Pioneers*. University of Utah Press, 2012.

Child, Lydia Maria. *The American Frugal Housewife*. S. S. & W. Wood, 1838.

Civitello, Linda. *Baking Powder Wars: The Cutthroat Food Fight That Revolutionized Cooking*. University of Illinois Press, 2017.

Clayton, Bernard, Jr. *The Breads of France*. Bobbs-Merrill, 1978.

Clayton, Bernard, Jr. *The Complete Book of Breads*. Simon and Schuster, 1973.

Cooperative Whole Grain Education Association. *Uprisings: the Whole Grain Bakers' Book*. Revised edition. Book Publishing Company, 1990.

Cordasco, Francesco, ed. *Studies in Italian American Social History: Essays in Honor of Leonard Covello*. Rowman and Littlefield, 1975.

Cornelius, Mrs. *The Young Housekeeper's Friend*. Charles Tappan, 1846.

Covey, Herbert C., and Dwight Eisnach. *What the Slaves Ate*. Greenwood Press, 2009.

David, Elizabeth. *English Bread and Yeast Cookery*. Viking Penguin, 1980.

Davidis, Henriette. *Pickled Herring and Pumpkin Pike: A Nineteenth-Century Cookbook for German Immigrants to America*. Max Cade Institute for German-American Studies, 2002.

Davis, Adelle. *Let's Eat Right to Keep Fit*. Harcourt, Brace & World, Inc., 1954.

De Renzo, D.J. *Bakery Products: Yeast Leavened*. Noyes Data Corporation, 1975.

Diner, Hasia. *Hungering for America*. Harvard University Press, 2001.

Dodoens, Rembert. *A New Herbal, or Historie of Plants*. By Edward Griffin, 1619.

Dondlinger, Peter T. *The Book of Wheat*. Orange Judd Company, 1908.

Dorst, Sally. *The New York Food Book*. Workman Publishing Company, 1973.

Dragonwagon, Crescent. *The Commune Cookbook*. Simon and Schuster, 1972.

Drury, Clifford Merrill, ed. *The Mountains We Have Crossed: Diaries and Letters of the Oregon Mission, 1838*. University of Nebraska Press, 1999.

Dupaigne, Bernard. *The History of Bread*. Harry N. Abrams, 1999.

Ernst, Robert. *Immigrant Life in New York City, 1825–1863*. Columbia University Press, 1949.

Evans, Oliver. *The Young Mill-Wright's and Miller's Guide*. Printed for, and sold by the author, 1795.

Factory Investigating Commission. *Preliminary Report of the Factory Investigating Commission*. Vol. 1. Argus Company, 1912.

Field, Carol. *The Italian Baker*. Harper & Row, 1985.

Fisher, Abby, and Karen Hess. *What Mrs. Fisher Knows About Old Southern Cooking: Soups, Pickles, Preserves, etc.: in facsimile with historical notes.* Applewood Books, 1995.

Galanakis, Charis M., ed. *Trends in Wheat and Bread Making.* Academic Press, 2021.

Gerard, John. *The Herball or Generall Historie of Plants.* John Norton, 1597.

Gerhard, Albert F., ed. *Handbook for Bakers.* The Century Co., 1925.

Giedion, Siegried. *Mechanization Takes Command.* Oxford University Press, 1948.

Ginsberg, Stanley. *The Rye Baker.* W. W. Norton & Company, 2016.

Ginsberg, Stanley, and Norman Berg. *Inside the Jewish Bakery: Recipes and Memories of Jewish Baking.* Camino Books, 2011.

Glezer, Maggie. *Artisan Baking Across America.* Artisan, 2000.

Goodfriend, Joyce. *Before the Melting Pot: Society and Culture in Colonial New York, 1664–1730.* Princeton University Press, 1991.

Grabe, Gordon and Phyllis. *The Hippie Cookbook.* Paisley Shawl Publishing Co., 1970.

Graham, Sylvester. *A Treatise on Bread, and Bread-Making.* Light & Stearns, 1837.

Graham, Sylvester. *Lecture to Young Men on Chastity.* Crocker & Brewster, 1837.

Graham, Sylvester. *Lectures on the Science of Human Life.* Fowler & Wells, 1858.

Hale, Sarah Josepha. *The Good Housekeeper.* Weeks, Jordan and Company, 1839.

Hamelman, Jeffrey. *Bread: A Baker's Book of Techniques and Recipes.* Wiley, 2013.

Harland, Marion. *Common Sense in the Household.* Charles Scribner's Sons, 1882.

Harris, Jessica B. *High on the Hog.* Bloomsbury, 2011.

Harris, Jessica B. *Iron Pots and Wooden Spoons: Africa's Gifts to New World Cooking,* New York: Athenaeum, 1989.

Hess, John L., and Karen Hess. *The Taste of America.* Grossman Publishers, 1977.

Hitchcock, Edward. *Dyspepsy Forestalled.* J. S. & C. Adams, 1831.

Hooker, Alan. *Vegetarian Gourmet Cookery,* San Francisco: 101 Productions, 1970.

Horsford, E. N. *Report on Vienna Bread.* Government Printing Office, 1875.

Horsford, E. N. *The Theory and Art of Bread Making.* Welch, Bigelow and Company, 1861.

Horsman, Reginald. *Feast or Famine, Food and Drink in American Westward Expansion.* University of Missouri Press, 2008.

Hui, Y. H. *Bakery Products: Science and Technology.* Blackwell Publishing, 2006.

Hunt, Thomas F. *The Cereals in America*. Orange Judd Company, 1904.
Hurt, R. Douglas. *Indian Agriculture in America*. University Press of Kansas, 1987.
Jacob, H. E. *Six Thousand Years of Bread: Its Holy and Unholy History*. Doubleday, Doran, 1944.
Jago, William. *The Technology of Bread-Making*. Bakers' Helper Company, 1921.
Jameson, J. Franklin, ed. *Narratives of New Netherland*. Charles Scribner's Sons, 1909.
Johannessen, Sissel, and Christine A. Hastorf. *Corn and Culture in the Prehistoric New World*. Westview Press, 1994.
Johnson, Edward. *Wonder-Working Providence of Sions Saviour in New England*. Warren F. Draper, 1867.
Kaplan, Steven L. *The Bakers of Paris and the Bread Question*. Duke University Press, 1996.
Kauffman, Jonathan. *Hippie Food*. William Morrow, 2018.
Kellogg, John Harvey. *A Household Manual of Hygiene, Food and Diet*. The Office of the Health Reformer, 1877.
Kelso, William M. *Jamestown: The Truth Revealed*. University of Virginia Press, 2017.
Klieger, Christiaan P. *The Fleischmann Yeast Family*. Arcadia Books, 2004.
Lahey, Jim. *My Bread: The Revolutionary No-Work, No-Knead Method*. W. W. Norton and Company, 2009.
Leader, Daniel, and Judith Blahnik. *Bread Alone*. William Morrow and Company, Inc., 1993.
Leonard, Leah. *Jewish Cookery*. Crown Publishers, 1949.
Leslie, Eliza. *Directions for Cookery in Its Various Branches*. Carey & Hart, 1844.
Lipman, Andrew. *The Saltwater Frontier*. Yale University Press, 2015.
Longgood, Wiliam. *The Poisons in Your Food*. Simon and Schuster, 1960.
Lo Pinto, Maria. *The Art of Italian Regional Cooking*. Doubleday, 1963.
Lyon, J. B. *Report on Bakeries and Bakers in New York City, 1912*. J. B. Lyon, 1912.
Mangione, Jerre. *Mount Allegro*. Columbia University Press, 1981.
Marcy, Randolph B. *The Prairie Traveler*. Harper & Brothers, 1861.
Markham, Gervase. *The English Hus-wife*. Printed by Iohn [*sic*] Beale, for Roger Jackson, 1615.
Marks, Gil. *The Encyclopedia of Jewish Food*. Wiley, 2010.

Matson, Cathy. *Merchants & Empire: Trading in Colonial New York*. Johns Hopkins University Press, 1998.

Matz, Samuel A. *Bakery Technology and Engineering*. Third edition. Van Nostrand Reinhold, 1992.

Matz, Samuel A. *Bakery Technology and Engineering*. The Avi Publishing Company, Inc., 1960.

Matz, Samuel A. *Equipment for Bakers*. Pan-Tech International, Inc., 1988.

Matz, Samuel A. *Formulas and Processes for Bakers*. Pan-Tech International, Inc., 1997.

McCance, R. A., and E. M. Widdowson. *Breads White and Brown*. J. B. Lippincott Company, 1956.

McCay, Clive, and Jeanette B. McCay. *The Cornell Bread Book*. Dover Publications, 1980.

McCollum, E. V., and Nina Simonds. *The Newer Knowledge of Nutrition*. Third edition. Macmillan Company, 1925.

McGrath, Maria. *Food for Dissent: Natural Foods and the Consumer Counterculture Since the 1960s*. University of Massachusetts Press, 2019.

McMahon, Sarah F. "A Comfortable Subsistence: The Changing Composition of Diet in Rural New England, 1620–1840." *William and Mary Quarterly* (January 1985): 26–65.

Miller, Henry. *The Intimate Henry Miller*. Signet/New American Library, 1959.

Moulton, Gary E. *The Journals of the Lewis and Clark Expedition*. University of Nebraska Press, 1983–2001.

Mourt's Relation, or Journal of the Plantation at Plymouth. J. K. Wiggin, 1865.

Mrozowski, Stephen A. "The Discovery of a Native American Cornfield on Cape Cod." *Archaeology of Eastern North America* (Fall 1994): 47–62.

Nadel, Stanley. *Little Germany: Ethnicity, Religion, and Class in New York City, 1845–80*. University of Illinois Press, 1990.

Neill, Edward D. *The History of the Virginia Company of London*. Joel Munsell, 1869.

Nissenbaum, Stephen. *Sex, Diet, and Debility in Jacksonian America: Sylvester Graham and Health Reform*. Greenwood Press, 1980.

Numbers, Ronald L. *Prophetess of Health: Ellen G. White and the Origins of Seventh-Day Adventist Health Reform*. University of Tennessee Press, 1992.

Olmsted, Frederick Law. *A Journey in the Seaboard Slave States*. G.P. Putnam's, 1904.

Opie, Frederick Douglas. *Hog & Hominy: Soul Food from Africa to America.* Columbia University Press, 2008.

Ortiz, Joe. *The Village Baker.* Ten Speed Press, 1993.

Panschar, William G. *Baking in America.* Northwestern University Press, 1956.

Parloa, Maria. *Miss Parloa's New Cook Book.* Estes and Lauriat, 1881.

Patterson, Betty Benton. *Mammy Lou's Cookbook.* R.M. McBride, 1931.

Peabody, Joel R. *A World of Wonders.* Robert S. Davis, 1838.

Perry, Charles. *The Haight-Ashbury.* Rolling Stone Press, 1984.

Philbrick, Nathaniel. *Mayflower: A Study of Courage, Community, and War.* Viking, 2006.

Pirrie, Peter G. *Modern Bakery Production.* American Trade Publishing Company, 1928.

Pyler, E.J. *Baking: Science and Technology.* 2 vols. Siebel Publishing Company, 1973.

Randolph, Mary. *The Virginia House-Wife.* Davis and Force, 1824.

Raven, Ralph. *Golden Dreams and Leaden Realities.* G. P. Putnam & Co., 1853.

Reinhart, Peter. *The Bread Baker's Apprentice: Mastering the Art of Extraordinary Bread.* Ten Speed Press, 2001.

Reinhart, Peter. *Crust & Crumb: Master Formulas for Serious Bread Bakers.* Ten Speed Press, 1998.

Richard, Lena. *Lena Richard's Cook Book.* Rogers Printing Co., 1939.

Richards, Paul. *Paul Richards' Book of Breads, Cakes, Pastries, Ices and Sweetmeats.* Hotel Monthly, 1907.

Riley, Glenda, ed. *Prairie Voices.* Iowa State University Press, 1996.

Robertson, Chad. *Tartine Bread.* Chronicle Books, 2010.

Robertson, Laurel, with Carol Flinders and Bronwen Godfrey. *The Laurel's Kitchen Bread Book.* Random House, 1984.

Rohrbaugh, Malcolm J. *Rush to Gold: The French and the California Gold Rush.* Yale University Press, 2013.

Rose, Peter G. *History on Our Plate: Recipes from America's Dutch Past for Today's Cook.* Syracuse University Press, 2019.

Rose, Peter G., ed. *The Sensible Cook: Dutch Foodways in the Old and the New World.* Syracuse University Press, 1989.

Rountree, Helen C. *The Powhatan Indians of Virginia: Their Traditional Culture.* University of Oklahoma Press, 1989.

Rubel, William. *Bread: A Global History*. Reaktion Books, 2011.

Rundell, Maria. *American Domestic Cookery*. E. Duyckinck, 1823.

Rundell, Maria. *A New System of Domestic Cookery*. M'Dermut & D. D. Arden, 1814.

Sambrook, Pamela, and Peter Brears. *The Country House Kitchen, 1650–1900*. A. Sutton Pub., 1997.

Scherber, Amy, and Toy Kim Dupree. *Amy's Bread*. Morrow, 1996.

Shorto, Russell. *The Island at the Center of the World: The Epic Story of Dutch Manhattan and the Forgotten Colony That Shaped America*. Vintage Books, 2005.

Silverton, Nancy, in collaboration with Laurie Ochoa. *Nancy Silverton's Breads from La Brea Bakery*. Villard Books, 1996.

Simmons, Amelia. *American Cookery*. Hudson & Goodwin, 1796.

Slater, Charles C. *Economic Changes in the Baking Industry*. American Bakers Association, 1958.

Smith, Captain John. *A True Relation of Virginia*. Wiggin and Lunt, 1866.

Smith, Captain John. *The Generall Historie of Virginia, New England & the Summer Isles*. J. MacLehose & Sons, 1907.

Sokolow, Jayme. *Eros and Modernization: Sylvester Graham, Health Reform, and the Origins of Victorian Sexuality in America*. Fairleigh Dickinson University Press, 1983.

Stavely, Keith, and Kathleen Fitzgerald. *America's Founding Food: The Story of New England Cooking*. University of North Carolina Press, 2004.

Stavely, Keith, and Kathleen Fitzgerald. *Northern Hospitality: Cooking by the Book in New England*. University of Massachusetts Press, 2011.

Steen, Herman. *Flour Milling in America*. T. S. Denison & Company, Inc., 1963.

Stokes, I. N. Phelps. *The Iconography of Manhattan Island*. 6 vols. Robert H. Dodd, 1915–1928.

Storck, John, and Walter D. Teague. *Flour for Man's Bread*. University of Minnesota Press, 1952.

Sugihara, T. F., Leo Kline, and M. W. Miller. "Microorganisms of the San Francisco Sour Dough Bread Process." *Applied Microbiology* (March 1971): 456–458.

Sultan, William J. *Practical Baking*. Avi Publishing Company, Inc., 1965.

Swanson, C. O. *Wheat Flour and Diet*. Macmillan Company, 1928.

Ticknor, Caleb. *The Philosophy of Living*. Harper & Bros., 1836.

Tipton-Martin, Toni. *The Jemima Code: Two Centuries of African-American Cookbooks*. University of Texas Press, 2015.

Tompkins, Kyla Wazana. *Racial Indigestion: Eating Bodies in the Nineteenth Century*. New York University Press, 2012.

Trall, Russell. *The Hygeian Home Cook-Book*. S. R. Wells, Publisher, 1874.

Twitty, Michael. *The Cooking Gene: A Journey Through African American Culinary History in the Old South*. Harper Collins, 2017.

United States Senate. *Bakery Combines and Profits*. Government Printing Office, 1927.

United States Senate. Reports of the Immigration Commission. *Immigrants in Industries, Part 24: Recent Immigrants in Agriculture*. Government Printing Office, 1911.

Weld, Theodore. *American Slavery As It Is: Testimony of a Thousand Witnesses*. American Anti-Slavery Society, 1839.

Whorton, James C. *Crusaders for Fitness: The History of American Health Reformers*. Princeton University Press, 1982.

Wihlfahrt, Julius. *A Treatise on Baking*. Fleischmann Division, 1935.

Wilcox, Estelle W. *The New Practical Housekeeping*. Home Publishing Company, 1890.

Williams, Jacqueline. *Wagon Wheel Kitchens, Food on the Oregon Trail*. University Press of Kansas, 1993.

Williams, Phyllis H. *South Italian Folkways in Europe and America*. Yale University Press, 1938.

Winthrop, John, Jr. "The Description, Culture and Use of Maiz." *Philosophical Transactions* 12 (1677–78).

Witty, Helen, and Elizabeth Schneider Colchie. *Better Than Store-Bought*. Harper & Row, 1979.

Zhou, Weibiao. *Bakery Products: Science and Technology*. Wiley, 2014.

Index

CALIFORNIA STUDIES IN FOOD AND CULTURE

Darra Goldstein, Editor

1. *Dangerous Tastes: The Story of Spices,* by Andrew Dalby
2. *Eating Right in the Renaissance,* by Ken Albala
3. *Food Politics: How the Food Industry Influences Nutrition and Health,* by Marion Nestle
4. *Camembert: A National Myth,* by Pierre Boisard
5. *Safe Food: The Politics of Food Safety,* by Marion Nestle
6. *Eating Apes,* by Dale Peterson
7. *Revolution at the Table: The Transformation of the American Diet,* by Harvey Levenstein
8. *Paradox of Plenty: A Social History of Eating in Modern America,* by Harvey Levenstein
9. *Encarnación's Kitchen: Mexican Recipes from Nineteenth-Century California: Selections from Encarnación Pinedo's* El cocinero español, by Encarnación Pinedo, edited and translated by Dan Strehl, with an essay by Victor Valle
10. *Zinfandel: A History of a Grape and Its Wine,* by Charles L. Sullivan, with a foreword by Paul Draper
11. *Tsukiji: The Fish Market at the Center of the World,* by Theodore C. Bestor
12. *Born Again Bodies: Flesh and Spirit in American Christianity,* by R. Marie Griffith
13. *Our Overweight Children: What Parents, Schools, and Communities Can Do to Control the Fatness Epidemic,* by Sharron Dalton
14. *The Art of Cooking: The First Modern Cookery Book,* by the Eminent Maestro Martino of Como, edited and with an introduction by Luigi Ballerini, translated and annotated by Jeremy Parzen, and with fifty modernized recipes by Stefania Barzini
15. *The Queen of Fats: Why Omega-3s Were Removed from the Western Diet and What We Can Do to Replace Them,* by Susan Allport
16. *Meals to Come: A History of the Future of Food,* by Warren Belasco
17. *The Spice Route: A History,* by John Keay
18. *Medieval Cuisine of the Islamic World: A Concise History with 174 Recipes,* by Lilia Zaouali, translated by M. B. DeBevoise, with a foreword by Charles Perry
19. *Arranging the Meal: A History of Table Service in France,* by Jean-Louis Flandrin, translated by Julie E. Johnson, with Sylvie and Antonio Roder, with a foreword to the English-language edition by Beatrice Fink
20. *The Taste of Place: A Cultural Journey into Terroir,* by Amy B. Trubek
21. *Food: The History of Taste,* edited by Paul Freedman

22. *M. F. K. Fisher Among the Pots and Pans: Celebrating Her Kitchens*, by Joan Reardon, with a foreword by Amanda Hesser
23. *Cooking: The Quintessential Art*, by Hervé This and Pierre Gagnaire, translated by M. B. DeBevoise
24. *Perfection Salad: Women and Cooking at the Turn of the Century*, by Laura Shapiro
25. *Of Sugar and Snow: A History of Ice Cream Making*, by Jeri Quinzio
26. *Encyclopedia of Pasta*, by Oretta Zanini De Vita, translated by Maureen B. Fant, with a foreword by Carol Field
27. *Tastes and Temptations: Food and Art in Renaissance Italy*, by John Varriano
28. *Free for All: Fixing School Food in America*, by Janet Poppendieck
29. *Breaking Bread: Recipes and Stories from Immigrant Kitchens*, by Lynne Christy Anderson, with a foreword by Corby Kummer
30. *Culinary Ephemera: An Illustrated History*, by William Woys Weaver
31. *Eating Mud Crabs in Kandahar: Stories of Food during Wartime by the World's Leading Correspondents*, edited by Matt McAllester
32. *Weighing In: Obesity, Food Justice, and the Limits of Capitalism*, by Julie Guthman
33. *Why Calories Count: From Science to Politics*, by Marion Nestle and Malden Nesheim
34. *Curried Cultures: Globalization, Food, and South Asia*, edited by Krishnendu Ray and Tulasi Srinivas
35. *The Cookbook Library: Four Centuries of the Cooks, Writers, and Recipes That Made the Modern Cookbook*, by Anne Willan, with Mark Cherniavsky and Kyri Claflin
36. *Coffee Life in Japan*, by Merry White
37. *American Tuna: The Rise and Fall of an Improbable Food*, by Andrew F. Smith
38. *A Feast of Weeds: A Literary Guide to Foraging and Cooking Wild Edible Plants*, by Luigi Ballerini, translated by Gianpiero W. Doebler, with recipes by Ada De Santis and illustrations by Giuliano Della Casa
39. *The Philosophy of Food*, by David M. Kaplan
40. *Beyond Hummus and Falafel: Social and Political Aspects of Palestinian Food in Israel*, by Liora Gvion, translated by David Wesley and Elana Wesley
41. *The Life of Cheese: Crafting Food and Value in America*, by Heather Paxson
42. *Popes, Peasants, and Shepherds: Recipes and Lore from Rome and Lazio*, by Oretta Zanini De Vita, translated by Maureen B. Fant, foreword by Ernesto Di Renzo
43. *Cuisine and Empire: Cooking in World History*, by Rachel Laudan
44. *Inside the California Food Revolution: Thirty Years That Changed Our Culinary Consciousness*, by Joyce Goldstein, with Dore Brown
45. *Cumin, Camels, and Caravans: A Spice Odyssey*, by Gary Paul Nabhan
46. *Balancing on a Planet: The Future of Food and Agriculture*, by David A. Cleveland

47. *The Darjeeling Distinction: Labor and Justice on Fair-Trade Tea Plantations in India*, by Sarah Besky
48. *How the Other Half Ate: A History of Working-Class Meals at the Turn of the Century*, by Katherine Leonard Turner
49. *The Untold History of Ramen:* How Political Crisis in Japan Spawned a Global Food Craze, by George Solt
50. *Word of Mouth: What We Talk About When We Talk About Food*, by Priscilla Parkhurst Ferguson
51. *Inventing Baby Food: Taste, Health, and the Industrialization of the American Diet*, by Amy Bentley
52. *Secrets from the Greek Kitchen: Cooking, Skill, and Everyday Life on an Aegean Island*, by David E. Sutton
53. *Breadlines Knee-Deep in Wheat: Food Assistance in the Great Depression*, by Janet Poppendieck
54. *Tasting French Terroir: The History of an Idea*, by Thomas Parker
55. *Becoming Salmon: Aquaculture and the Domestication of a Fish*, by Marianne Elisabeth Lien
56. *Divided Spirits: Tequila, Mezcal, and the Politics of Production*, by Sarah Bowen
57. *The Weight of Obesity: Hunger and Global Health in Postwar Guatemala*, by Emily Yates-Doerr
58. *Dangerous Digestion: The Politics of American Dietary Advice*, by E. Melanie DuPuis
59. *A Taste of Power: Food and American Identities*, by Katharina Vester
60. *More Than Just Food: Food Justice and Community Change*, by Garrett M. Broad
61. *Hoptopia: A World of Agriculture and Beer in Oregon's Willamette Valley*, by Peter A. Kopp
62. *A Geography of Digestion: Biotechnology and the Kellogg Cereal Enterprise*, by Nicholas Bauch
63. *Bitter and Sweet:* Food, Meaning, and Modernity in Rural China, by Ellen Oxfeld
64. *A History of Cookbooks: From Kitchen to Page over Seven Centuries*, by Henry Notaker
65. *Reinventing the Wheel: Milk, Microbes, and the Fight for Real Cheese*, by Bronwen Percival and Francis Percival
66. *Making Modern Meals: How Americans Cook Today*, by Amy B. Trubek
67. *Food and Power: A Culinary Ethnography of Israel*, by Nir Avieli
68. *Canned: The Rise and Fall of Consumer Confidence in the American Food Industry*, by Anna Zeide

69. *Meat Planet: Artificial Flesh and the Future of Food*, by Benjamin Aldes Wurgaft
70. *The Labor of Lunch: Why We Need Real Food and Real Jobs in American Public Schools*, by Jennifer E. Gaddis
71. *Feeding the Crisis: Care and Abandonment in America's Food Safety Net*, by Maggie Dickinson
72. *Sameness in Diversity: Food and Globalization in Modern America*, by Laresh Jayasanker
73. *The Fruits of Empire: Art, Food, and the Politics of Race in the Age of American Expansion*, by Shana Klein
74. *Let's Ask Marion: What You Need to Know About the Politics of Food, Nutrition, and Health*, by Marion Nestle, in conversation with Kerry Trueman
75. *The Scarcity Slot: Excavating Histories of Food Security in Ghana*, by Amanda L. Logan
76. *Gastropolitics and the Specter of Race: Stories of Capital, Culture, and Coloniality in Peru*, by María Elena García
77. *The Kingdom of Rye: A Brief History of Russian Food*, by Darra Goldstein
78. *Slow Cooked: An Unexpected Life in Food Politics*, by Marion Nestle
79. *Yerba Maté: The Drink That Shaped a Nation*, by Julia J. S. Sarreal
80. *Wonder Foods: The Science and Commerce of Nutrition*, by Lisa Haushofer
81. *Ways of Eating: Exploring Food Through History and Culture*, by Benjamin A. Wurgaft and Merry I. White
82. *From Label to Table: Regulating Food in America in the Information Age*, by Xaq Frohlich
83. *Intoxicating Pleasures: The Reinvention of Wine, Beer, and Whiskey After Prohibition*, by Lisa Jacobson
84. *The Quinoa Bust: The Making and Unmaking of an Andean Miracle Crop*, by Emma McDonell
85. *On Hunger: Violence and Craving in America, from Starvation to Ozempic*, by Dana Simmons
86. *The Pierogi Problem: Cosmopolitan Appetites and the Reinvention of Polish Food*, by Fabio Parasecoli, Agata Bachórz, and Mateusz Halawa
87. *Nile Nightshade: Tomato, A Kitchen History of Modern Egypt*, by Anny Gaul
88. *Food Justice Undone: Lessons for Building a Better Movement*, by Hanna Garth
89. *Sugar Coated: Unboxing the Hidden Forces Shaping America's Favorite Breakfast Food*, by Marion Nestle and Lisa Sutherland
90. *America Bread: A History*, by Andrew Coe

Founded in 1893,
UNIVERSITY OF CALIFORNIA PRESS
publishes bold, progressive books and journals on topics in the arts, humanities, social sciences, and natural sciences—with a focus on social justice issues—that inspire thought and action among readers worldwide.

The UC PRESS FOUNDATION
raises funds to uphold the press's vital role as an independent, nonprofit publisher, and receives philanthropic support from a wide range of individuals and institutions—and from committed readers like you. To learn more, visit ucpress.edu/supportus.